A Path From Rome

An Autobiography

ANTHONY KENNY

W0006929

Oxford   New York

OXFORD UNIVERSITY PRESS

Oxford University Press, Walton Street, Oxford OX2 6DP

Oxford New York Toronto
Delhi Bombay Calcutta Madras Karachi
Kuala Lumpur Singapore Hong Kong Tokyo
Nairobi Dar es Salaam Cape Town
Melbourne Auckland

and associated companies in
Berlin Ibadan

Oxford is a trade mark of Oxford University Press

First published 1985 by Sidgwick and Jackson Limited
First issued as an Oxford University Press paperback 1986
Reprinted 1986, 1988

British Library Cataloguing in Publication Data
Kenny, Anthony
A path from Rome: an autobiography
1. Kenny, Anthony 2. Philosophers — England — Biography
I. Title
192   B1646.K/
ISBN 0-19-283050-3

Library of Congress Cataloging in Publication Data
Kenny, Anthony John Patrick.
A path from Rome.
(Oxford paperbacks)
Includes index.
1. Kenny, Anthony John Patrick. 2. Ex-priests,
Catholic — England — Biography.   I. Title.
BX4705.K39A36 1986 282'.092'4 [B]   85-31068
ISBN 0-19-283050-3 (pbk.)

Printed in Great Britain by
The Guernsey Press Co. Ltd.
Guernsey, Channel Islands

To my mother

Contents

Preface 9

Preface

This book is in several ways a very partial autobiography. It tells the story only of part of my life: that part which ended twenty years ago, when, at the age of thirty-two, I left the priesthood in which I had served for seven years and returned to the lay state. Even of that part of my life I have not told the complete story. Cardinal Heenan, in whose diocese and under whose authority I served as a priest, called his own autobiography *Not the Whole Truth*; the title is likely to be an apt one for the story of any priest's life. I have tried to report that part of my story that I have chosen to record as fairly as I can, though it includes many things which I said and did and left undone which I now find painful to recall. But what I have told is only my own story; others involved in the events I record might well have a different tale to tell. If the book gives the impression that I was unhealthily self-absorbed, the impression may not be incorrect; but it will be exaggerated because I have deliberately chosen to leave out any account of private dealings with any person now living. Such memories are other people's property as much as mine; and I have not yet reached the advanced age which seems to confer on autobiographers the privilege of making free, in this way, with the pasts of others.

I am indebted to Margaret Willes and Marigold Johnson for thoroughly revising the manuscript, and to Paul Johnson for suggesting the title.

Anthony Kenny
30 ix 84

– I –

Childhood, 1931–43

It was a family joke that I ought to be the best Catholic in Liverpool, since I had been baptized into the Church not just once but three times. No one, according to Catholic teaching, can be baptized more than once, and what really happened was this. My birth was a difficult one, and when born I was judged unlikely to live more than a few hours. A priest was sent for to baptize me, but he took some time to arrive. My grandmother, fearing that he would be too late, poured water over me and pronounced the baptismal formula so that I should not die unqualified for Heaven. When the priest appeared, my grandmother feared to give offence by explaining that she had anticipated his function (though according to Catholic doctrine anyone, man, woman or child, is empowered and entitled to baptize in cases of necessity) and so he went through the rite again, in the abbreviated form used in an emergency. Later, as customary in such cases, I was taken to the church and the remainder of the christening rites were performed.

It was in my grandmother's house, 15 Sandhurst Street, Liverpool, that I was born on 16 March 1931. It was my mother's wish that I should be christened Anthony, the name I was to be known by, and John, after my father; but she was too exhausted to play any active part in the hurried ceremony, and my grandmother added, of her own initiative, the name Patrick. It would be a scandal, she thought, if a child born the very day before St Patrick's feast should not bear his name.

I do not remember my grandmother being as determinedly Irish as this story suggests. She was born Margaret O'Brien in Armagh but had lived in England at least since her marriage in 1894. She had caused great scandal to her Catholic family by eloping with a non-Catholic rigger, James Jones, and marrying him in a Protestant church in Toxteth, three months before the birth of their first child, James. But by the time I was born she had become a model of

11

Catholic respectability, recently widowed and highly revered in church circles. It was only long after her death that I learned of her adventurous adolescence.

My grandfather, though I never met him, was to have a great influence on the way I grew up. He earned his living by the sea: in youth as a rigger aboard ship; by the time of his retirement, as a quay foreman on the Liverpool docks. Though he ran away from school to sea in his early teens, he was in adult life a self-taught intellectual of a kind that has become rare since the great widening of educational opportunity in the present century. He was devoted to history and literature, would read Plato in Jowett's translation, and built up a library of solid, tough-bound volumes such as Green's *History of the English People* and Stobart's *Glory That Was Greece*, and massive *Cyclopedias of English Literature*. I grew up surrounded by his library and even at the age when my main reading was provided by A. A. Milne and Arthur Ransome I loved to browse through these ponderous Victorian works.

My maternal grandparents had five children, of whom my mother was the second. The eldest son was killed in the Royal Flying Corps in 1918, having earlier won a Military Medal for gallantry. Another son and a daughter died of disease shortly before I was born. The only survivor of my mother's siblings was the youngest, Alexander ('Alec'), in 1931 a 25-year-old student for the priesthood at the English College in Rome.

It was my mother's, and not my father's, family that provided the background to my childhood. My father, John Kenny, was an engineer on an Elders and Fyffe's steamship, engaged in the banana trade sailing out of Liverpool, Avonmouth, and sometimes Rotterdam. My memories of him are fragmentary as he was only a shadowy presence during the eight years of my childhood that he was alive. Not only was he constantly away at sea, but by the time I was old enough to take notice he and my mother spent less and less time together even when he was in England. I was only two years old when my parents sold their matrimonial home in Crosby and made a formal agreement of separation. I cannot recall a time when they lived together, and in all my earliest memories my mother is living at my grandmother's home. My father, on his visits to Liverpool, would stay with his sister at Wavertree; I would be collected for an afternoon's outing with him and then be returned in time for bed. Once I was taken to see his cabin aboard the S.S. *Sulaco*, and was exhibited to his fellow-officers. I recall the pulsing, gleaming brass of the engine room where he worked and the heat of the metal gratings underfoot. I never knew him well enough to discover what kind of person he was; nor did I ask myself whether he suffered because his son was such a stranger to him. My mother, after the separation, supported us by returning to her former profession of librarian. My daytime rearing fell to my grandmother; it was she to whom I looked for meals and clothes and from whom I feared punishment for misbehaviour. My mother would appear in the evening, often after bedtime, and at weekends; she was an occasional playmate, a provider of extra treats, rather than an enforcer of discipline.

The principal male influence on my childhood was my uncle Alec, once he returned to England from his clerical studies in Rome. For the first two years of my life our only contact was the stream of rhymes he wrote to be read to me and drawings to be shown to me; but when I was two and a half I was taken as the youngest member of a family party to attend his ordination in Rome in November 1933. The religious significance of this event was naturally above my head, but for years I treasured a clockwork sparrow bought in the Campo dei Fiori, which ate the cake crumbs at the ordination breakfast. During the ceremony itself I was kept quiet on bread and jam in the rooms of one of Alec's colleagues, later to be Rector of the English College when I became a seminarist there myself. When we had a private audience with Pope Pius XI, I howled with rage and horror at the black veil which my mother was obliged to wear. Apparently I quietened down sufficiently to be presented to the Holy Father and to be asked my age. (In later childhood I puzzled over this — why did he have to ask; didn't he already know, being infallible?)

I long believed I remembered these events, but I now realize that what I recall is really their repetition as part of family folklore. I first concluded this when I paid attention to the mental images in which the memories have come to be embodied: what is doing duty for the toy stall in the Campo dei Fiori is a Liverpool street market, and the scene over the black veil takes place, unaccountably, in a tram parked by the Liver Building.

My earliest real memory is of the family's departure from Sandhurst Street in 1935; and the most vivid part of the image is the smell of the horse which drew the removal van.

The move from the Sandhurst Street house was, we all thought, a move for the better. It was a small terraced house of red brick, with a flagged back yard, built in the 1890s. The new house, 40 Ryegate Road, was a mile or two further south from Liverpool centre, covered with the pebbledash then much affected by suburban builders, with lawns before and behind. Sociologists have remarked that if you ask Liverpool Catholics in what part of the city they live, the reply which comes most naturally to them is to name a Catholic parish. So, for us, the move was not so much a move from Aigburth to Grassendale, or from a working-class district to a lower-middle-class one, as from St Charles's parish to St Austin's parish. Ecclesiastically, the principal difference between the parishes was that while St Charles's was run by the normal diocesan ('secular') clergy, St Austin's was staffed by Benedictine monks on secondment from the great Abbey of Ampleforth. This meant a difference not only in details of the ritual used, and the vestments worn, but in the general ethos of the parish. 'Pax' was the Benedictine motto, and serenity rather than bustle was the keynote of the monks' ministry.

A year after the move to St Austin's I was sent to school — not to the parochial school, but to a fee-paying convent school called La Sagesse run by the French order of the Daughters of Wisdom. Like many convent schools, La Sagesse was primarily a girls' secondary school, but at the preparatory level took boys as well as girls. The polish which the sisters were believed to impart to their pupils was prized by Protestant as well as Catholic families; indeed my memory is that we Catholics were in a minority, and were segregated to receive full-blooded 'Religious Instruction' while the Protestant majority remained in the large classroom to listen to 'Bible Stories'. It must have been at La Sagesse that I first heard many of the New Testament episodes; my mental image of, for instance, the Agony in the Garden and the Kiss of Judas, however hard I try to alter it, is set in the playground of the convent. My most vivid recollection of the school is the smell of starch on wimples, and the prickliness of serge on the nuns' breastplates.

The major event of my two years at La Sagesse was my first Communion, on Corpus Christi day 1936, and my first confession in preparation for this. Weeks of preparation and coaching preceded the first visit to the confessional and the well-rehearsed words 'Bless me, father, for I have sinned. This is my first confession . . .' followed by a list of sins, classified, in theory, in accordance with the order of the ten commandments. Most lists no doubt resembled pretty closely my own 'I have been naughty in church and fought' (this would be against the first commandment), 'I have been disobedient to my mummy and cheeky to my teacher' (against the commandment which, according

to the Catholic count, is the fourth), and so on. The first confession
was a nervous affair; the first Communion far more festive, an
occasion for dressing up, for presents, and for jelly and
blancmange. To the child of a devout Catholic family, to be allowed
to receive the true body of our Lord Jesus Christ was an enormously
important thing; in the calendar by which a child measured his
progress towards adulthood it was the biggest event between one's
christening and one's twenty-first birthday.

In 1938 I was moved to the preparatory school of St Francis
Xavier's College run by the Jesuit fathers at Salisbury Street in
the middle of Liverpool. The five-mile journey into the city, which
involved two different tramcars, was quite an adventure for a seven-
year-old to undertake alone. In the preparatory school we saw little
of the Jesuits, of whom we were much in awe; we were taught
mainly by lay schoolmistresses. But twice a week we trooped into
the church of St Francis Xavier, once for Benediction and once
for confession. I later came to revere the church as the one where
Gerard Manley Hopkins used to preach; and recently I have
watched the efforts of preservation societies to save it from
demolition. But as a child I found it a cold, dark, frightening place;
very different from the small and welcoming church of St Austin
where the family went to Sunday Mass.

At S.F.X. I discovered that school work came easily; I was
usually first in class in the prep. school and my first report read
'Anthony is *very* promising and already has a University scholarship
in his pocket — if he keeps up his spirit of industry.'

My childhood had always been a solitary one, and became more
so after I moved to S.F.X. My classmates travelled in from afar,
as I did; we lived too far from each other to meet out of school
since few of our parents had cars. My grandmother would not allow
me to play in the streets with neighbouring children for fear, I
imagine, that I would be contaminated with non-Catholic
influences. Having no brothers and sisters I was dependent either
on the company of adults, or on my own solitary fantasies. In my
earlier years I had an imaginary companion named Honor Bonor.
All I now recall about him was that he came in useful when I
wanted to claim an extra sweet ration for him. Later I remember
re-enacting, usually in the cloakroom under the stairs, episodes
from the lives of Robin Hood and Captain Scott. I also had a
complete set of the Winnie the Pooh animals, and wrote plays in
which I impersonated each of them in turn. But most of my
childhood leisure was spent reading. I wallowed in Arthur Mee's

Children's Encyclopedia— all but the sections on the Bible, which I was warned off because Mee was not a Catholic.

Holidays were similarly solitary. Each year my grandmother spent a month at Ballaqueeney Hydro in Port St Mary, a small fishing village in the south of the Isle of Man. For some reason this holiday would always be taken in the month of June, and I was taken out of school to accompany her. Missing school was no problem, but there was a shortage of juvenile company when we got there. My earliest surviving letter, written to my mother in June 1937, complains, 'You talk about any children I know here. Well well I suppose you don't understand I am the only child here.' But Port St Mary was a pleasant place and I enjoyed exploring the rock pools and wandering along the craggy coastline. It was always a treat when my mother could join us for a week or so at the end of the holiday. We went to the Isle of Man every year until the war, when holidaymaking at Port St Mary ended abruptly and the hotels along its promenade were turned into internment camps for enemy aliens.

In the summer of 1938 there was an exceptional treat: a Continental holiday, or rather pilgrimage, to Lourdes. My grandmother, mother, uncle and I joined a group of ten to travel by boat-train to Paris and then drive across France towards the Pyrenees. I remember the two cars in which we travelled racing each other from point to point across the country in the style of Dornford Yates. At Lourdes we fulfilled the pilgrim's duties: visited the grotto where St Bernadette had her vision of the Virgin Mary, had ourselves dipped by burly *brancardiers* in baths full of the spring's miraculous waters, ascended the open-air Stations of the Cross on our knees, sweltered in the afternoon sun amid the rows and columns of stretchers at the Benediction for the sick, and marched in the torchlight procession singing the Lourdes *Ave Maria*. During the procession I was fascinated by the number of flies which plunged to their deaths in the cupped wax candles we held. We took the opportunity to visit the Spanish frontier, but we were halted at Irun since tourists were not allowed into the country where civil war was still raging.

Shortly after our return from Lourdes, I was given a book which affected my life for several years. It was the life of Guy de Fontgalland, by Mgr L. L. MacReavy. Guy de Fontgalland was a boy of a noble French family who had died of diphtheria at the age of twelve in 1930. He had been a very pious child who believed himself to be in constant conversation with the child Jesus. In particular, he believed that he had been told at his first Communion, and at Lourdes, that he was destined to die young; a secret which he passed on to his parents at the onset of diphtheria. His life was much read by Catholics, and his 'cause' was introduced in Rome: that is to say, he was proposed to the Vatican for beatification and canonization as a saint. Years later, I came to know one of the judges who decided such cases: he told me that it took no long time for the panel to decide that de Fontgalland's childhood piety did not amount to the heroic virtue of the saints. But at eight years old I found the book deeply impressive. I was particularly struck by passages such as the following:

> [Guy] used to ask people to listen if Jesus was in his heart. One day his mother said 'No, you've been too noisy! You've roused your baby brother with your trumpet. Little Jesus is gone from your heart.' Guy, crestfallen, hurled away his toy, and remained stock still for a moment or two. A tear glistened in his great blue eyes. Gone! Jesus, his Jesus whom he loved so much, his best and closest friend. Oh no! He must have come back . . . 'Yes, he is mama . . . Jesus is back in my heart. You don't hear him, no! But I — I feel him there.'

I soon convinced myself that I too could feel Jesus constantly in my heart, and could talk to him in interior dialogue. And I came to believe that by an extraordinary coincidence one of the things he had told me was that I too was to die young. I communicated this secret immediately to my mother.

The prospect of death did shortly come closer to all of us, in 1939. I had not long begun to take notice of events in the larger world. On 1 September 1939, my mother came home from work at lunchtime, in itself a sign that something had gone terribly wrong. I spread out on the floor the newspaper she brought, and lay on it, reading of the invasion of Poland.

Three days later we gathered round the wireless to listen to Chamberlain's declaration of war. We expected almost immediate bombardment, air raids, perhaps invasion. For weeks, all seemed strangely peaceful. But most schools in urban areas were evacuated into the country. The junior part of S.F.X. was removed to the small cathedral city of St Asaph in Wales. With two other boys from St Austin's parish I was billeted in a house called Trewyddon, on Mount Road, which belonged to a Colonel Watts, who lived in what appeared to me rather grand style. The Colonel had two living-in maids, whose quarters we three boys were to share. We ate well from the pies and puddings that were brought back from the dining room, and slept in a long and airy attic. The maids introduced us to detective stories and romances which our families would have thought unsuitable, and we listened with bated breath to not always fully understood backstairs gossip. Being away from home for the first prolonged period in our lives, we had to learn the art of letter writing:

> Dear Mummy,
> Can you buy me a Meccano boiler with ends please? Thank you very much for the parcel. We had a lovely walk to Tremerchion this morning. The Air Port looks grand set up with the Balloon Barrage. We have a holiday today. Leonard and Lily are going to marry, and Lily has false teeth. I don't think there's any more so goodbye.
> > Tony Kenny

Not only did Lily have false teeth; she had an operation scar which, after great oaths of secrecy, she exhibited to us boys in her bedroom: an exciting, and troubling, and long-remembered occasion of conspiracy. She also lent me Agatha Christie's *ABC Murders*, which reduced me, for the first time in my life, to sleepless terror one wet weekend.

Sad and homesick, we evacuees would walk down to the rivers Elwy and Clwyd, which bounded St Asaph, and gaze into their dark waters while counting the days until Christmas. Sometimes I was troubled by the thought that I was living in a Protestant household, and once I lamented to the local priest that I was not in a Catholic billet. However, when he showed me the cramped labourers' cottages which were the alternative, I decided I was well enough where I was. I tried to share with my classmates the fervour which I had acquired through meditating on the life of Guy de Fontgalland. Guy gave one an alibi for idleness in school; realizing, no doubt, the worthlessness of earthly endeavour he had been a daydreamer and an indifferent scholar. I wrote to my mother:

> I think my school motto is 'Fontgalland always in the moon' for Miss Horner often says 'Kenny, you're in the moon' or 'Kenny, you're dreaming . . .' Jeff (one of my housemates) and I have decided to be foreign missioners, and spend our time planning churches, inventing

aeroplanes to fly over in, or make holy storys to tell the [heathen]. Here is a plan for a church in africa or america or wherever I'm going.

But the sojourn in St Asaph cured me of the Fontgalland delusion. My companions were at first impressed, or pretended to be, when I related to them my daily conversations with Jesus, and indeed, they emulated my interior dialogues. Then one of them told me that the inner messages were merely the echoing voice of imagination. Shocked and wounded at first by this blasphemous suggestion, I gradually came to realize that it might, after all, be the truth.

The war brought my parents closer together. The submarine offensive against British shipping lanes made the life of a seaman like my father one of constant danger. British merchant ships were declared part of a 'Merchant Navy' and their officers were given naval rank, my father becoming a lieutenant commander. He and my mother came together to visit me in St Asaph; their letters of the period show that they were considering resuming life together. But they had not done so when, in December, I returned to Liverpool; brought home, like many other evacuees, because the inactivity of the phoney war made the separation of child from parent seem a pointless exercise.

At the end of October 1940 we were informed by Elders and Fyffe's that the *Sulaco* had been sunk, and that there were no more than one or two known survivors. 'Whilst there is no definite news regarding survivors from the vessel,' wrote the Superintendent Engineer on 1 November, 'there is still ground for hope that some of them may have been picked up by a passing steamer outward bound, and with no means of communication until reaching land, and personally I will cling to that hope until I am reluctantly bound to abandon it.' Like all families of missing persons we were not ever to receive any definite news of my father's death, only a succession of less and less optimistic letters at longer and longer intervals.

In late 1940 our own deaths seemed as if they might be very close. The German night raids which succeeded the Battle of Britain made life in Liverpool, as in many British cities, a precarious affair. My mother and I would sleep each night in the tiny cupboard where once I had been Robin Hood escaping from Guy de Gisborne. Nightly I prayed that I would live until Christmas, so that I would be able to discover what my presents were. Each new morning, on the way to school, one would find some landmark missing, or charred papers from some burnt office blown about the streets.

Parents disliked sending children into the city for the whole day, with the possibility that they might be caught by an air-raid warning and have to spend the evening at school in improvised shelters. So, for a period, school was reduced to a tutorial hour at midday, when one would hand in massive homework assignments and be given the next day's ration. My first attempts to master Latin declensions and conjugations were made in this way. On days when trams had ceased to run I recall reciting paradigms while picking my way on foot through the torn-up streets.

The second great air onslaught on Liverpool was in the spring of 1941. Several weeks of persistent raids were followed by a second evacuation: not of schoolchildren, this time, but of whole families. My family moved out to a lorry-driver's house in Roby Mill, a village near the seminary of Upholland where since returning from Rome my uncle Alec now taught. I attended the village school there for some months, a strange creature with more book-learning than most of the children, but ignorant of the simplest things about rural life; an urban alien with an absurd slipshod way of talking the language (never using 'thou'), and the strangest ideas about vocabulary (thinking, for instance, that 'moggy' meant a cat when everyone in Roby Mill knew it meant a mouse).

Each Monday morning the children were asked if they had been to Mass the day before; those who admitted to missing were upbraided and punished. I remember being rather shocked by this: at the other Catholic schools I had attended, the enforcement of Mass attendance had been thought to be a matter for parents, not teachers. Not that I was ever embarrassed by the question myself, for I had now begun to go to Mass not weekly but daily. Our billet was next door to a convent of Carmelites: nuns who lived their whole lives within a narrow enclosure, sealed off from contact with the outside world, and passing their days in prayer, contemplation and penance. I would rise at 6.30 to serve the chaplain's Mass: he and I and one or two villagers gathered in the chilly public chapel, the community heard but not seen on the other side of a spiked and curtained grille, squatting on an icy floor and accompanying the Mass in monotone. Occasionally I would speak through the grille to the sister sacristan, but I never saw her and passed things to her only through an elaborately sealed drawer of the kind now seen in high-security banks. I became expert at following the complications of the liturgy, proud of my new gold-edged Daily Missal with its four broad, coloured markers, one for the common parts of the Mass, one for the Mass proper to the day, one for the commemoration of any saint that might have been trumped by some superior feast, one for special prayers like the prayer for peace that had now become part of the daily routine.

My second evacuation, like my first, did not really take me out of any danger. The air bombardment ended at about the time we went to Roby Mill. After some weeks, we crept back to Liverpool, and then back again to another village near Roby Mill when bombing resumed. This time I attended the Catholic Grammar School at St Helen's, half an hour's trolley-bus ride away from our billet. It was not until the autumn of 1941 that I resumed normal schooling.

At St Francis Xavier's, now in the main school, I had a solid experience of Jesuit educational methods. Discipline was severe, but rigidly controlled. Corporal punishment was given on the hand with a special strap called the 'ferula'; the master who ordered the punishment was never allowed to administer it. Instead he must write the name, the offence, and the number of strokes on a white sheet of paper (a 'white bill') which the delinquent had to present, at the end of the school day, to an apprentice Jesuit ('scholastic'). There were also red bills, which acquired credit which could in theory wipe out the debit on white bills. But as red bills awarded for good academic performance (which I acquired quite often) were not allowed to count against white bills for disciplinary offences (which I acquired equally often) I found the system of little personal advantage.

In 1942 my grandmother died of cancer, after many months of illness at home. Her death meant much more to me than my father's; she had taken a much greater part in my life, and watching an invalid waste away at home was very different from learning by letter of a distant drowning. She was a woman of unusually upright and graceful carriage; she invariably wore, long after such things had gone out of fashion, a black neckband of watered silk, with long-drop amethyst earrings. When in charge of me she was very firm and stern; only when my mother was about would she relax, and would sometimes sing comic songs for me in quite a girlish way. She always scorned to take any shelter when air-raid warnings sounded but was eventually persuaded to pack an emergency bag. We discovered, at her death, that it contained just two things: a spare black neckband and a pair of white kid gloves.

My mother, for the last few years, had been librarian of the Liverpool branch of the Catholic Truth Society, but on my grandmother's death she felt obliged to give up her full-time job.

She took a post as school secretary to a convent school in Mount Pleasant, run by the sisters of Notre Dame, which gave shorter hours and longer holidays. We must, by this time, have been quite poor: my father was no longer there to pay my school fees, and my mother's salary was reduced with her hours. I remember it as a period when we ate very simple meals, but this may well have been the result of rationing as much as poverty. At all events it was a relief when in 1943 I won a scholarship from the Local Education Authority, even though its value was no more than six pounds a year. But I had by then decided that I wished to become a priest, and this meant that I should leave S.F.X. and go to the junior seminary of the Liverpool archdiocese, Upholland College.

Junior Seminary, 1943–9

No one, I imagine, was surprised when I announced at the age of twelve that I wanted to be a priest. The decision was, above all, in admiration of the uncle I had idolized since 1935. After a year of graduate studies at the Biblical Institute in Rome, Alec had been appointed to teach Scripture in the Liverpool seminary at Upholland, near Wigan. St Joseph's College was an ample, and in parts handsome, sandstone building in wide grounds with two lakes and an extensive farm and orchards. There were congregated all the candidates for the priesthood in the Liverpool archdiocese, youngsters from eleven to eighteen in the junior seminary, and adults studying philosophy and theology in the senior seminary. Alec was one of a staff of twenty priests who catered for about 200 boys and young men: as Scripture professor, his duties were mainly with the divines in the upper house. He lived in the College during term time, as did all the staff, and had one day off a week; he always spent it with us, and chose Saturday, so as to find my mother home from the library. During the vacations he lived with us all the time.

Alec was, throughout his life, the kind of person who takes children with the most complete seriousness. (For this reason, adults some-times thought him a little frivolous.) He entered into my games and fantasies more, it seemed to me, than such companions as I had of my own age. His visits were the climax of every week, and it was his company which really made the holidays worth looking forward to. When I was eleven he bought me a bicycle, and from then on for many years we spent much of the vacations cycling together in the Lancashire countryside (which at that time of petrol rationing was full of quiet motorless lanes). From time to time we went on longer expeditions to Wales or the Lake District; and the climax of my last holiday before going to the seminary was a cycling trip to Stratford and a week of nightly visits to the Memorial Theatre.

It was a visit from a great-aunt in the summer of 1943 which triggered my decision to become a priest. Elizabeth Whelan was an elderly, shrill, and pious lady who lived in a depressed village in Wales and, by her own account, more or less ran the Catholic parish there. She was never taken altogether seriously by any of our family, including myself; yet, for some reason which I have never understood then or since, it was her devout chatter during this visit which made me suddenly decide that I was called to be a priest. The authorities at the seminary were willing to accept me without the normal examination and interview, presumably on my school record and my uncle's recommendation. So in September 1943 I began to board at St Joseph's, where I was to remain for the next six years.

The junior seminary was divided into seven classes, which followed the normal course of grammar school education, leading through the Oxford and Cambridge Board School Certificate to the Higher Certificate (the examinations now replaced by 'O' and 'A' levels). The classes had names which went back to the days when recusant schoolboys were trained in Jesuit schools on the Continent: Underlow, Low Figures, High Figures, Grammar, Syntax, Poetry, and Rhetoric. Since I already knew some Latin and French I was admitted into Low Figures without passing through Underlow.

The three lower classes formed a division of the school called Lower Line; the other schoolboys were in Higher Line; and the students in the senior seminary, who wore cassocks and were students of philosophy or theology, constituted the Upper House. Any fraternization or conversation between members of one division and another was strictly forbidden and punishable by instant expulsion. The purpose of the rule, obvious to any adult but puzzling to an innocent twelve-year-old, was to prevent the formation of homosexual attachments. Conversation with the maids who did the cleaning was likewise visited with expulsion. The regime was an austere one, though physically perhaps no tougher than in other boarding schools in wartime. Most of the College rose at 6 a.m. and went to chapel at 6.30 for half an hour's meditation; the younger boys in Lower Line were allowed an extra half-hour's sleep and joined the community for Mass at seven each morning. Breakfast was at 7.45, followed by twenty minutes of compulsory fresh air. Study began at 8.35 after we had made our beds (each of us had a small wooden cubicle, open at the top, in a vast sixty-bed dormitory running across the vaulted top floor of the Lower Line wing). There were then classes until lunch, followed by organized games, soccer in winter and cricket in summer, with the alternative of walks in small groups around the grounds or in large supervised crocodiles through the Lancashire countryside. Tuesdays and Thursdays were half-holidays; on other days, including Saturdays, there were classes in the afternoon, and on all days, half-days or not, there was an hour and a half's study period from 5.30 to 7, after communal recitation of the rosary in the chapel. Between study and supper at 7.15 there was a period for silent reading of a work of devotion; after supper, recreation until night prayers in chapel at 9.15. From then until breakfast the following morning there was a rule of absolute silence, the *magnum silentium*, which was almost as strictly enforced as the rule against 'communicating'.

The food during my years at Upholland was Spartan, partly out of policy and partly because of wartime rationing. For breakfast there was tea and bread and butter and porridge, sometimes with milk and sometimes with syrup; for tea there was simply dry bread; for supper there was bread and butter with some small relish, cheese, or fish paste, or a sausage. The midday dinner was the one substantial meal, with a meat dish followed by various heavy puddings to which we gave dramatic names such as 'boiled baby' and — in all innocence — 'stiff Dick'. The midday and evening meals were eaten in silence while a book was read aloud from a high lectern: a chapter of the Gospel, or of the *Imitation of Christ*, followed by a secular book such as the memoirs of Maurice Baring or the history of Wingate's raiders.

Shortly after my arrival, there was a sudden stiffening of the regime. It was a regular rule that food parcels from home were not allowed, but the rule was not well kept; I recall that some contraband jam of mine, hidden in my football boots, gave itself away by fermenting and exploding in the bootroom. A few weeks after my arrival a dawn raid by the priest who was Prefect of Discipline revealed large quantities of illicit foodstuffs. The contraband was confiscated, our sweet rations (normally sold to us by the College once a month on 'buy-day') were stopped for the rest of the term, and supper was cut down to bread and a single pat of butter. The refectory reading was changed from *Three Men in a Boat*, which had been going down rather well, to an account of the sufferings and death of the Jesuit martyrs in Canada (which also became quite popular with the boys, once we reached the bloodthirsty bits).

Junior seminarists were allowed home only twice a year, for two
weeks at Christmas and eight in summer; during term-time there
were no exeats, or visits from parents, except in emergencies. Many
of us, in our first years, knew quite a lot of homesickness. I,
perhaps, had particular problems in adjusting to the long periods
of boarding, coming from a house in which I was the single child,
and combining intellectual precocity with an immature clumsiness
in relating to my own age group. I was, to begin with, cut off from
most of my peers in several ways. Entering the class in its second
year with two other boys, I found most relationships already formed
among the thirty or so who had started at the bottom. Most of
the candidates in the seminary were working-class boys. My own
antecedents gave me no reason to feel at any social distance, but
I found that my accent (which no doubt would have seemed very
provincial to someone from another part of England) was mocked
as snobbishly affected. I found I was unusual in having attended
fee-paying schools and in coming from a family where most of the
previous generation had received tertiary education. I was also
easily the worst of the class at organized games, the last to be picked
for any team. It did not help to endear me to my peers that I had
an uncle on the teaching staff. Alec, in a well-meant attempt to
temper the rigours of life away from home, would bring sweets
and cakes from home which he would feed me during my weekly
visits to his study. Some twenty years later, one of my school
companions of those days, hearing, as a priest, of my laicization,
said, 'Ah well, it's not surprising he came to a bad end: Alec has
been spoiling him ever since he was twelve years old.'

All such things considered, I received remarkably little bullying.
There was, indeed, less bullying at Upholland than in most other
schools I have heard or read about. Cold baths and beatings with
billiard cues were more often threatened than inflicted, and it was
comparatively rarely that we had to run a gauntlet of cold wet
towels flicked against our naked legs in the washrooms. Teasing
was commoner than bullying. A slab in the churchyard bore a worn
inscription beginning *'Beatae Ecclesiae'*, and older boys would tell
newcomers that this was the grave of Betty Eccles, a walled-up
nun who returned annually to haunt the dormitory. On 28 October
(known officially as Founder's Day, but unofficially as Betty Eccles
night) the High Figures boys would dress up in white sheets in an
attempt, usually quite ineffective, to terrify the Underlow boys.
During the war years some of the College playing fields were used
to graze cattle; these fields were surrounded with an electric wire

which gave off a pulsing shock every two seconds. Older boys would greet new arrivals by shaking their hands while grasping the wire with their own left hands behind their backs. The shock communicated to the victim was of course less than that received by the teaser; a convincing proof that, to the schoolboy, the positive value of inflicting pain is greater than the negative one of suffering it.

Year by year, particularly during later adolescence, a number of boys who had come to the seminary as children decided that they did not 'have a vocation to the priesthood'. Each year, too, one or two in a class were likely to be expelled, either for misconduct, or because they were clearly not going to reach the academic standard necessary for philosophical and theological studies. During parts of the war, seminarists were also conscripted for military service or for the mines, and when I arrived into a Low Figures of some thirty boys, there were only three in Rhetoric, the top class in the junior seminary.

The priests who taught us were mainly Cambridge graduates. Looking back, I realize we were educationally very privileged to be taught by highly qualified teachers in such small classes. The system must have been very expensive to the archdiocese: even though the priests on the staff received only a token payment (I think £60 p.a.) in addition to their keep, the institution was in effect providing free education, board, and lodging for ten boys at the bottom of the school for every one who would emerge, thirteen years after entry, as a priest. There was one year in which only one of the original entrants survived to the priesthood; it was calculated he had cost the diocese some £30,000 to produce. I heard the calculation being made when, two years after ordination, he left the priesthood without permission to marry the secretary of the Children of Mary in his parish.

There were two ways in which the academic studies differed from those in non-seminary schools. First, and most obviously, religious instruction played a larger part in the syllabus; secondly, the emphasis was on arts throughout the school, rather than on science, and within the arts an enormous weight was placed on Latin. For priests this was to be not only the language of prayer and liturgy, but also the medium of study and a means of international communication. The place in which we sat in class, ate at table, knelt in chapel, and qualified for any privileges was governed by our academic ranking, but it was our ranking in Latin, not in any other subject, that counted. The results of the termly examinations were announced publicly in the gymnasium which doubled as school hall: the ranks in each subject were read out by the headmaster in Latin. The members of each class would shuffle out to the front of the hall and line out in the order of the previous term's Latin examination, and the headmaster would begin, '*In prima classe literarum humaniorum, in Latinis, primus A.B., secundus, C.D.*' As one's name was called out one returned to one's seat; so that someone who went down in Latin in any given term was left alone and ashamed while his colleagues departed right and left.

Religious instruction took the form of commentary on the catechism, the cycle of questions and answers on Catholic doctrines with which we had been familiar from infancy. The textbook was a depressing manual entitled *Perry's Instructions*. Its detailed descriptions of the various ways in which one could fall into sin had the effect of inducing in quite a number of us, at the age of twelve or thirteen, a neurotic form of scrupulosity. Concern with sin no doubt forms a major part of any Christian education; what is peculiar to Catholic education is the attention paid to the distinction between mortal and venial sin. Mortal sin, according to Catholic teaching, is sin which is so serious that anyone who dies after committing it (unless they have repented and, in the normal course of events, confessed) will suffer the torments of Hell for all eternity. Venial sin, at worst, will condemn the soul not to Hell but to the pains of Purgatory, and since Purgatory, however painful, will have an end, while Hell lasts for ever, the difference between venial and mortal sin is of literally infinite importance for a Catholic believer. Sins were classified — principally for mnemonic purposes in confession — as being against one or other of the commandments. Sins against most of the commandments could be either mortal or venial; thus perjury would be a mortal sin against the second commandment ('Thou shalt not take the name of the Lord thy God in vain') while a casual swearword in the playground would be only a venial sin; against the seventh commandment ('Thou shalt not steal') a substantial theft would be a mortal sin, a minor theft would be venial — the boundary between the two was, if I remember rightly, fixed at a value of £2, but no doubt inflation will have altered that in the intervening years.

With sins against chastity, however, the case was very different. Any violation of the Catholic sexual code was, of its nature, a mortal sin; a sexual sin could be venial only if there was some lack of knowledge or consent involved. This meant that a voluntary dwelling on a sexual fantasy put one in danger of Hell if not promptly repented and confessed. It became an agonizing question whether one had, on a given occasion, 'consented' to the fantasy; and consent seemed such an ethereal, elusive event, difficult for even the most intrepid introspection to pin down for certainty.

It was the practice for all the boys to go to Communion at each day's Mass; we would line out in order, bench by bench. One could not receive Communion without sacrilege, however, if one was conscious of an unconfessed mortal sin, or if one had broken one's fast since the previous midnight. Was it breaking your fast if you swallowed some water while cleaning your teeth? Or if you discovered some undigested food in a cavity? Or if a hair got on your tongue? For the scrupulous, the climax of each day's anxious concern was the moment when it was one's turn to go to Communion. Could one be sure one had not broken one's fast, or that one was not in a state of unconfessed mortal sin? All too often the answer 'No' suggested itself; and one would stand back, red-faced, while one's colleagues pushed past one to the altar.

A victim of scruples would feel the need to confess his sins almost daily, and sometimes more than once in a day. Confession, never a pleasant duty, was made more difficult in the seminary because instead of reciting one's sins anonymously in a confessional, one had to pluck up courage to knock on the door of one of the priests on the teaching staff and kneel all too conspicuously beside his desk. It did not lessen the ordeal that the confessors whom I frequented at Upholland were all gentle and kindly men, anxious to soothe rather than terrify the sinner.

As a child, I had been puzzled by the catechism's denunciation of 'the irregular motions of the flesh'; with the onset of puberty, I became a little clearer about *what* it was that the sixth commandment existed to stop me doing. However, though there were frequent exhortations to purity, clear information about what sex was and what it was for played no part in the syllabus. (That is not quite correct: sex instruction was imparted, along with the relevant part of moral theology, to 23-year-old divines the year before their ordination. The subject was popularly known as 'blacks'.) Nor, for me, was it easy to learn much about sex at home (though my mother, some years later, was to write a sex instruction book for the use of the girls at the convent school of which she was secretary). I remained ignorant of the nature of human reproduction until I was about fifteen. Then, one day during the vacation, I confessed to my parish priest that I had sinned by reading a pious book on the Virgin Birth for an unworthy motive, namely to discover about birth and conception. The priest, a mild, unconventional and very erudite Benedictine, was not as shocked as I expected. He gave me a very thorough explanation of the mechanics of sex and reproduction in a concrete but unprurient manner. I was much luckier than several of my companions at Upholland who remained ignorant of sex until eighteen or later; I refused rather priggishly to share with them my own information on the topic, believing that sex instruction should be given by a parent or a priest.

Very soon after my arrival at the seminary I was chosen as a choirboy, to sing treble in the *schola* which led the singing at the weekly High Masses and Vespers and at the liturgical ceremonies of Christmas, Holy Week, and the other major feasts. I was surprised to be picked, since I had no musical ear and a very poor voice—indeed, at my earlier schools, when I had appeared on the stage in musical performances, I had been instructed to open and shut my mouth in time but on no account to let any sound out. I later learnt that when the choirmaster, Mgr J. F. Turner, who was also the Rector of the College, was choosing choirboys from the new students, my uncle said to him, 'Don't waste your time with Tony; he hasn't a note in his head.' Mgr Turner, a man of great strength of purpose, had a conviction that there was nobody who could not be taught to sing perfectly, and he saw this as an opportunity to test his belief on an ideally unpromising subject. So I became the unwilling recipient of a great deal of individual musical tuition, but during my three years in the *schola* I did little to provide evidence in favour of his theory. But I did acquire a love for the church music I was so indifferently rendering.

In most weeks of the year the choir's performances were restricted to Sundays at High Mass and Vespers; the liturgy was sung almost entirely in plainsong and polyphony was allowed only for the offertory motet. I never came to enjoy the elaborate melismatic chants of the graduals; but after a while I came to revel in singing some of the simpler and finer pieces of chant, especially hymns such as the *Te Deum, Vexilla Regis, Pange Lingua* and some of the masterpieces of the great feasts, such as the Christmas invitatory *Christus Natus Est*, the *Gloria Laus* of Palm Sunday, the *Ubi Caritas* from the washing of the feet on Maundy Thursday, the Reproaches of Good Friday and the sequence *Victimae Paschali Laudes* on Easter Sunday.

The offices of Holy Week and of Christmas were the climax of the year at Upholland. The Christmas office lasted from 10 p.m. on Christmas Eve until about 2 a.m.: first the Christmas Matins (nine psalms, lessons and antiphons), then the Midnight Mass, and immediately afterwards the Christmas Lauds (five psalms, a hymn and a canticle). Members of monastic orders rise in the middle of each night to sing Matins and Lauds; for us the liturgy was especially solemn because it was the only day in the year on which we sang the night offices. The psalms had been selected many centuries ago to express the spirit of the feast: psalms glorifying the Davidic kingdom and voicing the hope of a Messiah. My favourite was, and remains, the eighty-eighth psalm in which the psalmist from exile reproaches God for failing to fulfil his promises to the Davidic kingship; a lament turned into triumph by the Christmas antiphon, which sees the fulfilment of the promises in the birth of Christ. From one year's end to another I would look forward to this office with as much ardour as to the turkey and Christmas pudding and the presents and pantomime.

But for overall dramatic effect the Christmas office was far outdone by the ceremonies of Holy Week. The entire week before Easter Sunday was given over to religious observances. On Palm Sunday we re-enacted in the procession of psalms the welcome of the children of Israel to Christ entering Jerusalem; we sang the Byrd and Vittoria settings of the texts and carried in our hands palms and olives (or wartime substitutes like pussy willows). There followed the Mass of which the most solemn moment was the singing of St Matthew's Passion. The Gospel text was divided among three deacons in the sanctuary, representing the evangelist, Christ, and the 'synagogue'; we choristers sang, to Vittoria settings, the crowd parts, the *turbarum voces*. In the evening, after Vespers, we went into three days of retreat.

In retreat periods—there were two a year, the other being at the beginning of the academic year in September—all conversation was forbidden, and strict silence had to be kept. Every hour or so there was some pious exercise: a sermon, a meditation, the recitation of some traditional prayer such as the rosary or the Stations of the Cross. A retreat, we would be told, was a time of spiritual stocktaking: we should examine ourselves and see how far we had progressed or fallen behind during the preceding six months.

Retreat ended on the morning of Maundy Thursday. On the Wednesday, Thursday and Friday of Holy Week we sang Matins

and Lauds for the following day, an office popularly known as
'Tenebrae'. A fifteen-branched candlestick was lit at the beginning
of the office; as each of the nine psalms of Matins and the five
psalms of Lauds ended, one of the candles was extinguished. The
final candle was taken behind the altar at the end of the office and
when it was extinguished the church was kept in total darkness,
and all those in church banged their books on the benches for a
few moments to symbolize the rending of the temple veil at the
death of Christ. It was a slightly risky piece of symbolism; if
anything went wrong, it could turn out silly and comic; if all went
well, the dying echo of the *strepitus* followed by silence and total
darkness could strike a note of poignant desolation.

On Maundy Thursday the day began with the solemn Mass in
memory of the Last Supper, at the end of which the Blessed
Sacrament was carried to an altar specially decorated with candles
and flowers in a separate chapel ('the altar of repose'); a rota of
volunteers kept watch on prie-dieux in front of it for the next thirty-
six hours. Some years there was also an extra ceremony at which
the Archbishop of Liverpool would bless, for the coming year, the
sacred oils which are used to anoint babies at christening, priests
at their ordination, and the dying in the sacrament of extreme
unction. He brought with him a great train of clergy: seven pairs
of priests, for instance, would process up to the vat of oil, kneel
and then sing in succession *'Ave Sanctum Oleum'* to it; then the same
with the chrism, singing *'Ave Sanctum Chrisma'*. Privately I thought
the ceremony tedious and overloaded; I wondered if it didn't smack
of the idolatrous.

Good Friday was the one day in the year when the Mass, the
sacramental re-enactment of Christ's passion, was omitted. Instead,
there was held a unique ceremony called the 'Mass of the
Presanctified': after the *St John Passion* and the ancient custom of
'Creeping to the Cross' the celebrant received Communion from
the host which had been consecrated on the previous day, brought
in procession from the decorated altar where they had remained
overnight. At Tenebrae on Good Friday, despite the dismal
trappings, the psalms and antiphons made continual reference
to the conquest of death, 'as if,' I wrote one year just after
the ceremony, 'they couldn't keep the secret of the Resurrection
any longer.'

The Resurrection was, in fact, celebrated on the morning of
Holy Saturday. We rose early in the morning to bless the new
fire, to sing a dozen 'prophecies' from the Old Testament, and

to bless the paschal candle with the triumphant chant *'Exultet'*, a cento of quotations from Augustine and other ancient authors. At the *Gloria in Excelsis* of the Holy Saturday Mass, the bells, which had been silent for the last three days, were all rung out, large bells in the tower and tiny bells in the hands of the altar boys; the organ sounded for the first time since the beginning of Lent; and the black and purple vestments gave place to white and gold. After this moment of exultation, the official Easter High Mass on the following day, Easter Sunday, often seemed something of an anti-climax.

At Upholland, the Holy Week ceremonies were performed with great precision; we rehearsed carefully not only for the music but for the liturgical movement around the altar and up and down the processional cloisters. The rites were set in a graceful and airy church built in the Decorated style by one of the Scott dynasty. Later, when I had the choice of all the churches in Rome to attend the Holy Week services, I could never find one where they were enacted with such dignity.

Unlike the great ceremonies, the prayers of the daily seminary routine were often just a necessary chore to be got through. From Grammar onwards, each day began with half an hour of meditation: we would read a book, very slowly, and think over its content; or we would reconstruct in imagination an event from the life of Christ and seek to draw a moral for our own lives. Meditation was often painful and sleepy; the half-hour would drag out, and the sound of the Angelus bell at its end was a great relief. The daily Mass which followed was for most of us much more appealing, with its careful balance between parts common to each day and prayers for particular feasts and seasons.

For me, throughout the whole of my Catholic life, the most difficult form of prayer was the Rosary. This prayer consisted of fifteen repetitions of a cycle of prayers, each cycle or 'decade' consisting of one Lord's Prayer, ten Hail Marys and one *Gloria Patri*. One passed the beads through one's hand to count the prayers, and during each decade one was supposed to meditate on one of fifteen 'mysteries' of the lives of Jesus and Mary, beginning with the Annunciation by Gabriel and concluding with the Crowning of our Lady in Heaven. Even in my most pious periods I found this monotonous and irritatingly distracting.

I did indeed have pious moods when I would add many devotions to those prescribed by the College rules, rising early in the morning to perform the Stations of the Cross before meditation, giving up

recreation in the evening to recite the Little Office of the Blessed
Virgin. But these rarely lasted for very long, and by the high
standards of the seminary I was not a particularly devout person,
observing in general the obligatory minimum and not over-
scrupulous about keeping the College rules.

I do not know when I first began to be conscious of any doubts
about Catholic teaching. I find an entry in my diary for May 1947:
'All the old troubles — scruples, doubts against Faith etc — have
cropped up again.' The substance of the doubts was not, I think,
anything metaphysical about the existence of God or the reality
of the sacramental system; I was afflicted at this time rather with
doubts of a Protestant kind, partly inspired by the reading of
Macaulay. I wondered whether the pomp and deference shown
to the Catholic hierarchy was really compatible with the bishops
being the successors of the Apostles who led such simple lives. The
Archbishop of Liverpool at that time, Archbishop Downey, was
a man whose aspect was calculated to inflame rather than calm
such doubts. He was small, round, and pompous, and looked as
if he lived rather well. (Some years later he died, leaving in his
will, to the great scandal of the faithful, the then enormous sum
of £63,000.) He visited the College on great occasions, such as
the feast of the solemnity of St Joseph; and I was always
uncomfortable at the amount of deference which the liturgy called
for. A diary entry for one such solemnity shows distaste struggling
with respect:

> At 6.30 there were Pontifical first Vespers of St Joseph. The ceremony
> went off quite well. I wouldn't like to take a Protestant to see it, though,
> because the Archbishop looks rather ridiculous when gasping for
> breath. I feel very sorry for him; I'm sure he does more work than
> other men of his age; it's a pity that he's so fat. He has quite a dignity,
> though, and is extremely patient while they're dressing him, though
> I must admit I laughed at one or two of the things he did and the
> expressions on his face.

I have written at length about the Christmas and Passiontide
liturgies because when I look back their memory remains the most
vivid of those I have retained from the years at Upholland. No
ceremonies, sacred or secular, which I have ever witnessed since,
no theatrical or operatic performances however magnificent or
sophisticated, have ever compared in dramatic impact with the
re-enactment of the last week of Christ's life. This remains true
when I look back on those ceremonies from a secular and agnostic

standpoint; at the time, of course, we believed that we were not merely playing a part in a pageant of great antiquity and beauty, but mystically making present, in a way which we did not claim fully to understand, the redeeming events which restored mankind to divine grace and favour.

Beside the solemn and sacred drama of the liturgy, we took considerable pains at Upholland over more profane performances. The College hall could be turned into a theatre with a very well-equipped stage. Each term there was a major dramatic production; once a year a performance of a Gilbert and Sullivan opera; and at Christmas a home-made pantomime packed with topical songs and insider jokes. In this we were no different from any other school except that we were not allowed to represent women on the stage so that all female parts had to be written out, and the plots adapted to exclude all love interest. This produced some striking alterations to the Gilbert and Sullivan repertoire; the maids from school in *The Mikado*, I recall, were converted into a football team, and to the tune of 'Braid the raven hair' the chorus sang 'Bind the ankle round'. In *The Pirates of Penzance* Major-General Stanley's daughters became his nephews, a rather priggish group of midshipmen whom the pirates were bent on enslaving; and while his brothers sang 'How beautifully blue the sky' Fabian (*né* Mabel) sang:

> *Did ever hero quail before the night of duty*
> *But saw its daylight break in all-exceeding beauty?*
> *Did ever knighthood draw the sword for all uprightness*
> *That did not sheathe its blade new-forged with nobler*
>   *brightness?*

For some years I was more familiar with the bowdlerized versions than with Gilbert's libretti.

My own part in Upholland dramatics was mainly restricted to operating the lighting; I had a keen interest in electricity and wireless, building a dozen or so radios, half of which worked. On one occasion, however, near the end of my course, I produced a performance of *Trial by Jury*; I managed to convince the authorities that there was no way in which this could be rewritten without female parts and without any reference to breach of promise and so, for the only time during my years there, female impersonation was permitted.

It will have already become obvious that at Upholland we were a very inward-looking community: we knew little of what was happening in the outside world, and most of it had no effect on our lives at all. We were not allowed newspapers or radios — even when I built a radio myself I was not supposed to listen to programmes on it. Naturally, during the war years we were anxious to know how the war was going, and at the beginning of a class we would ask the teacher, and often be told, what the latest war news was.

The war affected us, of course, in some ways. At crucial seasons of the agricultural year we worked a day a week on the College farms to replace labourers who had been conscripted. These days were generally popular as a change from school routine, but in themselves could range from the almost wholly delightful (haymaking) to the backbreakingly awful (lifting mangel wurzels). Also, there was food rationing, and we youngsters were, at first, more conscious of sweet rationing than of anything else. We were allowed to buy our month's ration on a single day of the month, and for most of us it would not last more than a day or two. The ration was usually sold to us on a feast day; one year the tuckshop was not opened on Holy Saturday, as usual, because we were due to broadcast Easter Sunday Vespers on the B.B.C. and the choirmaster was afraid we would all eat our voices away.

It was bread rationing, not imposed until after the war, which really affected us, since bread was the central staple of our diet. The breadboard at the centre of the table was guarded by a special carver; since, during reading, we were not allowed to speak, we had a system of hand signals to ask for bread to be cut: four fingers extended for a whole round, two for a half, one for a quarter. Consequently, a round of bread was known as 'a four'; and I can recall the glum faces in winter 1945 as the news was passed round, 'They're going to ration us to four fours a day.'

We must have had some celebrations in College to celebrate VE-day, but I can hardly recall them. VJ-day, the final end of the war with the surrender of Japan, occurred during the vacation; I was on holiday in Ambleside with Alec and another priest but any jubilation was quenched by the way in which it had been brought about. Brought up in the just war tradition, Alec and his friend could not see the slaughter at Hiroshima and Nagasaki as anything but a violation of the prohibition on the deliberate killing of non-combatants.

The General Election of 1945 remains clearly in my memory. At breakfast the Rector came into the refectory and announced that those who were old enough would be allowed to leave the

College to cast their vote in the Ormskirk constituency. 'You may vote for anyone you like,' he said, 'but the Pope has ruled that no one may vote Socialist.' 'Does that mean,' incredulous students asked him, 'that we can't vote for the Labour Party?' 'I don't know what the Pope *means*', he said, 'I've told you what the Pope *said*.' With or without the votes of the Upholland students the Labour candidate was elected in Ormskirk: his name was Harold Wilson.

I was too young to have a vote; if I had had one, it would be unlikely to have been cast for Labour. My mother's family had been keenly Conservative ever since coming from Ireland, and my mother was at this time working in the Liverpool Exchange ward in the Conservative candidate's interest. It was not for some years yet that I thought of questioning my family's political judgement: it was also to be a dozen years before I was to be in Britain again on an election day.

The isolation of Upholland from the outside world was extreme even among seminaries: this was largely due to the character of its Rector. He was the most upright man I have ever known, totally undeflected by fear or favour, pain or pleasure, vanity or human respect from pursuit of the good as he perceived it. He was a Cambridge graduate with a deep love of the classics and of music; but both passions were rigidly integrated into his ideal of the priestly life. A seminary, he believed, should be an 'enclosed garden'; Upholland provided all that was necessary for boys to grow up in learning, virtue, and piety, and the concerns of the outside world could only be a distraction. One year he carried our insulation to the length of refusing to allow the College to adopt daylight saving time; he simply moved our entire timetable one hour backward on the day on which the Government had told us to put our clocks one hour forward.

Many times in my life I have started to keep a diary; never have I succeeded in doing so for more than two consecutive months. One of my most prolonged efforts began on my sixteenth birthday, when I was in the middle of the class of Syntax, having completed School Certificate in the previous year. I had just discovered the poetry of G. M. Hopkins. He was the first poet I had ever come to appreciate. The Catholic sacramental themes of his major poems had an obvious interest for a seminarist, and I was just beginning to wake up to the kinds of natural beauty which he describes with incomparable art. I found that my own life had been lived in the same physical as well as spiritual surroundings: Stonyhurst, where Hopkins made his noviciate, was in a nearby part of Lancashire;

at St Francis Xavier's in Liverpool where he had been a curate
I had been a schoolboy; St Asaph, whither I had been evacuated,
was in the heart of the Valley of the Elwy where he had written
some of his best-known verses.

The diary which I started in March 1947, then, was begun in
conscious imitation of Hopkins' early notebooks and papers. It
was not at all a successful imitation. The descriptions of natural
phenomena, such as the budding of the chestnut trees, are
unoriginal and leaden. The religious remarks exhibit an em-
barrassingly self-conscious piety; so do the draft poems, most of
them very obviously derivative. One of the most elaborate
described Christ's last look from the Cross before dying, surveying
the parts of his own body and the different sections of the crowd
at the gibbet's foot:

> . . . *He saw his mother, she who had flesh'd him, rear'd him,*
> *Suffered sorrow's sword in her heart for man's sin . . .*
>
>   . . . *He saw and read*
> *The hearts of all the crowd; their mocking tongues at rest*
> *Hush'd into sullen silence at God's death . . .*

Various syllables were given stress marks to show that the poem
was in sprung rhythm.

The principal secular concerns of the diary were the rehearsal
and management of the lighting for a performance of *I Killed
the Count*, and the planning and arrangement of a summer
holiday in Stratford with one of my companions from Syntax.
Much of the book consists of reviews of the books I was
reading during recreation: a Batsford book on English church
craftsmanship; *Richard III*; Ruskin on the deteriorative power
of conventional art (which I argued bitterly against for three
pages); *Caesar and Cleopatra*; Guedalla's *The Duke*; Jerome's
Three Men in a Boat; Pevsner's *European Architecture*; Leacock's *Short
Circuits*; Sitwell's *English Architects and Craftsmen*; and Chesterton's
Everlasting Man. The latter alternately fascinated and infuriated me:
'GK,' I wrote angrily, 'will go to the end of the world to be able
to make a statement like this: "Peter Pan belongs to the world
of Peter rather than the world of Pan".' But my favourite that
spring was F. J. Sheed's *Theology and Sanity*. An entry in my diary
for 13 April 1947 suggests that I had begun to take an interest
in philosophy as well as theology:

At present everything is in a rather shadowy state and I feel quite insane owing to having had several arguments on existence. I have almost been convinced that everything else is a mere figment of my imagination. Makes you feel quite queer.

As the reading list shows, I had a strong curiosity about architecture, particularly ecclesiastical architecture, at this time. I was a passionate Goth, and had the contempt for post-Renaissance architecture of a Gilbert Scott or a Banister Fletcher. One April Tuesday I tried to define the reasons:

> Externally, rustication makes a house look gloomy, vulgar and dull. The classical orders are ugly in themselves, especially if fluted, and get terribly monotonous if repeated; they have not the variety of Gothic caps. The whole effect is heavy, dark and sombre, instead of light and airy like Gothic buildings . . .

The hatred was almost entirely at second hand; I had seen hardly any of the masterpieces of Renaissance or Baroque building except in photographs. Still, I was better informed about architecture than about painting. The only history of painting which I possessed had lost half its illustrations; the nudes had been cut out by the Prefect of Studies, who censored all books coming into the College.

My six years at Upholland fell into two distinct parts: the first three years when I was often bored, miserable, and homesick, a victim of depression and scruples; and the three years beginning with Syntax in which I was generally cheerful and happy. One reason for the change was that I began to be more at home with my classmates. Those whom I regarded as persecutors gradually left, having come to believe, or having been told, that they had no vocation to the priesthood. I became less awkward in relating to my peers and less dependent on adult support. I made a number of very good friends, and when, in the final year of Rhetoric, the time came for one of our year to be chosen Censor of Higher Line (the equivalent of Head Boy) I was elected. This was not necessarily a sign of popularity — what was needed was someone who was good at handling the beaks — but at least meant I was no longer seen as an outlandish freak.

Equally important, from Syntax onwards I began to enjoy literature, and especially classical literature. I had now acquired enough Latin and Greek to be able to read the works of classical authors as books, without losing track of the story in the constant reference to Smith's dictionary or Liddell and Scott. The first classics

I enjoyed were the third book of Xenophon's *Hellenica* and the fifth book of the *Aeneid*. I followed the Greek campaigns with fascination, marking the positions of armies and navies with flags as I had earlier marked the position of Russian and German armies in the Second World War; I placed bets on the candidates in the games described by Vergil. The long evening periods in the study hall under the new blue neon lights became something to look forward to rather than to dread. My Syntax diary is full of reviews of the classical works we were reading, as well as of the English books I chose myself: I was bored by the end of Aeschylus' *Persae*, and found I needed to use the crib ('cog' was our word) too much; but I preferred it to Euripides' *Hecuba*. More interesting than either was Plato's *Apology*, or the Latin book we were reading concurrently, the first book of Horace's *Odes*.

There were eleven of us remaining in Syntax at the end of the year. The academically more gifted were put into Group I and prepared to take the Latin and Greek and Ancient History options; they were no longer taught in classes (except for subsidiary subjects) but were left almost entirely to work alone, apart from weekly composition tutorials in Greek and Latin prose. Each student was encouraged to draw up his own reading list in Greek and Latin literature, and once it had been approved by the tutor, he was on his honour not to make undue use of the crib. All he had to do was to make notes on his reading and in due course discuss it in a tutorial. During most of the day, the Group I students had the vast study hall to themselves, reading unsupervised. It was a most enlightened and humane method of instruction.

As I had hitherto always been first in the termly examinations, I was not surprised to be promoted to Group I. Examination standards now became higher. The annual examination results were printed each year; everyone's grade ('H' for 75% or over, '1' for 60%, '2' for 45%, 'P' for 33%) was recorded and the printed results were circulated to the parents of all boys. Hitherto, I had had an unbroken record of Hs. In Group I the honours mark was raised to 90%, and I began to get 1s as well as Hs; and when the Certificate examinations came, I failed to get a distinction in Greek to match the distinctions in Latin and Ancient History.

The writing of Greek prose had always been a drudgery for me, and in Latin prose too I never achieved elegance. But the liberty to range over the whole of classical literature which Group I conferred was an unmixed delight. During the years of Poetry and Rhetoric I read in Greek all of Homer, Herodotus, Thucydides,

Aeschylus, Sophocles and Euripides, and in Latin all of Vergil, Horace, Tacitus, and a fair amount of Cicero and Livy. I did not realize at the time that the Upholland system enabled one to get through almost as much reading as a university course; and I have never since been as well-read, in the sense of retaining so much literature in my head at the same time.

Homer (the *Odyssey*, not the *Iliad*) was my favourite Greek reading; of the prose writers I liked Plato best, and was particularly fascinated by the *Phaedo*. Thucydides I found hard going, and Pindar impossibly difficult; Sophocles was my favourite tragedian, and I was glad that the *Oedipus Rex* was one of our set books. Among the Latins I enjoyed the patriotic parts of Vergil and Horace. Livy was slow to plough through, the narrative always interrupted with tedious speeches; Cicero was a pompous windbag, except when writing letters, and my favourite prose author was Tacitus. I would memorize and recite some of his setpieces, especially the exordium to the *Histories* which concludes that the moral of history is that the gods care nothing for our peace but only for our punishment . . . *non esse curae deis securitatem nostram, esse ultionem*.

Apart from academic delights, promotion to Poetry brought with it certain disciplinary freedoms. Instead of having to go for walks in long supervised crocodiles, Poets were allowed to go for walks in threes. We valued this privilege particularly for the opportunity it gave for supplementing College food. On a walk of eight miles or more we were allowed to take refreshment; so we would walk the long roads to St Helen's, or Chorley, or Ashton-in-Makerfield for the pleasure of tucking in to a high tea of fish or sausage and chips.

In the final year, Rhetoric, we had some duties as prefects, though not as much as in most schools, since selected divines from the Upper House had the responsibility of disciplining the schoolboys, under a priest who was Prefect of Discipline. In addition to the Censor's duties of representing the students to the authorities, I had to ring the handbell summoning everyone to each of their daily duties and to ring the bell in the chapel tower thrice daily for the Angelus. For one of my light weight this was not a trivial task; if one muffed one's preparatory back-swing one would be carried up with the rope, and the bell would make an extra muffled clang which would echo round the quadrangles to put one to public shame.

After the Higher Certificate examinations which ended Rhetoric, most of the students expected to move into the Upper House, where they would wear the cassock and start their six years of professional studies in philosophy and theology. But from time to time some were selected for higher studies elsewhere, in particular at the Gregorian University in Rome. In some years the selection of students for Rome was made by a national scholarship, in which students from the half-dozen local English seminaries would compete. In our year, 1949, there was no Roman scholarship, but from early in the year there were rumours that some of us were to be sent to Rome. In the end, two of the three of us who sat Group I together were told that we were to do our professional studies in Rome, and the third was sent to the English College in Valladolid.

This was very exciting news. It meant a chance to see at close hand the ruins of the Rome we had spent so much of the last three years reading about. It meant that we would see the Pope and the major shrines of the Catholic Church. For me it meant above all that I would go to the English College where Alec had been trained and which, throughout his life, he remained convinced was the best college in the world.

– III –

The Gregorian University, 1949–52

My companion and I journeyed to Rome at the end of September 1949. We travelled by slow stages, staying in Paris and Venice, dutifully admiring the Victory of Samothrace and the mosaics of San Marco. The arrival in Rome itself was something of a shock. It was clear that however exciting the Eternal City, life would be more constricted and less comfortable than it would have been in the Upper House at Upholland. St Joseph's had been surrounded by playing fields, lakes, orchards and woods; the English College in the Via Monserrato was a cramped, decaying palazzo backing on to an area which one with no eye for the picturesque would have called a slum. The ground floor and *piano nobile* of the College provided the staff with an environment of mild grandeur; but the upper floors where the students lived were seedy warrens of ill-shaped rooms, sparsely equipped with gimcrack furniture and peeling enamelware. I rushed out to buy some pictures to cover the worst patches and cracks on my walls: a Raphael madonna, and Botticelli's *Birth of Venus* (the head of Venus only). I comforted myself that from the window, above the terrace laundry-lines and cats' alleys of the Via dei Capellari, there could just be seen the top storey of the Palazzo Cancellaria. The food, cooked by Italian nuns, was to the initiate more appetizing than that at Upholland; but for the first few months I found it hard to cope with the quantities of pasta, and I would give away to my neighbour the little third-of-a-litre carafes of Marino wine which were provided with each of the two main meals of the day.

Of course, there was the city of Rome to explore; but at first there was little time or freedom to do so. We were allowed to leave the College only in *cameratas* of four, and on an ordinary weekday for just over an hour. St Peter's was just within brief walking distance; but when first taken there I decided that it was a cold, oppressive, vulgar, unchristian building, and I did not much care whether I saw it again.

43

It was not easy, at first, to walk abroad in a cassock without self-consciousness. Roman cassocks, being meant for outdoor as well as indoor use, were several inches shorter than their English counterparts, so that they would not collect mud and dust. To go out, one put on over one's cassock (or *sottana*) a sleeveless black cloak (or *soprana*) with slender tails hanging from the shoulders, and a round beaver hat covered with fur, which dandies could polish to a fine domed shine, but which if neglected (as it usually was by me) took on a resemblance to a birds' nest. Beneath the cassock we wore white canvas underpants (*mutande*, usually abbreviated as *'tande*) specially designed by the nuns who supervised the domestic arrangements of the College (and therefore known as '*madre 'tande*'). Later, I would cheerfully sing, as a verse of one of our innumerable mountaineering songs:

> *We climbed the Corno Grande*
> *In a pair of* madre *'tande*
> *While the boys were drinking grappa*
> *In the valley down below*

But to begin with I found the wearing of bare legs beneath a cassock very uncomfortable; I never was able to bring myself to put on *madre 'tande*, and wore instead white tennis shorts.

The University term left little opportunity for sightseeing, except on Thursdays which were a whole-day holiday. The general routine was not unlike that at Upholland. We rose at 5.25, but this was not a great hardship in the Mediterranean climate, and during the summer months there was an official daily siesta of an hour and a half. Meditation and Mass were over by 7.15, and at 8.10 we would take the fifteen-minute walk to the University for four lectures at half past each hour. After lunch, followed by siesta in season, the rest of the day until supper was spent in private study except for the daily walk. Lights out was at ten, and the *magnum silentium* was observed as at Upholland.

The University course at the Gregorian lasted seven years: three years leading to a licentiate in philosophy followed by four years leading to a licentiate in theology. This was a year longer than the course would have been at Upholland: a disadvantage to be weighed against the attractions of Rome, since it meant that ordination to the priesthood was likely to be postponed by up to a year. Moreover, we soon discovered that after the enlightened academic freedom of our last years at Upholland we were now to be subjected to a narrow and rigid regime.

Instruction at the Gregorian was in Latin lectures delivered through a microphone to classes of hundreds of students packed into tiered benches. We sat, like delegates at the United Nations, in national or regional groups. Students from some of the colleges were marked out by the distinctive colour of their cassocks: the Scots, for instance, wore violet; and the students of the Germanicum-Hungaricum were resplendent in red. There was an official order of seating, based on the antiquity of the different colleges; we English, notwithstanding, always grabbed the seats nearest the windows, in the chauvinistic belief that other nations did not appreciate the virtues of ventilation. All lectures were compulsory, and checks were made by the University bedels to see that all were present and correct. But many of us for a long time, and all of us for some time, found the Latin of the lectures incomprehensible. It was quite common to see students, like jurors at the Pétain trial, or delegates at a dull political conference, whiling away the time by openly reading newspapers, or playing 'battleships' with their neighbours. The course information could be made up by buying, from more diligent students, cyclostyled copies of the notes they had taken.

The textbooks and lectures followed a common, well-defined form. The material was divided not into chapters but into theses. A theological or philosophical doctrine would be stated—as, for instance, the seventh thesis in our psychology course stated that the powers or faculties of the soul were really distinct from the essence of the soul. The terms of the thesis were then explained: what was a power, what a faculty, what an essence, what was it for two things to be really distinct. This was giving the *status questionis*, the state of the question. Then were listed the adversaries of the thesis: namely, in this case, the pantheists, the nominalists, the Scotists, and (I quote) 'the moderns in general, namely Descartes, Locke, Leibniz and Gerdil'. The supporters of the thesis might also be cited: here Aristotle, Albert the Great, St Thomas and Suarez were enlisted in favour. After this the thesis was proved by a lengthy syllogism, objections were answered by syllogistic distinctions, and supplementary points were treated in appendices called *scholia*.

The examinations at the end of the year corresponded to this method of presentation. The principal examinations were oral, conducted, like the textbooks and lectures, in Latin. The candidate

faced the examiners across a green baize tablecloth on which lay a
list of theses. The examiner would point to the thesis list: take thesis
number fourteen, he would say. Then the candidate had to explain
the terms of the thesis, list its adversaries, prove it by syllogism and
be prepared to answer objections. Marks were out of ten: six was a
pass, nine *cum laude*, and ten *summa cum laude*. More discreetly than
at Upholland, marks were mailed confidentially to the Rector of each
college and then communicated to the candidate alone.

The Latin spoken by most examinees was halting and incorrect;
that of the lecturers and examiners was fluent but far from classical.
The accent of an Englishman, an American, a Spaniard, a
Frenchman and a German differed so much from each other that
it took some time to realize that the lecturers were not all speaking
different languages. Lecturers did not scruple to translate the idioms
of their own tongue literally into Latin, leaving foreigners to make
what they could of them. Thus a Frenchman would speak of a
far-fetched interpretation of a Scripture text as being *'ad usum
delphini'*, while an American would drawl *'haec theoria non tenet
aquam'*. When dealing with matters of contemporary science,
lecturers would struggle valiantly with the Latin of antiquity: thus,
discussing the 'complementarity' of particles and waves in quantum
theory, our textbook said:

> *Inter duo photona numquam datur collisio, nec aliquid simile collisioni; si sese
> tangunt in suo motu, possunt sese penetrare; sunt sine interactione, ad tempus
> potest adesse 'superpositio'. Interactio inter corpusculum et photon (effectus
> Compton) describi et calculari potest ut collisio, sed ideo nondum* est *collisio;
> simili modo functio adhibetur in calculo ut functio coordinatarum in spatio 3n
> dimensionum, sed non ideo id est realiter; et ita saepissime adhibentur in physica
> entia rationis mathematica, cum fundamento in re. Photon et electron manent
> igitur fundamentaliter diversa.*

Though Latin was the official language of communication at the
Gregorian, it was hardly ever used for spontaneous conversation
between students of different nationalities. The ten-minute breaks
between the lectures gave, instead, a great opportunity for would-be
linguists ('spekkers') to practise foreign languages. But most
remained resolutely Anglophone. This was particularly so of smokers.
Smoking was not allowed officially in the Gregorian, but it was
tolerated in the (fortunately rather spacious) lavatory areas. So,
being then a heavy smoker, I spent most of the gaps between lectures
beneath a cloud of nicotine beside the urinals, rather than learning

Italian from future diplomats in the Capranica College, or
discussing philosophy in Spanish with a South American from the
Collegio Pio Latino.

The philosophy course was divided into three years, and its
subjects had to be taken in a prescribed order, beginning with
minor and major logic and metaphysics. Minor logic was the
'Aristotelian' formal logic which had been on the curriculum of
most European universities since the Renaissance; it owed little
first-hand to Aristotle's own logic, or to the developments of that
logic in the Middle Ages, but was a truncated torso of the genuine
medieval logic, dealing with 'simple apprehension', with
'judgement', and with 'syllogism'. Much importance was attached
to learning the moods and figures of syllogism with the aid of the
mnemonic 'Barbara Celarent', and modern mathematical logic
was dismissed in a brief *scholion* 'De logistica Russellii et Whiteheadii'.

Major logic, for which the textbook had been written by the
lecturer Morandini, was essentially epistemology. It was very much
a post-Cartesian subject: the refutation of scepticism, relativism,
idealism and anti-intellectualism, and the vindication of the power
of sense and intellect to achieve truth. Much energy was spent on
the problem of universals, and we were encouraged to reject
nominalism, conceptualism, and exaggerated realism, and to
embrace moderate realism. Morandini was an energetic, genial
figure, who spoke incomprehensibly rapid Latin, waving his arms
like a traffic policeman. Very different was Dezza, the Professor
of Metaphysics; sitting totally motionless, he enunciated rheumily,
in a barely audible voice, theses about the analogy of being and
the varieties of potentiality and actuality. He had a reputation for
holiness, and was alleged to have a saint in the family; he seemed
to us immensely old and was slowly going blind. It was a surprise
to me to learn in 1981 that Pope John Paul had brought him out
of retirement to rule the Society of Jesus.

The Gregorian was an international university, and Jesuits were
summoned from all over the world to teach there. In our second
year we were taught by a Dutchman, a Belgian, and a Frenchman.
Cosmology—the metaphysics of space, time, motion and the
methodology of physics and chemistry—was taught by Peter
Hoenen, a difficult and irascible lecturer who had been, the senior
students would tell us, an intimate of Einstein. Scholastic
psychology—the philosophy of mind and of organic nature—was
taught by the Belgian, Georges Delannoye, a pink-cheeked
Anglophile who simpered with delight when English students

brought him a red rose on St George's Day. Natural theology, the proofs of the existence of God and the philosophical derivation of God's attributes, was taught by a very senior priest, Père René Arnou, a long cadaverous figure whose French accent made his Latin the most impenetrable of all.

The philosophy which was imparted in these lecture courses was officially scholastic philosophy. But it was very different from any philosophy that would have been taught in the Middle Ages. It was an eclectic mixture of items from different periods and styles, including recent developments in the sciences of biology, physics, and experimental psychology. Thus it was through scholastic Latin that I learnt much of what little I know — and much more that I have forgotten — about evolutionary mechanisms and quantum physics.

To relate ancient and medieval wisdom to contemporary problems is a reasonable, indeed an admirable aim; it is one to which I have devoted a good deal of my own working life. The difficulty was that both the ancient wisdom and the contemporary problems were brought to our acquaintance in a derivative and second-hand manner. The teaching of wave mechanics in scholastic Latin was — to adapt Johnson — like a dog standing on its hind legs: it was not well done, the surprising thing was that it was done at all. Not only the modern sciences, but medieval philosophy too was presented through a distorting medium. We were supposed to be learning Aristotelian philosophy *ad mentem Sancti Thomae*, according to the mind of St Thomas; but we never opened a book of St Thomas until our third year of philosophy, when the set book was the brief and juvenile *De Ente et Essentia*. Similarly, it was only in the third year that we met anything of Aristotle at first hand.

The third year was less academically frustrating since we were encouraged to take some initiative on our own. As part of our licentiate examination we presented an *exercitatio practica*, or small thesis, on a topic chosen by ourselves. This thesis, unlike examination papers, could be written in the vernacular, and we were encouraged to write on authors in our own national tradition. I chose to write on Austin Farrer's *Finite and Infinite*. Farrer was then Chaplain of Trinity College, Oxford: I found his book one of the richest works on natural theology I had encountered. It was not an easy book to understand, but I found the author most generous with his time and trouble in correspondence when I wrote to ask questions. The principal lecture course, in the third year, was also an improvement: a synoptic history of philosophy by a

German Jesuit, Alois Naber. It was whispered, in shocked tones, that he was a secret Kantian.

A list of 100 theses, drawn from our five main subjects, was published on 1 March. During the spring months we revised so as to be able to expound and defend these theses to the examiners at the end of the year. It was agreeable to be dispensed from the daily burden of lectures; but as the weather became warmer and the examinations came closer, nerves became taut and sleep became harder. On our summer evening walks we examinees would struggle up the hill to the courtyard in front of S. Onofrio, textbook under arm, to get in an extra half-hour's revision in the comparative cool of the Janiculum Hill.

I passed the licentiate examination *summa cum laude*, so presumably I imbibed what I was supposed to from the Gregorian philosophy course. But those three years remain in my memory as the least satisfactory of all my academic experiences. It was not that the professors who lectured us lacked dedication or erudition or kindness, however much we might revenge ourselves for our boredom by mocking them in song in the Christmas pantomime:

> *My name is Father Charley Boyer*
> *And I am Père René Arnou*
> *My aim in life is to annoy yer*
> *And I am quite annoying too*
> *We're very fond of all the students*
> *But when they're from the V.E.C.*
> *We put 'em down (we put 'em down)*
> *We put 'em down (we put 'em down)*
> *To show that we're the P.U.G.*

The Jesuits we jeered at were respected international scholars, Boyer an authority on Augustine, and Arnou well known in the world of patristics. But even the most learned scholar and the most gifted teacher must have felt his heart sink at the prospect of lecturing in Latin five days a week. Father Copleston, the author of a best-selling history of philosophy, was drafted to the Gregorian to teach metaphysics and modern British philosophy. His distaste at lecturing in Latin was no secret from his audience. It was permitted to lecture in the vernacular if the audience had a common language, and of course quotations could be read in the original. So Father Copleston would discourage non-English speakers in his course—an optional one—by reading out longer and longer quotations from Bradley, Bosanquet, Russell and others. Finally, there were only Anglophones remaining and lecturer and class could settle down with relief into English. Quite apart from the language problem, philosophy is not a subject which can be taught by a monolithic series of lectures. A pupil needs discussion, and a great deal of writing and criticism, if he is to learn to think philosophically, rather than simply to master jargon.

The system could not be blamed on the Gregorian professors, or the University itself; for it, like other pontifical universities throughout the world, had to work to a syllabus and to a method laid down in an encyclical of Pius XI, *Deus Scientiarum Dominus*. It was distressing to come from a provincial seminary to the central university of the Church and find that one had passed from an enlightened intellectual regime to an academic monstrosity. Those who came to the Gregorian having already taken an Oxford degree suffered even more from the change. One of them, a pupil of Farrer, wrote to his former tutor to lament the hardships of studying in a university ruled by *Deus Scientiarum Dominus*. The Pope, replied Farrer, 'should be persuaded to write a new encyclical: *Deus Artium Magister.*'

During my three years I did manage to learn some philosophy, but most of it away from the Gregorian. The English College, like the other national colleges, employed a *Ripetitore* or tutor; an English priest who did not, as his title suggests, merely repeat what had been said in the lectures, but who organized philosophy discussions and made us write occasional papers. Our *Ripetitore* was Alan Clark, now a bishop in England. He made a great effort to arouse our reluctant interest, and introduced us to books far removed from the Gregorian syllabus, including Gilbert Ryle's recent *Concept of Mind*. But the man who really kindled my interest in philosophy was Patrick FitzPatrick, a student three years ahead of me who had come to Rome from the other northern seminary at Ushaw. He was a person of keen and independent intelligence and enormous patience; we would have lengthy philosophical arguments—I had almost written 'interminable'—but they always ended with him winning. He gradually cured me of any illusion that the scholastic system taught at the Gregorian could provide a description of the 'metaphysical works' which made things tick at the deepest level; the illusion that the system, if it worked at all, was calculated to produce.

In 1950 and later there arrived a lively group of former Oxford Greats men who also provided energetic philosophic companionship. One of them, C. J. F. Williams, was prevented by illness from becoming a priest, and is now Reader in Philosophy at Bristol University, just as FitzPatrick, a priest in the Newcastle diocese, is now Reader at Durham. It was Williams who introduced me to the works of Russell and Wittgenstein, and to the ideas of his former Balliol tutor, R. M. Hare. We often argued at cross-purposes, because the scholastic notions which I had ingested hardly seemed to belong to the same discipline as the philosophical topics which appeared to be the centre of concern at Oxford. Ironically, it was not until I went to Oxford myself that I came to appreciate the philosophical genius and permanent value of Aquinas and Scotus and other medieval Schoolmen.

– IV –

The English Romayne Life, 1949–55

Despite the unsatisfactory academic environment, my years in Rome were not unhappy. We English seminarists made a sharp distinction in our lives between the University and the College, between the Gregorian and the Venerabile. For most of us the Gregorian was a tedious chore each weekday morning; the Venerabile, on the other hand, enriched our lives and enlisted our loyalties.

The Venerable English College was old and proud. The seminary had been founded by Pope Gregory XIII in the buildings of the English Hospice, a medieval hostel for English visitors to Rome which outlived its usefulness when the Reformation dried up the supply of pilgrims. The Roman seminary began as an overflow institution for the English College at Douai founded by Cardinal Allen to send missionary priests into Elizabethan England; but by the twentieth century the seminary at Douai had long since been dismantled, while the College in Rome continued. Other national seminaries had been founded in Rome in the fervour of the counter-Reformation; but none of them claimed the title 'Venerable' and few of them remained, as the English College did, on their original site. Life in the College had changed remarkably little since it was first described by the Elizabethan poet and spy, Antony Munday, in his book *The English Romayne Life*. The College carefully preserved a number of traditions which exhibited its antiquity. The priests in the College, for instance, were always called 'Mister', never 'Father': that was what secular priests had been called when the College was founded, and no one was going to kowtow to the vulgar nineteenth-century innovation of using 'Father' in imitation of the religious orders.

A few years after the College was founded, the statute of 1585 made it high treason for anyone ordained abroad to return to England. For long after, every seminarist from the English College who 'went on the English mission', as all swore to do when they entered the College, took his life in his hands when he crossed the Channel. Between forty and fifty alumni of the College — forty-four was always the official figure — were executed under the penal laws, and the memory of their martyrdom sustained the ethos of the College. The names of the forty-four hung outside the chapel; on the days of their deaths we would invoke them: Blessed John Shert, pray for us, Blessed Thomas Pormort, pray for us, and so through the litany. The title 'Blessed' meant that they had received official beatification, the halfway house to sainthood; several have since been canonized and are now saints. The protomartyr, Ralph Sherwin, who was martyred along with Edmund Campion on 1 December 1581, shone out of a stained-glass window on the main staircase, and his response to the missionary oath was often quoted: he was ready to set off for England and martyrdom today rather than tomorrow (*potius hodie quam cras*). Each 1 December the College chapel was open to the public for the veneration of the martyrs' relics, and leading figures of the English community were invited to a banquet.

Since the removal of Catholic disabilities and the restoration of the Roman hierarchy in England in 1850 the Venerabile had been more distinguished for the production of bishops than of martyrs. Cardinal Wiseman, the first Catholic Archbishop of Westminster, had been Rector of the College before his flamboyant pastoral letter 'From out the Flaminian Gate' aroused the no-Popery riots in the days of Lord John Russell. Cardinal Hinsley, a bluff Yorkshireman whose energetic patriotism during the Second World War had made him a popular national figure, had been Rector of the College in the 1920s; his successor as Rector, William Godfrey, was himself to become Apostolic Delegate in London and then successively Archbishop of Liverpool and of Westminster. The young student who arrived at the English College was not there long before he heard the old joke about the three conditions necessary for being made a bishop: one, he must be a baptized Catholic, two, he must be male, and three, he must be an alumnus of the Venerabile. The first two conditions, we were told, were sometimes dispensed with, but the third never.

It would be wrong, however, to think that a young seminarist entered the English College with his heart set on a career as a bishop. None of us thought of ourselves as having a crosier in our knapsack. We were, in a sense, interested in power: but it was sacramental power, not jurisdiction or management. The powers

of the priesthood—the power to forgive sin, to consecrate bread
and wine and turn them into the body and blood of Christ—they
were a goal glorious enough in all conscience, and a goal that
seemed still so distant that we had no eyes to look further. Middle-
aged clergy are no doubt as vulnerable to ambition as those of other
callings; but we young seminarists, though proud that the College
had produced so many martyrs and so many bishops, no more
thought we would ourselves become bishops than we thought we
would become martyrs.

However dreary the daily trudge to the Gregorian, the English
College was an interesting and often exciting place to live. The
student community numbered seventy: small enough for intimacy,
large enough for variety. Not that we were encouraged to choose
our company; 'particular friendships' were frowned on. When one
arrived in the hall to form a *camerata*, or group of four, for the daily
walk, one was supposed simply to announce one's destination and
take the first companions that offered. But the student body was
a far more varied one than that at Upholland. There were alumni
from regional schools and seminaries, Ushaw for the north-east,
Ware for London, Prior Park for the West Country and so on.
Academically, too, the students were more lively; the junior
seminaries had, after all, usually picked their more scholarly seniors
to export, and we smirked deprecatingly when journalists would
describe the College as containing 'the cream of the English
seminaries'. There were also in most years a number of university
graduates, especially from Oxbridge. The English College probably
represented fairly accurately the social mix of English Catholics
as a whole: a large body of descendants of Irish immigrants, usually
second or third generation, with a sprinkling of members of the
old recusant families who had never accepted the Reformation,
plus intellectual converts from Anglicanism.

The goals of the College were explicit: we were in training for
the conversion of England, conceived as the reconciliation of each
individual with the Church of Rome. Like all priests, of course,
most of us would be working in parishes where most of our time
would be devoted to the pastoral needs of the already Catholic.
But what marked the English College from the other seminaries—
one of the elements of the 'Roman spirit' or *'Romanità'* which we
believed to be the unique essence of the College—was its emphasis
on conversion. One of the most businesslike expressions of this
emphasis was the Catholic Missionary Society, a group of priests
dedicated full time to proselytizing, by preaching, street-corner

meetings, and correspondence courses. The society was run by two former English College men, John Heenan and George Dwyer, both later to be Archbishops. Many of us thought of this as the paradigm of what the English College stood for. Before going to Rome I read some of the letters which Alec had sent home during his student days in the thirties as a contemporary of Dwyer and Heenan. 'If Protestant England knew,' he wrote in one of his earliest, 'what a spirit there is here for the conversion of England, it would quake in its boots.' The conversion of England would be the completion of the task for which the martyrs had died.

Coupled with the conviction that the salvation of England lay in its conversion to Rome was the equally strong belief that the Catholic Church in Rome—and in the rest of the world for that matter—had much to learn from the Catholic Church in England. Coming from a country where the majority of Catholics were reputed to attend Mass each Sunday, we were shocked to find that in the Eternal City Mass attendance was less than ten per cent. We thought the performance of the liturgy in the average Roman church slipshod and slovenly, and we were astonished to discover that Roman priests very rarely visited their parishioners in their houses. Clergy in Rome, we soon discovered from our own experience, were not generally popular. As we walked through the streets in our black cassocks, we were sometimes followed by children hissing *'bagarozzi'*, an abusive word for a priest, whose polite meaning is 'black beetle'. (Our slang word for any clergyman was 'bag'; when the Rector welcomed the Archbishop of York I remember being told, 'The Boss is giving a party for some Anglican bag.') We certainly did not see it as the goal of the conversion of England to make English churches resemble Roman ones.

We were indeed exaggeratedly English in many things. It was not simply the extra patriotism of the expatriate: in every generation since the Gunpowder Plot English Catholics have been anxious to prove that, despite the penal laws and despite the Armada, they yield nothing to Protestants in patriotism and loyalty to the monarch. It was also the unthinking chauvinism of a young generation not yet sensitive to overtones of racism, not yet suspicious of national stereotypes. We spoke cheerfully of 'Dagoes' and 'Wogs', and the native seminarist who, each year, was supported by voluntary contributions from the students, was always known as 'The Nig', no matter what country he hailed from. It was one of the more absurd manifestations of our chauvinism that, speaking Latin at the Gregorian and English at home, few of us took the trouble to master the language of the country we lived in.

The constitution of the College was, by the authoritarian standard of that period, comparatively democratic. Since the teaching was in the hands of the Jesuits at the Gregorian, the resident staff was small: a Rector, a Vice-Rector, and the *Ripetitore* in philosophy. The staff made an effort to share in the students' lives, eating in the same refectory and joining the circles round the common room tables where, each evening, we took our joint compulsory recreation. The students enjoyed a measure of self-government, assembling at intervals in a public meeting chaired by a Senior Student, who was elected annually to serve as a sort of J.C.R. President. The Rector when I arrived was Mgr John Macmillan. He was prevented by illness—and, we unkindly suspected, hypochondria—from performing many of his duties; he was rarely able to rise in time to say the Community Mass. His Vice-Rector, Mgr Gerard ('Jock') Tickle, was in effect Rector for the first few years of my course, and later became Rector in name as well. He was a kindly, even-tempered man, devoid of pomp or pretension, suspicious of theology and theologians, most at home with concrete practical tasks like cooking, wall-painting, bricklaying, in many of which he had a surprising skill. He was a superb host, which was an important asset, since in the mid-twentieth century the English College had recovered much of the aspect of the medieval pilgrim hospice. Bishops and other ecclesiastics were constantly in Rome on business and many of them chose to stay in the College. Many alumni of the College would return from parishes in England to take their holidays in Rome, and British scholars working in the Vatican library or archives would often bring introductions to the College, so High Table in the refectory was rarely without its quota of guests; and in the common room afterwards we students had an opportunity to meet leading churchmen and scholars and learn something about the workings of the ecclesiastical establishment.

There was a flood of English visitors during the first year of my studies, for Pope Pius XII declared 1950 a Holy Year, or Year of Jubilee, when Catholics from all parts of the world are encouraged to make a pilgrimage to Rome. All the English bishops visited Rome at the head of their diocesan pilgrimages. On many days we students were let off to act as tour guides, escorting pilgrims round Rome's four major basilicas, instructing them in the history of the catacombs and the Christian shrines, accompanying them on day-trips to Assisi or Subiaco, sorting out their problems with passports, traveller's cheques or hotel bedrooms. For us first-year men it was salutary to have to learn up the history of the main Roman churches, and for all of us it was agreeable to pocket the often handsome tips which came our way. I was also employed during Holy Year as a special correspondent of the Liverpool diocesan magazine, the *Cathedral Record*, writing a monthly piece about the ceremonies which marked the jubilee.

The Holy Year began with the opening of the Holy Door of St Peter's — a door which is walled up for twenty-four years out of twenty-five and opened only in Holy Year for the pilgrims to enter. It was my first major Vatican ceremony, and it was something of a disappointment. 'From the Press correspondents' box' I wrote grumpily in the *Record* (which was not in fact sufficiently important to be assigned a place there): 'This must have been an enthralling spectacle and was rightly reported as such; but what few people in England must have realized was that the actual opening was visible only in the porch so that nine-tenths of those present in St Peter's could do no more than listen to the words of the ceremony through loud-speakers.' This was on Christmas Eve, 1949; two days later, on Boxing Day, I attended a more satisfactory ceremony, when the seminarists and clergy of Rome made their own jubilee visits. The visit to St Peter's was led by the Pope, and as he passed between us on the way out I had my first close look at Pius XII.

The most interesting of the ceremonies, to a newcomer in Rome, were the beatifications and canonizations, unusually frequent in Holy Year. Enormous pilgrimages would arrive to see the canonization of a regional or national saint; almost the entire body of a religious order would appear for the beatification of its founder.

A beatification fell into two parts. In the morning ceremony, which the Pope did not attend, the life of the candidate was read, the decree of beatification was proclaimed by a cardinal, and finally a *Te Deum* was sung during which a picture of the newly beatified was dramatically unveiled in the Holy Ghost window above St Peter's chair. In the evening the Pope came into the basilica to pay his respects to the new *beatus* and to bless the assembled congregation. The first beatification I attended was that of Blessed Vincent Palotti, a Roman priest who had lived a few hundred yards from the English College, and had been a confessor there in the nineteenth century.

The ceremonies of canonization were more elaborate and gorgeous, though they had been shortened to a mere three hours by Pius XII who found the traditional ceremonies too taxing. At a canonization the full panoply of Vatican pomp could be seen. The basilica was lined by the three corps of Papal guards: the Noble Guard, drawn from Italian aristocratic families, the professional Swiss Guard, and the Palatine Guard, a sort of Territorial Army of part-time soldiers. The diplomats accredited to the Holy See were in attendance *en masse*, and a score of cardinals and a hundred or so bishops were always to be seen in the Papal procession. The gigantic columns which support the dome were hung with tapestries illustrating the miracles which had been worked in answer to prayers to the new saint, to testify to his qualification for canonization. Those with a fancy for heraldry and pageantry could pick out the Papal orders of chivalry, the Knights of Malta led by their white-haired Grand Master, and the newly reconstituted Knights of the Holy Sepulchre in flowing white robes bearing a scarlet quintuple cross.

The postulators of the Cause—the lawyers and theologians who had had the task of presenting the case for canonization to a panel of cardinals—processed to present the Pope with a pair of doves in a gilded cage. (The English College treasured the cage which had been used to present the doves for the canonization of Thomas More and John Fisher.) The Epistle and Gospel at the canonization Mass were sung in both Latin and Greek, to stress the Church's claim to be Catholic and universal. At the central point of the Mass the Pope would turn full circle to show the consecrated bread and wine to the faithful in all four of the arms of the Latin cross of the basilica. Silver trumpets in the dome played a fanfare while the Swiss and Palatine Guards presented arms. For one who believed both in transubstantiation and in the divinely given office of the Pope there could hardly be a more moving piece of pageantry.

I was as moved as anyone by the high moments of Papal ceremonial, and was one of the keenest to attend every possible canonization or pontifical Mass, both in Holy Year and in the remaining six years of my Roman course. But it would be idle to pretend that I spent all the time during such ceremonies in a spirit of devout reverence. Admission to ceremonies in St Peter's was by ticket only: tickets could be obtained, without payment, at the Vatican chamberlain's office, and a number were issued regularly to the Roman colleges. But the standing-only enclosures for which very junior seminarians were given tickets were at a great distance from the Papal altar, and were so thronged with pilgrims that one was in some danger of being crushed. Within the enclosure it was astonishing how deftly sisters of the most respectable orders of nuns could use an elbow or an umbrella to carve their way to the best vantage points. The crush was too great, often, for a prayerbook to be held, and only the most resolute of meditators could have kept his mind on spiritual things in the middle of the mêlée. Mere physical survival called for great stamina.

A seminarist did not have to be long in Rome to discover that he did not have to remain cramped in his pen for the whole duration of a canonization. However dense the crush near the central aisle, it was always possible to wriggle out of the rear end of the enclosure and withdraw — for the length of a sermon, say — to the sacristy. In the sacristy of St Peter's there was a bar (designed for the convenience of priests who wanted a quick breakfast after saying Mass at one of the many altars of the basilica). There one could enjoy a leisurely coffee before fighting one's way back into the congregation in time for the more solemn parts of the ceremony.

But it was not really necessary to be resigned to the lowly accommodation provided for seminarists. The entrances to the basilica were guarded by Swiss Guards who checked the tickets to make sure that only those entitled entered the choicer tribunes. After a while one discovered that all they really checked was the colour of the ticket, which was changed on each occasion; they had no time to read the print which specified the nature of the ceremony. So it was worth while collecting tickets for past functions: a colour which entitled one to a third-class position on one day might be used to mark off the very best seats on another. So it was possible to get a ringside seat for the canonization of St Joan of Valois in 1950 by clutching one of the most inferior tickets for the canonization of St Thomas More in 1935. The more expert would possess so rich a collection of past tickets that not only the colour, but also the name of the place (e.g. 'Tribuna della Veronica') would match. Since the tickets were all free anyway, we felt able to practise this mild deception without qualms. But there was always the possibility of detection, and I was once expelled with ignominy from one of the plusher boxes I had entered irregularly, and frog-marched down the central aisle of the basilica between two Switzers.

There were more subtle methods of securing good seats. The tribunes on either side of the chancel were reserved for bishops and diplomats. Bishops entered in procession, and the tickets of diplomatic staff were rarely checked. One could enter therefore by insinuating oneself into the episcopal procession, or by posing as a member of an embassy staff. The bishops vested in the gallery of inscriptions in the Vatican museums; there one could almost always find the bishop of some tiny diocese who would be grateful for help in vesting, and who would then allow one to accompany him, as a *bona fide* member of the episcopal procession. To enter the diplomatic box all that was really necessary was a sufficiently confident manner. If one was pressed to say which embassy one was attached to, the safest way was to say that one was looking for the Welsh Ambassador, his Excellency Mr Llewellyn.

Many of the more sober students disapproved of this kind of activity, and would frown as we St Peter's buffs boasted of our exploits at a late lunch after a canonization. No doubt it was all very juvenile and indecorous; but it would be wrong to think that it was a sign of any disbelief or disrespect towards the Papacy or the central elements of the ceremonies. It was a response to something in Vatican ceremonial itself, such an odd mixture of religious sentiment, venerable tradition, and slightly absurd Ruritanian protocol.

Some of the canonizations during my seven years in Rome were indeed very moving occasions. I remember especially the canonization of St Maria Goretti. She was canonized as a martyr to chastity: she had been killed at Anzio, at the age of twelve, because she refused the amorous advances of a neighbouring youth, saying, 'It is against God's will' (*'Dio non vuole'*). The mother, brothers, and sisters of the new saint were present; so too was the murderer, now long penitent, and a lay brother in the Passionist Order. Very different was the canonization of St Joan de Valois: then the family box was occupied by members of the royal house of France; but the saint herself had been dead more than four hundred years. In a letter home I described the canonization of St Pius X, the Pope who in the early part of the century condemned Modernism and introduced Communion for young children:

... In the robing room I helped to vest a poor secretary-less Abbot who had his vestments and mitre tied up in a brown paper parcel with string. He was the Abbot of Prague, a friendly, humorous little Czech of 43 who had escaped over the border in civilian clothes after being for ages in a concentration camp; his monks are still there with other religious to the number of about 1,000. They were on hard labour, but not tortured, but with crushing restrictions such as that all the 1,000 must say Mass within an hour.

With the Abbot I walked in the procession from the Sistine Chapel, down the Scala Regia, through the Piazza to the Obelisk and then up to the temporary altar; the procession must have taken nearly an hour as mitres swept by without end. At the top we secretaries were put into a pen just behind the Cardinals, quite near the Papal throne. We had a good view of everything. The Pope looked very haggard and stumbled once or twice when going to kneel on the prie-dieu; another time he seemed to have fainted and a group had to stand around him for a while. For the sermon he was quite fresh. Monsignor Heard says that at one of his disappearances he was, he thinks, given an injection which might explain why he perked up. The Pope kept on making gestures and grimaces at the Master of Ceremonies, most unlike his usual impressive dignity. They say that one of his arms is paralysed and that he has to have injections in it if he wants to use it; certainly it dropped limp once next day when he was blessing the crowd.

After the ceremony came the unveiling of the picture (I thought it very ugly) and the *Te Deum*. We found that the two rows of lay people between us and the Cardinals were relations of the new Saint. There were two nieces, jolly little old ladies in their eighties, very friendly and simple who promised us that they would pray for us to their 'Zio Giuseppe' (Uncle Joe). There were several great-nieces and nephews, sixty relations in all but none of them named 'Sarto' as they are all descended from St Pius' married sisters. The proprietor of the inn called the Due Spade, the osteria in Riese, was there too. The inn kept by his brother used to be visited by Pope Pius who as a young priest used to go there for a glass of wine. There was also a great-nephew who had been a prisoner of war in Egypt for five years and had come back to find his little son of five (also present) determined to be — not a priest — but a Pope. (He is now studying engineering!) One of the great-nieces was an oldish lady with wonderful searching eyes and a powerful peasant face who gave an impression of real sanctity. She said, without it seeming at all affected, that she should ask for our prayers rather than *vice versa* because we were young and hadn't committed many sins yet.

During my period at the English College we kept hoping that some of our forty-four martyrs might one day be canonized, but it seemed then a distant and doubtful prospect: for one thing, two miracles had to be worked by a saint if he was to be canonized. Miracles seem rare in Anglo-Saxon countries: Thomas More and John Fisher were, indeed, canonized without miracles by special dispensation of Pope Pius XI ('I see,' said an Oxford wit of the

time, 'they have been dispensed from the practical part of the
examination'). But in time two cures were reported of patients
who had prayed to the English martyrs, and they satisfied the tests
which the Vatican requires before certifying a cure as a miracle.
So a company of the recusant martyrs, including several from the
Venerabile, were indeed canonized; but that was not until long
after I had left Rome.

Apart from the special ceremonies of Holy Year, Rome provided
every year an annual cycle of picturesque religious attractions. At
Epiphany you could hear children preaching in the church of the
Aracoeli; later in January you could watch the blessing of the lambs
at Sant' Agnese. Once Lent began, there was something to look
out for every day. All those who have used a Roman Missal know
that for each Mass during Lent there is indicated a 'Station' church.
On Ash Wednesday, for instance, we read 'Station at Sta Sabina'.
The Station church was the church at which, in the Middle Ages,
the Pope celebrated Mass. In the course of Lent he would go to
a different church each day, thus visiting most of the historic
churches of the city during the forty-day period. Nowadays on all
but the most solemn days a cardinal deputizes for the Pope, but
there is still a special gathering each day of Lent at the Stational
church. So, starting on Ash Wednesday at the beautiful Dominican
church of Santa Sabina on the Aventine, where St Thomas began
the *Summa Theologiae*, the devout tourist could start on a spectacular
round of all the city's most ancient shrines. Those who felt they
might not get through Lent if they gave up smoking or eating sweets
might resolve instead to visit the Station each day — no trivial
resolution, for it meant on some days a long, rushed walk, on other
days forgoing more attractive alternatives, such as watching the
College XV playing Rugby Roma.

One could make up for broken Lenten resolutions by a particular
frenzy of activity during Holy Week. On Palm Sunday, for
instance, the more athletically devout could make the pilgrimage
round the Seven Churches — the four major basilicas plus the other
three Constantinian basilicas of Santa Croce, San Lorenzo and
Santa Prassede. This was a walk of some sixteen miles, most of
it through busy city streets, which had to be taken at a stiff pace
if it was to be completed between lunch and dinner. Much of it
followed roughly the line of the walls of ancient imperial Rome,
but it was important not to mistake one of the surviving bits of
the Claudian aqueduct for the city wall, or one could find oneself
striding far out into the Campagna.

On Palm Sunday evening, in Rome as at Upholland, we went into retreat for three days; but the second half of the week was far more extrovert. Though we performed the morning ceremonies in our own chapel, we were encouraged to take part in the public ceremonies at St John Lateran or at Santa Croce later in the day, or to attend the Stations of the Cross which the Pope would lead in the ruins of the Colosseum on Good Friday. We did not sing Tenebrae, and those who liked the afternoon offices had a choice of tramping up to the Benedictine monastery of S. Girolamo to listen to the austerest plainsong, or assisting the Canons in the neighbouring church of San Lorenzo in Damaso in rumbustious bellowing of the Psalms. The climax of the week came on Easter Sunday morning when up to a hundred thousand people, from Rome and·from all over the world, would assemble in the Piazza S. Pietro for the Pope's Easter message and blessing *Urbi et Orbi*.

Some sixty days later the Piazza filled again for the procession of the Blessed Sacrament on Corpus Christi day. The Pope was carried round the circle of the piazza, carrying the Host in a monstrance; he was borne on the shoulders of the Swiss Guards on a prie-dieu ingeniously designed so that he appeared to be kneeling in adoration when he was in fact sitting. Later in the summer the Pope retired to his summer villa in Castel Gandolfo.

Of all the public ceremonies I attended in Rome the most memorable was the Pope's Definition of the Dogma of the Assumption in 1950. According to Catholic belief, the Pope was infallible: that is to say, when solemnly pronouncing on matters of faith and morals he was preserved from error by a special gift of the Holy Ghost. The charisma of infallibility attached only to the most solemn utterances: a mere sermon in St Peter's was not infallible and the Pope had to be speaking, as the phrase went, *ex cathedra*. There was much discussion among theologians as to how one could tell when the Pope *was* speaking *ex cathedra*, and in spite of various Vatican fulminations against modern errors in the last hundred years, it was generally held that there had not been any infallible Papal pronouncement since the infallibility of the Pope had been proclaimed at the Vatican Council of 1870. But Pope Pius XII was not one to feel overconstrained by precedent, and he welcomed occasions to exhibit special devotion to the Blessed Virgin, and it soon became known that he intended during Holy Year to make use of his infallible power to define the doctrine that Mary had been assumed into heaven, body and soul, without having to wait for the resurrection of the body at the end of the world.

This had been the common belief of Catholics for centuries — for *how many* centuries was a matter of dispute — but it had not been officially defined. Some theologians shook their heads. It was not the custom to define doctrines, they said, except to correct specific heresies; moreover, a definition of the Assumption would offend other Christian churches and stand in the way of reunion. But most of us young seminarians were simply excited by the prospect of attending the first infallible statement of the twentieth century.

I described the ceremonies in an article in the *Cathedral Record*:

As the wind howled and the rain drenched the Roman streets during the last week of October, we wondered if the definition of the Assumption would have to take place in poor weather similar to that prevailing at the time of the definition of the Infallibility of the Pope at the Vatican Council, when the dome of St Peter's was struck by lightning so that the glass panes of the lantern fell in splinters around the feet of Pius IX as he read the Bull. The event was seized upon by the Protestant papers as being a direct expression of 'the displeasure of Providence at the arrogant presumption of the Bishop of Rome'. Anyone who indulged in this childish form of historicism would have to admit that by the same reckoning, Heaven could be said to have showed to the full its joy at the proclamation of the Dogma on November the First, for not only was the actual day of the Definition warm and cloudless, with that strange sharpness of colour peculiar to early spring and late autumn in Rome, but even on the afternoon of the 31st the prevailing bad weather had ceased in time for the solemn procession which was to celebrate the end of the International Marian Congress. True, the wise wore a pullover under their cassocks, for even on the finest days a November evening can be cool if one has only a *cotta* over one's indoor clothes; but the rain had stopped, and stopped for good, and the procession was sure of an enthusiastic audience with its ardour undamped in every sense.

In this ceremony the famous painting of Our Lady (called 'Salvation of the Roman People', owing to the many deliverances from siege, famine and plague which Rome owes to her intercession) was carried from the Aracoeli, or Church of the Holy Child, on the Capitoline Hill, to the piazza of St Peter's basilica. Thus, by an intentional piece of symbolism, the route ran from the citadel of Pagan Rome to the centre of the Catholic world. The clergy of the city assembled in a nearby convent while the lay part of the procession moved off, and when it came to our turn to leave we were met by a tremendous splash of colour on the steps of the Aracoeli where the children taking part were standing proudly in sashes of every possible shade. Above, in Michelangelo's piazza, the standards of the different districts of Rome fluttered in the still strong breeze. The long line of clergy and the religious orders made quite an impressive sight, though, as always in these gigantic processions, the elaborate attempts to organize plainchant singing met with little success.

The cortège passed along the main road from the Capitol to St Peter's — for when there is a procession in Rome the life of that part of the city must stop and all traffic is diverted — crossing the Ponte Vittorio and marching up the new road to the basilica between its two lines of obelisks. As we approached the end of the two-hour walk the gigantic loud-speakers began to function and we heard the voice of the famous Jesuit preacher Fr Lombardi. Unfortunately the echo in that great area made his words almost unintelligible, though it added awe to the pool of dark flanked by two illuminated lines of Saints and Prophets above Bernini's colonnade.

When the end of the procession reached the centre of the Piazza, the Pope, from his private apartments, led the faithful in a prayer which he himself had recently composed in honour of Our Lady's Assumption. Finally, he appeared at the illuminated window of his study and gave his blessing to the cheering crowd.

(Next day), shortly after dawn crowds of people could be seen moving along the Tiber towards the Vatican; the police of Rome assembled at the Basilica to deal with the enormous multitude, and so many of them were needed that the tram conductors had to take over point duty, as we noticed as we hurried along amid the crowd. Though there was still an hour and three-quarters to go before the official opening of the ceremony, the inside of the church and most of the good places outside were already taken, so that the ticket which I had been so glad to obtain proved useless. In any case it had seemed rather strange having a ticket for the Definition of a Dogma; somehow, when learning the articles of Faith one had never connected them with admission by ticket; and then there was always a sort of irrational urge to wonder what would happen if the Pope changed his mind.

Eventually we succeeded in obtaining a good position in the Piazza in good time for the beginning of the ceremony, so that we had a fair view of the whole Definition. The ceremony was in form rather like that of a Canonization; after the long procession of clergy and nobility had passed, and the Pope, accompanied by six hundred and fifty Bishops and Cardinals, had taken up his position on the high dais at the top of the steps, the rite commenced with a solemn petition for the Definition of the Dogma, presented by Cardinal Tisserant, the Dean of the Sacred College. The Pope replied that he did not wish to proceed with the proclamation of the Dogma until all the faithful present had prayed for the guidance of the Holy Ghost. All, therefore, sang the *Veni Sancte Spiritus*, after which, amid a silence which was remarkable when one considered the immensity of the crowd, his Holiness read the important parts of the Bull which proclaimed the Dogma. As he neared the solemn words which contained the *ex cathedra* statement you could almost see the tension throughout the Piazza. The Holy Father seemed entirely calm, though the emotions of one who hears himself speaking with the voice of Peter must be indescribable. The only sign of nervousness which he betrayed was a slight quickening of the voice as he read the first part of the Bull, but his voice was measured and clear as he read the words 'We pronounce, declare and define that it is a divinely revealed Dogma that the immaculate and ever virgin Mary, Mother of God, when the course of her earthly life had ended, was assumed body and soul to heavenly glory.'

And then the silence was broken by a tremendous cheer. 'Viva Maria' they cried, and 'Viva il Papa' as well; until someone found a happy compromise with 'Long live the Pope of the Assumpta'. A great flock of doves was released symbolically at the actual moment of the proclamation, though many people's attention was caught rather by the aeroplane which swooped over the Piazza to take the official photograph for the Vatican newspaper. Other aeroplanes were flying all over Rome and dropping leaflets in honour of the Assumption, most of which were seized by the local children as soon as ever they touched the ground. A battery of guns on the Janiculum Hill which dominates Rome fired a salvo of twenty rounds.

The solemn proclamation over, Cardinal Tisserant thanked the Pope on behalf of the Church, and a *Te Deum* was sung by the massed crowds. The Pope then gave a sermon in Italian which he concluded with his own prayer in honour of the Assumption. The definition ceremony proper ended with the Apostolic Benediction which conferred a Plenary indulgence on all those who were present or who were listening on the radio. Then the Papal cortège moved into the Basilica to prepare for the celebration of the Mass, specially composed for the occasion. Meanwhile the loudspeakers broadcast recordings of hymns to our Lady in different languages which had been made by the various colleges; the hymn chosen to represent the English tongue was 'Hail Queen of Heaven' which we had recorded in the Vatican some days before.

And then, without waiting for the Papal Mass, which would be out of sight, inside the Basilica, the vast crowd began to disperse. It might have been more edifying had they stayed in that hot and overcrowded Piazza until the whole ceremony was concluded; but in one respect their instinct did not err. A Mass sung by the Pope is a great experience, but it can be attended many times a year; but what they had seen was an event of history that was not likely to be repeated during the lifetime of even the youngest of us. As the Pope had said in his allocution: 'This great day, so long awaited—at last it is ours, at last it is yours. Our voice, which with the assistance of the Holy Ghost has solemnly defined this wonderful privilege of our Heavenly Mother, is the voice of ages—nay, it is the voice of Eternity.'

V

Fides Quaerens Intellectum

What had all this pontifical pomp to do with religion? The question might be asked, not only by an evangelical Protestant but also by a devout seminarist. Most of us answered it something like this. Vatican ceremonies served to present in vivid form some of the doctrines of Roman Catholic belief. But it was not essential, or indeed particularly laudable, for a Catholic to attend a doctrinal definition any more than it was a necessary characteristic of law-abiding Englishmen to listen to the Master of the Rolls laying down the law in the Court of Appeal. Attendance at ceremonies was really not much more than a hobby, a religious hobby, no doubt, but away from the main course of our religious life; if it helped our progress in that life it was only incidentally. Hearing Mass, of course, was a serious business; but from a strictly religious point of view the Pope's Mass was no different from any Mass said in a side chapel in the most down-at-heel suburban church. The hours amid the pageantry of St Peter's did not take one any nearer to Heaven.

The serious pursuit of holiness, which was to be the essence of training for the priesthood, took place elsewhere: in the quiet of the College chapel, in the privacy of one's room, in the life of the College community and the observance of the College discipline. It was by the effort put into the daily period of meditation, the devotion with which one attended Mass and community prayers, the charity which one exhibited to one's brethren, the energy with which one resisted the temptations of the flesh, the assiduity with which one pursued one's studies and observed the College rules—it was by these things that one's spiritual progress was measured.

The meditation between six and six thirty in the morning was supposed to set each day in the appropriate spiritual context. We were left free to choose our own topics, though each night a passage was read in Latin from a meditation manual by one Avancinus

proposing themes for the following morning's consideration. Few
of us found the baroque rhetoric of this manual congenial, and
we turned to other texts. Some of us made use of a manual of
meditations, three pages or so for each day of the year, entitled
Intimità Divina, written by an Italian Carmelite, and based on the
works of St Teresa and St John of the Cross. In the time set aside
for spiritual reading each day we would familiarize ourselves with
the classics of devout and mystical writers: St Teresa's autobiography, St John of the Cross's *Dark Night of the Soul*, St Francis
de Sales' *Introduction to the Devout Life*, *Holy Wisdom* by Dom
Augustine Baker O.S.B.; the *Imitation of Christ* was read to us,
chapter by chapter, at the evening meal each day.

The message of St John of the Cross was a severe one. The
progress of the soul was a long and painful ascent through mystical
states which would lead to union with God. The ecstasy of the goal
was described in terms of incomprehensible rapture, but what was
absolutely clear was that the way towards it was through suffering
and self-discipline. First, one must enter the dark night of the senses;
but this was only the kindergarten of preparation for the dark night
of the soul, which was itself only the first stage of the mystical ascent.
The very first steps on the spiritual life were laid out by St John
in the following precepts:

> Strive always to prefer, not that which is easiest, but that which is
> most difficult;
> Not that which is most delectable, but that which is most
> unpleasing;
> Not that which gives most pleasure, but rather that which
> gives least;
> Not that which is restful, but that which is wearisome . . .
> In order to arrive at having pleasure in everything,
> Desire to have pleasure in nothing.
> In order to arrive at possessing everything,
> Desire to possess nothing.
> In order to arrive at being everything,
> Desire to be nothing.
> In order to arrive at knowing everything,
> Desire to know nothing . . .

It was a matter of debate among theologians and spiritual
directors whether these bleak precepts were intended for all
Christians, or only for those who had received a special call to the
mystical life; and if the latter, whether the fact of being a candidate

for the secular priesthood meant that one had received such a call. It was no easy matter to see how the rules were to be applied. The College regime left comparatively few things to one's free decision, and the College rules took precedence over applying the counsels of a mystical writer. If one should strive to prefer not that which was restful, but that which was wearisome, did this mean that one should stand, rather than sit, to study in one's room? Surely not, for that might make study less efficient, and that must be the overriding concern during study time. Did it at least mean that one should stand rather than sit during recreation time? No, because the College custom meant that we should sit round in circles in companionable conversation. There always seemed good reason why St John's rules should not be applied literally. At most it seemed that one should give up a cigarette from time to time, on the principle of preferring that which gave less pleasure to that which gave more.

But would not anyone who took St John seriously give up smoking altogether? Oddly, the College ethos pulled strongly in the opposite direction. These were days before the link was established between smoking and cancer, and smoking was regarded as a harmless activity. We were, however, allowed to smoke only in recreation time and in places of community recreation, such as the common room and the garden. Smoking in recreation time was thus seen as something positively valuable, which drew people towards the communal centre away from private relaxation in their rooms. High feasts were celebrated by the granting of extra smoking time, and visitors were expected to provide free cigarettes: the non-smoker felt cut off from the celebration of the festivities or the benefit of the munificence. Among many there was a suspicion that non-smokers were eccentric loners, not altogether to be trusted.

Smoking was not even a particularly costly form of vice, since we were able to buy British and American cigarettes at duty-free prices, imported from the Vatican City. Few smoked Italian cigarettes; it took a strong stomach to smoke even the more expensive Export brands, let alone the Nazionale. To this day the smell of a Nazionale always reminds me of Lent: on several Ash Wednesdays, too weak-willed to quit smoking altogether, I would switch to Nazionale, thus combining abasement before my addiction with homage to St John's principle of preferring the nasty to the pleasant.

St John's precepts haunted my imagination without having any real effect on how I lived. His poems fascinated and enchanted me: more I think for their allusive erotic imagery than for the mystical decoding which he provides in his prose commentaries. I know no other Spanish, but I still have by heart many of his stanzas. The *Spiritual Canticle* and the *Dark Night* contain, for the unbeliever as well as for the believer, some of the most magical lines ever written.

A spiritual writer who seemed to present a much more practical programme for virtuous living was St Francis de Sales. Writing for noble men and women in the courtly world of seventeenth-century Savoy, he put into his *Introduction to the Devout Life* almost as much worldly wisdom as other-worldly asceticism. Not that it would be easy to live up to his standards, but the virtues he inculcates seemed to be designed for the real world. I grew to enjoy reading his correspondence, particularly with his friend St Jane de Chantal, whom he alternately inspired and teased towards sanctity. I was fascinated, indeed, by the way in which many of the most austere saints, of unimpeachable chastity, seemed to come in companionable pairs: St Francis and St Clare, St John of the Cross and St Teresa, St Francis de Sales and St Jane de Chantal.

I discovered gradually — too gradually — that the reading of the classics of spiritual and mystical writers, with their warnings against self-indulgence, could itself be an insidious form of self-indulgence. It made one concentrate on elusive phenomena of introspection, inquisitive whether one's 'interior life' matched the descriptions of spiritual progress in the autobiographies or counsels of the mystical writers. It distracted one from looking at one's life as a whole.

To a seminarist the need to shape life to some overall purpose is masked in two ways. First of all, the daily details of life are laid out by the discipline under which he lives: his only contribution to the overall plan of his life is to remain in the seminary rather than quitting it. Most seminarists wonder, from time to time, whether they should abandon the project of becoming a priest, but for most of the time the question 'Should I be here at all?' is not one that occupies their minds. Secondly, the future is so bounded by the prospect of ordination that the relation of one's present actions to one's later life does not come up for question. The priesthood is a clearly desirable goal; the seminary life has been laid down by the authorities as the only possible way to achieve that goal; the thing to do is to get through the seminary as smoothly as possible. The life in Rome was congenial enough so that for most of us it did not often raise in any acute form the question 'Why am I doing what I am doing?'

It is only thus that I can explain why I was not struck at the time by something which with hindsight seems overwhelmingly obvious: namely, the mismatch between the training for the priesthood provided by the seminary, and the actual life of a secular priest for which it was alleged to be a preparation. A seminarist devotes himself to scholarship in a closed and companionable community; a priest in a parish lives a solitary life in which the place of studies is taken by administration and social work. Of course the life of prayer was intended to be a common thread linking the two stages of a clerical career; but even there, participation in the liturgy of the seminary was very different from the administration of the sacraments to a parish. In the seminary we lived a life similar to that of a novice in a religious order; but success or failure in a seminary is much less secure a test of suitability for the parish priesthood than a novitiate is of adaptation to a monastic life. In particular, the type of stress involved in the acceptance of a life of celibacy looks quite different from within the walls of a community of congenial fellow-celibates, and from the point of view of a solitary bachelor in a parish of families.

Seminarists in England were less cut off, during their philosophical and theological training, from the world in which they would work after ordination. They would spent at least two vacations each year at home in a non-clerical environment, though they were expected during vacations to attend church daily, and to avoid liaisons with women which might be regarded as 'endangering their vocation'. But during the Roman course, the seminarist returned home only once, during the break between the three years of the philosophy course and the four years of the theology course. Our summer holidays at a villa in the Alban Hills were delightful, but they increased our isolation from the outside world, and deprived some of us at least of acquiring greater self-knowledge before committing ourselves to a life in the priesthood.

As my philosophy course drew to its close, and the time came for me to take the licentiate and return for my mid-course vacation in England, I did indeed become depressed and worried about the prospect of continuing my studies for the priesthood. More and more of what I was taught seemed either muddled or incredible. The proofs we were offered for the existence of God all seemed to contain serious flaws; many of the philosophical theories we were taught seemed implausible constructions invented to shore up particular theological doctrines.

All material bodies, we were told, were made up of substance and accidents; the substance appeared to be an invisible metaphysical core around which the accidents clustered like a wrapping. The doctrine of substance was presented thus in order to make room for the doctrine of transubstantiation. According to that doctrine, in the Eucharist the substance of the bread and wine changes into the substance of the body and blood of Christ; the appearances of bread and wine remain but they are merely accidents inhering in no substance. The notions of substance and accidents were taken from Aristotle, and may well be coherent; but for Aristotle the notion of accidents adhering in no substance would be a contradiction in terms. The doctrine of the real presence I was, as a loyal Catholic, prepared to believe, however mysterious it might be. But the metaphysics we were taught appeared to save the coherence of transubstantiation only at the cost of calling in question our knowledge of every ordinary material object. For all I could tell, my typewriter might be Benjamin Disraeli transubstantiated; since all I could see were mere accidents, and I lacked any metaphysical eye to see through to the real substance.

In ways like this the philosophy we were learning came to seem less and less credible, and its incredibility connected directly with specific Catholic dogmas. In rejecting some of the philosophy I was not necessarily, yet, denying or disbelieving any of the dogmas. Scholastic philosophy, while favoured and sanctioned by the Church, was not imposed for absolute belief like the articles of the Creed or pronouncements of the Pope or General Councils. But the implausibility of the philosophy did strain the student's faith in the dogmas themselves: if they needed support from such ramshackle philosophy, how sound could they be in themselves? This thought, when it presented itself, was of course perceived as a temptation: a temptation to one of the worst sins, doubting the Faith. It was, I think, in my final year as a philosopher that I began to mention in confession more or less weekly that I had been tempted against faith and perhaps consented to the temptation. I was comforted, but not always completely so, by the reassurances of confessors that the saints had borne similar temptations. Cardinal Newman was frequently quoted to the effect that a thousand difficulties do not make a doubt.

My misgivings about the Gregorian philosophy did not prevent me from satisfying the examiners in the licentiate examination, and I went home for the summer of 1952 with a *summa cum laude*. But I was also full of foreboding about the life I was committing myself to; I began to realize what misery could lie in a life devoted to the spread of doctrines in which one only half-believed. I spent the vacation in a turmoil of indecision, kept to myself for most of the time. On the one hand, the goal of the priesthood was something on which I had set my heart for nine years; it was the dream of those I most loved and admired that I should achieve it; all my upbringing and all my advisers taught me to regard difficulties or doubts as temptations to be put aside. On the other hand, if one found unusual difficulty in accepting Catholic dogma, would it not be foolish to place oneself in the front line of the defenders of that dogma? The thought of giving up Catholicism altogether was no doubt a hideous temptation which one should fight by prayer and mortification; but no one was obliged to become a priest, and so there could be no sin, surely, in leaving the seminary and pursuing the life of a Catholic layman.

Or could there be? If one was called by God to be a priest, how could it be other than wicked to refuse the call and turn one's back on Him? Throughout my years in the seminary there ran a deep ambiguity in what we were taught about the notion of 'vocation to the priesthood'. The word suggested a special call from God; fail to answer it, and you could be like the man in the parable of the talents who kept his talent wrapped in a napkin. If you had a vocation, it was sinful to do anything which might lead to your failing to answer it: to keep company with a girl, with the risk of falling in love and wanting to marry her, was 'endangering one's vocation', and we were repeatedly warned against it. On the other hand, we were also told that a vocation did not mean a special vision or revelation from God: we were not to expect a visitation like the infant Samuel to assure us that we were, indeed, the chosen favourites of God. How, then, did one know whether one had a vocation? Pressed on this, spiritual writers and advisers were inclined to say that a vocation in the end amounted to no more than suitability of character, plus a rightly motivated intention to become a priest. But this was more puzzling than ever: how did one find out whether one's character was suitable without doing some of the things which could count as 'endangering one's vocation'? We were often told that it would turn out that some of us in the seminary did not have vocations at all; there seemed no way of discovering until it was too late whether our fugitive and cloistered virtues genuinely amounted to a vocation.

Had I been inclined to test, or endanger, my vocation by seeking the company of women I had little opportunity to do so even in the only three months I spent outside the seminary in seven years. At the age of twenty-one I not only had no female friends; I did not have a single male friend who was not a priest or a seminarist. Since my friends from Rome were, during the vacation, scattered in different parts of England, the holiday was altogether a lonely time. When in England, I found Alec my closest companion; I loved him as ever, but my doubts about the Faith and my uncertainty about the priesthood came as a barrier between us.

It was during this vacation that I paid my first visit to Oxford, and looked over the colleges and city. I thought ruefully how agreeable, in those congenial surroundings, would be a life of scholarship untied to a set of dogmas.

The three months passed, and I took no firm decision. I felt I could not go on much longer towards the priesthood in my state of half-belief; on the other hand, home was lonely, England seemed drab, and I wanted to return to Rome and discover if, in that more genial climate, my faith would rekindle. If the Faith is true, I argued to myself, I will be given grace to overcome my doubts, and courage to support the sacrifices of the priesthood. If it turns out to be false, then I will be free anyway of the obligations laid down by the Church, and can walk away before the life becomes stifling. But what matters most is to decide about the Church's claims to truth. I have, after all, studied no more than philosophy; theology will be the real test. There I can get to grips with the doctrines of the Church, and decide whether they are sublime and mysterious truths, or whether they are sophistry and illusion.

So I went back to Rome, to the English College and to the Gregorian, in the autumn of 1952. Perhaps I was wrong to do so; perhaps the wiser and more honourable thing to do would have been to write to my Archbishop and say I could not go any further toward the priesthood.

I cannot recall with any clarity how or when the doubts which troubled my last terms of philosophy abated. It was certainly not that the philosophical difficulties found a solution; it was rather that, as I took up the prescribed theological studies, my attention moved elsewhere. The theological course at the Gregorian was far superior to the philosophical course, even though the basic defects of the Roman university system continued. But even so, it was certainly not until the second year, when we began the study of dogmatic theology, that I began to look on the mid-course hesitations as a thing of the past. The first year was devoted to apologetics, the defence of the theological system as a whole against rationalistic and agnostic objections, and the defence of the Catholic, Papal and hierarchical system against the objections of Protestants and Presbyterians. The lecturers in this part of the course, Tromp on the concept of revelation and Zapalena on the nature of the Church, were no more inspiring than most of our philosophy lecturers; and the arguments which were used to establish the rationality of accepting the Christian revelation, and the Scriptural basis of the specifically Roman system, did not carry any more emphatic conviction than those offered in philosophy to prove the existence of God. Theology in the Gregorian, like philosophy, was too reliant on second-hand texts. Very little of the Bible was assigned for reading: one Gospel and a few psalms; we met Biblical texts principally as proof-texts in the course of apologetic arguments.

The *Summa Theologiae* of St Thomas, and the theological works of the great scholastics, remained more or less closed books. While we were given little encouragement to read the works of the great Catholic divines, we were positively forbidden to read theological works by any writer who was not a Catholic. The Index of Prohibited Books proscribed, of course, the classic works of all the great reformers; but more limiting than the Index were the general provisions of the Code of Canon Law, which forbade, under general description, many more books than had ever been listed by name. Thus the Code forbade all books written by non-Catholics on religious topics. It was possible to be exempted from the provisions of the Index, for good cause; hence our College library had a large collection of such forbidden books, but all were clearly marked with a red blob on the spine to show that they could not be read without a dispensation. Thus, when I needed to read Hume's *Treatise on Human Nature* for a philosophical dissertation, I had to get an express dispensation from the Rector of the University. Later, I secured general permission from the Holy Office to read all forbidden books necessary for my work, 'excluding frivolous and obscene ones', but not until after I had been ordained and was a graduate in theology.

The theology course lasted four years, with a bachelor's degree after two, and a licentiate after four; those who wished to proceed to the doctorate would have to return for a further year or two of graduate work. It was in the middle two years that we studied the central topics of speculative theology such as the Trinity, the

Incarnation, Grace and Redemption. And it was in these years that we followed the course of moral theology, ranging over the discipline of the sacraments and Catholic teaching on ethical topics such as justice, property, lying, drunkenness and (predominantly) sex. The only primary text with which we were really forced to get closely acquainted was the Code of Canon Law: it was published in handy pocket editions for examination purposes. For those who were later to be involved in ecclesiastical administration, proficiency in the Code was essential; and all of us, as parish clergy, would need to know it if we were to manage ecclesiastical property and see to it that our parishioners were validly married. Though later in life I came to be fascinated, in an amateur way, by the English Common Law, I look back on Canon Law as one of the few totally boring subjects I have ever been called on to study.

Most students found the moral theology course the most interesting to study. It dealt with concrete and practical matters, rather than scholastic or dogmatic abstractions; it was treated in a lively and casuistical, indeed anecdotal, style. A story would be told about fictional characters (commonly called Titius and Bertha); then we would be asked *'Quid de casu?'* Who, in the circumstances narrated, is the real owner of the house? Are the couple validly married? Is what Titius did a mortal sin? What restitution should Bertha make?

Our moral theology lecturers had the gift of holding the attention of their unwieldy and heterogeneous audience. One, Father Abellan, a Spaniard, would lean relaxedly over the lectern like a politician at the despatch boxes, and run through a *casus perplexus* in a tone of confidential bonhomie. The German Huerth, a shrivelled and rheumy man, sat motionless and never let his voice rise above a whisper. He it was who lectured on the sins against the sixth commandment, so it fell to him to explain the facts of reproduction to those of his audience who might be ignorant of them. We all long remembered the hush that fell over the tiered ranks of cassocked figures as he began: *'Et ipse actus sexualis consistit in hoc . . .'*

After a while Father Abellan was promoted to the Rectorship of the University and his place was taken by an American, Father Healey. He lectured in abominable Latin with a magnificent drawl. One day, in order to illustrate what degree of drunkenness counted as a mortal sin, he told in Latin the story of Pat saying to Mick, 'Here, you hold the door steady and I'll put the key in the lock.'

But it was in the lectures on dogmatic theology that we met two theologians of real distinction: Maurizio Flick and Bernard Lonergan. Flick, a bouncing Tyrolean, taught us the treatises on grace, salvation, predestination, and took us through the great Reformation controversies; Lonergan, a sardonic Canadian, had the task of making comprehensible the mysteries of the Trinity and the Incarnation.

Flick was the best lecturer I have heard in a lifetime of lecture-going: every sentence vibrated with curiosity, energy, and decision. He would bring to the rostrum a huge pile of books, decrees of councils, writings of Church Fathers, treatises of theologians; at the appropriate moment he would grab a text from the pile on his right, read it with the passion of an actor declaiming the last speech of Marlowe's *Dr Faustus*, and then place it on the growing pile to his left. His lectures were so popular that we would turn up voluntarily to attend them even on the English national days, like the feast of St George, when we were exempt from attending the University. I still preserve the notebooks in which I took notes of his course: the only complete set of lecture notes I have ever had the perseverance to take from a course. The only other lecturer I have ever listened to who could excite and hold the interest of an audience, on a similarly abstract topic, in a similar manner, was the Oxford philosopher J. L. Austin.

Lonergan's lectures were not so easy to follow: he was not at home in Latin and lectured with an air of boredom that quickly communicated itself to his audience. Many of us, rather than take regular notes, would purchase the cyclostyled summaries of the lectures sold by diligent stenographers from the Collegio Pio Latino to less assiduous lecture-goers. Lonergan was not then a famous figure; after his book *Insight* appeared he was hailed by some as the most distinguished Catholic philosopher and theologian of the century. He published the material of the lectures he gave us under the title *Verbum*. I now admire that book greatly, but at the time I did not fully appreciate his learning and originality.

It was, I think, the intellectual power of theologians such as Flick and Lonergan that led to the gradual disappearance of the worries which had previously plagued me. The subjects we were studying were of very great interest. From the Catholic point of view, we were seeking an understanding of the mysteries of faith which were the truths of supreme importance for the life of every human being. But even from the point of view of a secular historian of ideas, the Christian and Catholic system, if not a revelation from God, is one of the most fascinating inventions of the human spirit; a construction erected by the best minds of many generations. It was the treatises on the history of salvation, from the fall of man through the redemption to the final judgement, which gripped me most. In particular I was held by the tract on grace. Hitherto, the University course had mainly been a systematic exposition of items of Catholic doctrine whose main lines had been part of my life since infancy. On the topic of grace, however, I began to see that I had never known what Catholic doctrine really was. The first thesis of the treatise on grace went like this:

> Fallen man without grace cannot long keep all the precepts of the natural law. The free will of fallen man, however, is not completely extinct nor is it capable only of sinning . . . But for any act leading to salvation, even the first step of faith, grace is absolutely necessary. An adult should dispose himself for justification by freely assenting to grace, but he is justified entirely gratuitously; and God distributes graces to fallen human beings in an unequal degree.

Most of this was novel to me: indeed, on these topics, the theses presented sounded to me more like the kind of things Protestants believed. Others, too, were surprised by what we were taught: American students in particular were disgusted when we were taught that God's distribution of grace was not governed by a principle of equal remuneration for equal merit. But there was no doubt that the substance of what we were taught was the authentic official doctrine; it was clearly to be read in the decrees of the Council of Trent, with which we became familiar. We came to realize that we had been brought up in a mild version of the Pelagian heresy, and that even predestination was a Catholic doctrine as well as a Calvinist error.

Being totally ignorant of modern Protestantism, I did not realize that the differences between contemporary Catholics and Protestants on topics such as grace, justification, and free will are likely to be much less than those that separate both of them from the official positions laid out on either side of the Reformation controversies. Most Anglicans, for instance, now sit as lightly to the predestinarian Article XVIII as we had done to the corresponding parts of the Councils of Orange and Trent. This has now become a commonplace of the ecumenical movement. Among those who sat with me listening to Flick lecture on grace there was, in the red cassock of the Collegium Germanicum-Hungaricum, Hans Kung, who later wrote a book, *Rechtfertigung*, which was to be hailed as a landmark in the ecumenical understanding of the doctrine of justification.

Absorbed in the study of dogmatic theology, I felt the philosophical difficulties fade and I began to enjoy again with a clear conscience the genial and cultural aspects of life in the College and in the City. I found that prayer and the reading of spiritual writers began again to bring comfort rather than anguish. It was not until the fourth and final year of theology that we returned to topics which troubled me: the theme of tran-substantiation in the treatise on the Eucharist, and the logical justification of the Faith that we studied as the first and fundamental theological virtue. But by the fourth year of theology I had already been ordained as a priest, and I had found a temporary philosophical *quietus* for the problems which had troubled me in 1952.

VI

Outside Classroom and Chapel

Apart from the summer vacation spent in England between the three-year philosophy course and the four-year theology course, the summer months in other years were spent in a villa twenty miles to the south of Rome in the Alban Hills at Palazzola. It was a place of spectacular beauty, perched halfway up the steep wooded slope of Lake Albano which rises towards the extinct volcano of Monte Cavo. It stood like a fortress, with its formal garden, cloister, and swimming pool, on a table of rock hollowed out for a consular villa in imperial times, and later enlarged for a Cistercian monastery whose twelfth-century chapel now served the seminary. The villa, which housed about fifty students, had been bought for the English College, after a brief inglorious period as a home for alcoholics, by Mgr Hinsley in the 1920s. The few hundred feet which lifted it above the Campagna on the rim of Lake Albano made it ten degrees cooler than Rome, a perfect place to enjoy the brilliance of an Italian summer.

The regime at Palazzola was more relaxed than in Rome, though we were told that 'there is no holiday in the spiritual life' and we spent no less time in church. We rose at six, instead of five thirty; after meditation, Mass and breakfast there was a period of study from nine until ten thirty. We were free until 12.15, when a quarter of an hour's spiritual reading in chapel preceded lunch. There was a longer siesta than in Rome; I liked to take mine in a deckchair under the cypresses at the far end of the garden. Rosary at 3.45 formed a brutal awakening; but the period from four to eight was one of glorious freedom, the best time of day for exploring the nearby woods, hills and villages, or for playing golf on the improvised golf course on the Sforza meadow above the villa. Supper was at eight; there seemed something delightfully decadent about having a meal without prayers immediately before it. After supper there were not formal recreation 'circles' as in Rome; one could play cards, listen to records, or sit under the stars talking and smoking.

In Rome the rules forbade us to read works of fiction; at Palazzola this rule was relaxed and there was a 'blood library' of light fiction; too light, much of it, but it was at Palazzola that I first read through Jane Austen and still the opening pages of her novels call up a mental image of the garden wall and the humming of the *grilli* beneath the cypresses. The swimming pool at the end of the garden was larger and airier than the one in Rome, and was used more for athletic pleasure and less as a desperate means of cooling off. But the most delightful place to swim was Lake Albano beneath us. A twenty-minute scramble after tea would take one down to an isolated lakeside glen with a good diving rock. No one who has done it can forget the experience of lying back in the cool smooth blue water, watching the evening sun tint the fortress foundations and towering walls of Palazzola high above the woods. The one snag of swimming in the lake was the return scramble, which made one sticky enough to need a quick dip in the swimming pool ('tank') before sitting down to supper. Another way of spending the evening was to vary the College diet by taking a meal in a *trattoria* in nearby Albano or Rocca di Papa. As the College authorities did not approve of our eating out on these evening walks — except perhaps for a plate of strawberries and a glass of wine in neighbouring Nemi — one had to return in time at least to pretend to eat a normal supper in the College refectory.

A strip of concrete amid the humps and hollows of our would-be golf course enabled it to do double duty as a cricket pitch: the only one in Rome and perhaps in all Italy at the time. Twice a week there were house cricket matches, and from time to time we would play against visiting teams, battling for the Ashes with Australian seminarists from the Collegio di Propaganda Fide across Lake Albano, or competing with teams from the British Embassy, often led by the staunch veteran Sir Victor Mallett. The Embassy also sent a strong representation to the Gilbert and Sullivan operas which we performed towards the end of each *villeggiatura*. Practices for these operas took up many a morning. Before we had been long at the villa, a beery voice would confide to the *cortile* that he was a Pirate King, he was, and heavy-footed choruses would tramp their dance routines. The Venerabile was less hostile to transvestism than Upholland, and only those who were already in Holy Orders were forbidden to play female parts. Accordingly we worked through the Gilbert and Sullivan repertoire unbowdlerized, and

I found myself in successive years a *contadina* in *The Gondoliers*, one of the Major-General's daughters in *The Pirates of Penzance*, a Japanese schoolgirl in *The Mikado*, and a lovesick maiden in *Patience*.

Wednesdays were free days ('*gita* days') and we could wander where we wanted, in groups of three; though in the hotter weeks of July we had to return in the middle of the day for a picnic on the Sforza (at which the unlimited supply of wine meant that we usually spent much of the rest of the day in a prolonged siesta). On all-day trips it was possible to visit the sea at Anzio or exchange visits with seminarists from the other national colleges, scattered in *villeggiatura* around the Castelli (the Scots at Marino, the Americans in Albano, the Germans at San Pastore).

A favourite expedition from Palazzola was to Tusculum, a hill above Frascati where, above the ruins of a pagan theatre and the site of Cicero's villa, a Christian altar and cross had been erected. We rose early and walked through the woods via Rocca di Papa in time for Mass in the open air there. I wrote in a diary, for the College magazine, in 1951, during a holiday visit to Palazzola by Alec Jones:

> 25th (July) Wednesday. Fifteen of us rose at 5.30 and journeyed to Tusculum, accompanied by a refractory donkey carrying vestments, altar linen, and breakfast utensils. When we reached the summit at 8.00 Fr Jones said Mass beneath the giant cross, with chasuble billowing in the wind and altar cloth and pall weighted down by prayer books. As we stood round the altar to shelter it from the gale, we realized why the Hebrews were always wanting to worship in high places. Cavo and Faette above us seemed to take rank with Tabor and Hermon; below us lay the Holy City and for a brief half-hour this pagan hilltop was itself a Holy Mountain. *Magnus Dominus et laudabilis nimis; in civitate Dei nostri, in monte sancto eius.*

The Alban Hills form two concentric circles: the summit of the inner circle is Monte Cavo, one of the claimants to the site of Alba Longa, with an undoubtedly authentic paved Roman road leading to the summit; the highest point of the outer circle is Monte Faette. This, which presented the most splendid eastern view in the vicinity, we would ascend early in the morning to watch the sun rise. The Latin vale which ran between the inner and outer rim we believed (on what authority I do not know) to be the scene of the epic fight between Aeneas and Turnus which closes the *Aeneid*.

Early in September we were allowed to escape briefly from the community to take a holiday in a smaller group, always in Italy or near its borders. The youngest students, in their first *villeggiatura*, had to go together: they hiked in a body to Subiaco, St Benedict's mountain retreat north-east of Rome; a blistering trek which took two days with an overnight stop at the house of the Irish Augustinians half way. The second-year students were allowed to venture further, to Florence or Siena, as they chose; I chose Florence for my *gita*, and have been in love with the city ever since. During the theology course we could chose our own destinations, and we could also take a holiday at Easter. During the spring break I would visit cities such as Siena, or southerly resorts like Capri and Amalfi, but the summer *gitas* were always spent in the mountains.

One evening in my first villa I timidly followed one of the seniors up the lakeside practice rock which we called 'Jock's tooth'. From that moment, though never an expert and often a nervous climber, I found rock-scrambling and snow-climbing incomparably the most satisfying vacation.

The first peak of any size which I ascended was the Gran Sasso d'Italia. With two companions I climbed it in Easter 1953 while it was still covered with snow and ice. It was not difficult, though it involved a night in a refuge (the famous one where Mussolini had been imprisoned between the fall of Fascism and the Republic of Salò) and a long early-morning haul up snowfields. In summer, I imagine, there must be an easy path to the summit, but we needed to rope up and make frequent use of ice-axes. I am told climbers don't cut steps any more on steep snow slopes; but cutting steps up the steep sides below the top ridge under an ultramarine sky at six in the morning was most exhilarating.

In the summer of 1953, with three companions, I set off to climb the Matterhorn (Monte Cervino, as we called it in our Italian way). The four of us did not feel experienced enough to climb without a guide; but we were doubtful whether poor students like ourselves would be able to afford to pay Alpine Club rates for the pair of guides which the rules would require. At Breuil, at the top of the Val d'Aosta, at the foot of the Italian slope, we found a young guide, Berto, who had only just graduated after the five-year training period as *portatore*. He offered to take us all up, alone, for 20,000 lire, which was well within our resources. He was the great-great-nephew of Jean Antoine Carrel who was the first ever to climb the Italian side of the Matterhorn. Our plan was to walk

over into Switzerland and ascend the easier Swiss ridge; but while
we stayed the night at the Carrel house Berto persuaded us it would
be pleasanter to go up the Italian ridge and then descend to Zermatt
from the summit. So on the following day, with a huge sack full
of ready-cooked chops, boiled eggs, cheese, bread and spaghetti
packed by Mother Carrel, we set off at about 9.30, Berto carrying
in his water bottle a most surprising mixture of tea and wine. We
lunched at the Oriondé refuge. Here, one of our party spilt a glass
of wine. 'Better than break a leg,' said Berto, with satisfaction. We
noticed that whenever anything was dropped or broken, he seemed
to regard it as an offering to the gods. Whenever we finished a bottle
of anything, he would pick it up, throw it over the side of the ridge
saying *'Domino Nostro'* and then, as it tinkled to pieces in the valley
below, say *'Amen'*.

An hour from the Oriondé, after zigzag walking and scrambling
towards the left-hand ridge of the Matterhorn, we roped up. This
part of the climb was a mere scramble; there was rarely need to
belay and the rope was as much of a hindrance as a help. Traversing
the Colle di Leone was straightforward, with magnificent views
to the south and south-west of the Breithorn, and the shimmering
top of the Gran Paradiso range. One had to choose resting-places
with care, to avoid avalanches. Above the saddle between the Colle
di Leone and the main massif, slab-climbing began. On the Italian
route up the Matterhorn there are a number of fixed ropes; some
short ones to give you a chance to swing with a leap to a shoulder-
high foothold, others as long as sixty feet, in angles of smooth rock
where there are pressure holds for the feet but nothing that tourists
like us would consider a handhold. The fixed ropes enable you
to move fast up pitches where it would take an hour to climb the
face or make a detour. We reached the top of the longest rope at
about 6 p.m. From there it was only fifteen minutes up the
causeway-like rocks to the platform which holds the Rifugio Savoia
where we were to spend the night. It was a small hut with a single
room, half of which comprised two bunks, one on top of the other,
each to hold five; the rest contained a table, a stove, a chimney
and some shelves. At the back, in the open, was a lavatory with
a sheer drop. We put on the wooden clogs provided as
(astonishingly comfortable) slippers; another guide and his client
arrived and the two guides prepared supper, asking us to do no
more than occasionally belay them as they went out into the glacier
to get clean snow to boil. After supper we went outside to wave
a lighted newspaper as a signal to the families in the valley below

to tell them we were safe; we believed we saw a pinpoint of light flicker in reply.

We rose at five in the morning, and were glad enough of Mother Carrel's hard-boiled eggs before venturing into the icy grey-blue air. The only way up from the refuge was a fixed rope, leading up the jagged face which rose from the hut's tiny plateau, formed by layer after layer of stratified rock; each layer projected a different amount from the main massif, so that sometimes they made stairs, and sometimes overhanging upside-down stairs. The climbing was not very difficult, but you might have to belay from a cramped position with your body wedged between two pieces of rock or your head and shoulders pushed outward by a jutty halfway up your back. We traversed the foot of the Pic Tyndall, a forbidding-looking spur named for the Victorian agnostic scientist who first climbed it, and then went along the narrow ridge which joined it to the Col Félicité and the final summit ridge of the Matterhorn. I described this part of the journey in a letter home:

> The first part of the ridge was a knife-edge of snow not more than three inches wide at the top; one side (the west) dropped sheer to the glistening Tiefenmatten glacier; the other fell away sharply over broken and angry towers of rock. As it was out of the question to walk along the top of this ridge, you had to place your feet in a set of recently-kicked steps on the west side, facing east into the ridge, which fitted into your armpits, as it were; you held on to the east side by pressure. It was only a short traverse, and quite easy when you were shown the method, but delightfully spectacular. The last people to cross were wondering how much longer the snow would hold — because the ridge was made entirely of snow, the rock ridge ending at about one's knees and on the wrong side.

At the final bit, before the Col Félicité, there was a fifteen-foot drop where you had to jump from one rock to another with a minor abyss between the two. Once across you could see the final tower of the Matterhorn for the first time. The longest of the Matterhorn ropes, the Corda Grande, comes at this stage. It was too long for the guide to reach the top of it before the other two of us started; we had to string out across the face, all three of us at different levels. With the fixed rope this was not dangerous, and it was exhilarating to be standing on a tiny ledge with one hand nonchalantly on the fixed rope and the other controlling the paying out of the climbing rope. The fixed rope ended with a Robin Hood-like leap to the left to cover the final pitch; here at least there was a colossal stanchion around which to take belays.

We went on at a great rate up the summit ridge, chasing in and out of boulders, each turn rewarded with a new view, an upward and eastward zigzag until we came to the notorious rope-ladder. It has been described thus by Frank Smythe, the Everest climber:

> Presently we came to the well-known rope-ladder, which enables the climber to surmount an otherwise impassable overhang. It does not ascend the overhang direct, but bends to the right over and round it. The lower end of the ladder has been pulled inward and fixed to a sloping niche under the overhang: if left to hang down it would be impossible to reach it, so pronounced is the outward bulge of the precipice. Thus the ladder also overhangs, and the climber must ascend on the inside of it until the lip of the overhang is reached, and then transfer himself to the outside, a movement complicated by the lateral slant of the ladder. It is a sensational manoeuvre, and takes place on the face of a precipice 5,000 feet high.

Nowadays, no doubt, a serious climber would take in his stride not only the ladder but the impossible overhang it was meant to circumvent. It did not occur to us to start on the inside of the ladder, and then transfer to the outside as Smythe did, so we climbed outside all the way with the ladder overhanging at first and our heads further back than our heels. Berto, who usually strode the mountain as if walking along the village high street, puffed and grunted as he went up; my colleague, a better climber than I, took thirty minutes to get up twenty feet: he was, we later discovered, in the early stages of a hernia. When it came to my turn I found it quite bad enough. As I wrote home:

> After the first few steps up the ladder there was no hope at all of getting any footholds on rocks beside the ladder; you were left dangling in mid-air with a 5,000 foot drop below; not that I remember thinking of the drop, but merely of the fearsome strain on the muscles. The ladder, besides having half its rungs missing, seemed possessed of a malicious spirit: whenever you raised a foot to put it on the next rung, the ladder would shoot forward away from you, or curl round, turning you with it and threatening to smash you against the rock. There didn't seem any way of getting up it other than hauling with hands alone; and after four hours of strenuous previous climbing, your fingers refused to grip. By the time I got to the top of the ladder I was whimpering like a child.

At the top, a simple slope, with a fixed rope as a balustrade, led to an alcove where we could rest, and drink wine-and-tea, and smoke a cigarette, and listen to Berto's reproaches at our slow progress. At this rate, he said, we would have to spend the night at the Solvay (the emergency hut on the Swiss ridge) instead of returning to Breuil, or going to the Hornli hut at the foot of the Swiss route.

But from there it was only ten minutes, up easy slopes and comfortable rocks, to the Italian summit. In the gap between the Swiss and Italian summits was a metal cross; there, on the frontier, we had our first view of the Swiss ranges. I felt no elation — that came later — only thankfulness to be no longer on the ladder. But after a sandwich and a drink and a smoke, we perked up, to take photographs and watch an inquisitive Swiss Customs plane fly past. As we moved to the Swiss summit we found company: two elderly but efficient Germans, and a man, whom we later learnt to be a wine-merchant from the Valois, called Joseph, who was working along the ridge between the two summits on his hands and knees. Behind him were two climbers from the Dolomites who we thought must have brought him up; but later we discovered he had come up alone, God knows how. 'You wait for me,' he shouted as we went past; 'I give you chocolate. Wait for me: I have no rope.' 'Then why did you ever come up the Matterhorn?' muttered Berto: this was the kind of person who got the Alps a bad name. But my colleagues were softer hearted and let him use their rope as a fixed rope.

The descent began with an alarmingly steep snow slope. Berto rebuked me for wanting to descend it facing inwards, like a companion ladder on shipboard; gradually I learnt to move fast facing forwards, lurching down the cut steps in rhythm with the others. Berto alternated between telling us to go faster *'Forza, forza'* and not to be foolhardy *'piano piano e sicuro'*. We had to keep the rope taut between us in case anyone slipped. Joseph was handed down from rope to rope. In the end the Dolomiters took responsibility for him with great good humour. They were experienced, and he was constantly doing the most foolish things. They would discipline him by threatening to untie him from the rope if he did not behave.

I have much less clear memories of the Swiss descent than of the Italian ridge. Even when I wrote home, a few days later, I had begun to forget:

> I do remember that on some of the Swiss fixed ropes my fingers wouldn't grip, and I had just to slide down them, hoping I wouldn't

hit anything jagged at the bottom. There were numerous pitons, some
of them great stanchions like capstans almost, with curls at the top into
which you wound your rope. This made you feel very safe, but wasted
quite a bit of time. The difficult patches, so far as I remember, were
caused by ice-covered rocks; the climbing itself was all easy, and even
monotonously so in places. We all agreed it must be dull coming up the
Swiss side: it is a uniform ridge and you don't get the variety of view or
of technique which you do on the Italian side. At one difficult crossing
over a snow-patch the Dolomiters stopped and let us travel down their
rope. Joseph and I got entangled in the middle because he was stuck and
would not move any further, and I couldn't get past him without getting
the two ropes entwined; I had to go back in the end, untwine the ropes,
and descend on the other side, Joseph explaining in a half-scared, half-
amused manner that his limbs wouldn't move.

Eventually we were all at the bottom of the ropes, removed *ramponi*,
and drank wine-and-tea. This improbable drink was wonderful
stuff for climbing. The wine warmed you and the tea stopped it
making you drunk. I have tried it since and it tastes like poison
at sea level, but then it was nectar.

We belied Berto's prophecy that we would not make the Solvay
until nightfall. We reached it at three o'clock, a dismal, filthy place
with old crusts on the floor, mouldy straw on the bunks, and a
notice threatening a ten-franc fine if you slept in the hut outside
an emergency. Here we lunched on bread and cheese and jam,
and Ovaltine provided by Joseph, who handed round his visiting
cards and invited us to visit his winery.

We had intended to stay the night at the Hornli; but when we
reached there, we found that the price of tea and beer was such
that we would clearly never have enough money to be able to pay
for beds. We felt too tired to go back over the pass into Italy to
Breuil, but decided to push on down to the lower hotel at the
Schwarzsee, which was reputed to be cheaper.

We had the good fortune to meet, on the way, two cheerful
smugglers. Don't worry about the Hornli people rooking you, they
said; we do it to them when they go into Italy. Their trade was
to smuggle Chianti from Italy into Switzerland, and Swiss cigarettes
(Players) into Italy; they lent us 5,000 lire, which we promised
to pay back via Berto, and introduced us to the hostess at the
Schwarzsee who fed us handsomely in a servants' hall, and
provided wonderful beds with red blankets in a beautifully clean
pine-smelling hut. The drinking water was deliciously sharp,
effervescing as it came from the tap.

Next morning I bathed in the dark lake which gives the Schwarzsee hut its name; the water was not as cold as I feared, and I could lie back and survey the incomparable panorama. We did not leave until midday, when our smuggler friends returned from cigarette shopping in Zermatt. Our journey was not a difficult one, over the eastern pass into Italy. We roped up as we crossed the edge of the glacier; it was an almost level walk, but there were crevasses to be leapt over, and it was comforting to be attached to two other people in case one stepped into a concealed one. We had a very cheerful lunch, with the smugglers playing their mouth organs, smoking huge cigars from their contraband packs, and singing ribald Italian alpine songs.

At the top of the ridge, where the snow began, was the frontier, with its little Customs house. Shortly before this, we said goodbye to the smugglers, who wished to make a slight detour of their own at this point. The frontier guard in the Customs house was not, I should have thought, a great danger to their livelihood. When we returned to ground level in Breuil that evening, and completed our expedition, I discovered that though it was 1 September 1953, my passport had been clearly stamped to show that I had crossed the Theodul on 1 September 1955. I was proud of that stamp for the next two years. It occurred to me that if I needed to murder anyone, 1 September 1955 would be a good day, since I would have a cast-iron alibi for anywhere except the Matterhorn. But fortunately the occasion did not arise.

The Matterhorn *gita* was the first of a series of summer mountaineering holidays. In 1954 we climbed in the Dolomites, staying at Ortisei with a hospitable family of wood-carvers, the Stuflesers (best known in this country as the carvers of the stalls of Downside Abbey). In 1955 it was the turn of the Monte Rosa area: a snow climb predominantly. We now felt experienced enough not to need a guide, and once again crossed from Italy to Switzerland over the Alpine summits, sleeping in the Margherita hut on the Signalkuppe, which is the highest hut in Europe, higher than the summit of the Matterhorn. From Zermatt we attempted to climb the Rothorn; but steady rain forced us back into Italy, where we hitchhiked back to Rome via Milan, Bologna and Florence. It was not always easy to hitch lifts in those days, and we had run out of money. I remember vividly one day, when we were exhausted, going with a companion (now a bishop) into the mainline station and attempting to beg the price of a ticket to Roma Termini.

It was always one of the most agreeable parts of the *villegiatura* when the community reassembled after their *gitas* and exchanged stories of their adventures. We had a *gita* book, with the cities of Italy arranged in alphabetical order, in which we entered the names of good and cheap hotels, warnings against expensive restaurants, and such information as 'At Vallombrosa the Parocco hates Englishmen', 'At Piediluco there is a crazy count who lives in the osteria and will buy you unlimited drinks.'

As the September nights drew in we were no longer allowed to prolong our afternoon walks until supper time: we must be home when the Ave Maria bell rang, a fraction earlier each night. There was still opportunity for all-day walks. One option was to walk the twenty-odd miles round the Castelli Romani (Albano, Marino, Frascati, Monte Compatri, Monte Porzio, and so on) and sample the wine in each of them. To make sure of finishing the journey, we would have only a quarter of a litre among four of us at each vineyard town; on the way to the next we would make up a verse describing the wine, to a chorus which was a mnemonic for the names of the sixteen Castelli. When I did the tour, Rocca Priora was awarded the palm by a unanimous vote. Twenty years later, that tiny village has started to export wine to England—but under the label 'Frascati'.

One of the final activities of the villa was the production of an illustrated satirical magazine called *Chi Lo Sa?*, strictly for internal consumption. This was already an ancient institution when I arrived at the English College: it had been produced roughly thrice yearly since the 1920s. I edited several issues. We would stay up late into the night on the days before its appearance, working with panic fervour in an atmosphere of flowing vino, green eye-shades and clouds of smoke. This was all strictly illegal at a time of night when we were supposed to be observing the *magnum silentium*; but there was a kind of unofficial dispensation for the staff of *Chi Lo Sa?* The Rector and Vice-Rector kept well away from the part of College where it was being produced, though they reserved the right to censor it before it was finally brought into the common room. The volumes of *Chi Lo Sa?* since its inception had been placed in an archive which was passed from editor to editor: by now it contained a good deal of irreverent information about the student days of many who now occupied senior positions in the hierarchy or the curia. Each editor had to make an explanatory diary to illuminate the cryptic jokes, and explain which eccentricity or obnoxious feature of which person was being mocked.

There was also, of course, a serious college magazine, *The Venerabile*, which appeared twice yearly; it contained historical articles, about the past of the College or other items of recusant history; poems and essays on aspects of College life; a substantial day-to-day diary of the College life, and book reviews. I edited three issues of it, and was one of its most regular writers, usually contributing historical articles on the College during the sixteenth century.

At the end of the long *villeggiatura* we did not look forward to the return to Rome and the University. On the last night, as we drank mulled wine and ate chestnuts by a pergola below the Sforza, we would sing:

> *I leave Palazzola with a tear in my eye*
> *The Villa's been lovely in spite of the pi*
> *And though I like swotting and bricking in Rome*
> *I prefer Palazzola, the inebriates' home!*

Words written, I was assured, by Bishop Heenan when a student.

One way to make sure that the holiday ended with a bang rather than a whimper was to return to Rome on foot, rather than by the trams which clattered downhill from Rocca or Albano. We rose at two in the morning to arrive in Rome in time for Mass at the catacombs of St Callisto. The moonlight shining on the surface of Lake Albano added a touch of magic to one's departure from the villa. A stony path round the lake in the unusual cool took one past the carabinieri who guarded the Papal villa at Castel Gandolfo, and then we descended to join the tracks of the Via Appia Antica at Frattochie — once the Bovillae which gave birth to the Caesars. For the first few miles the road was a muddy cart track with paving stones hidden by weeds. As the daystar came up, and the sun rose from the mists, we would see on either side the shells of Roman villas and tombs, and fragments of magnificent friezes beside shattered inscriptions which testified to the greatness of forgotten Roman nobles. Our journey ended at the catacombs, where, near the chapel where St Cecilia's body was found, one of the priests would say Mass for us and we would consecrate our return to the Holy City.

– VII –

Orders and Priesthood

Ordination to the priesthood in the Roman Catholic Church was preceded by a number of preliminary steps. The New Testament mentions bishops, priests, and deacons; and the Roman Church regards the diaconate as the most junior of the sacramental orders of the priesthood, but below it there were several degrees of ordination. The subdiaconate, though not a sacrament, entitles those ordained to it to wear elaborate coloured and embroidered vestments similar to those of priests and deacons. Priesthood, diaconate, and subdiaconate are Major Orders; below these are four Minor Orders. In ascending order these are: porter, lector, exorcist, and acolyte. No doubt these four titles once represented serious duties in the service and worship of the church community; but for centuries they had entirely fossilized. Others besides lectors and acolytes read or carried candles, and the College porter was a paid servant, not an ordained divine. Exorcists were expressly forbidden to attempt to cast out devils, a task which was held to be highly dangerous; if one attempted it without being very holy, and having a special licence from the bishop, the devil might move out of his current victim into the exorcist himself. So though the old ceremonies of promotion to these orders were carried out, though keys, book, and candle were ceremonially handed over as in bygone centuries, the only function of these Minor Orders now was to mark the gradual approach of the priesthood, and to serve as a means of discipline for the seminary authorities — for those who had misbehaved were likely to have their Minor Orders postponed. They were conferred in pairs, portership and lectorate together in one's second year of theological studies, and promotion to exorcist and acolyte early in one's third.

The first step in the life of a cleric was the conferring of the tonsure. Though we had been wearing the cassock throughout our period in philosophy, we remained, according to canon law, laymen, not subject to the discipline or privileges of clerics. As anyone who has looked at medieval painting knows, the tonsure used to be a shaving of the whole scalp, which left a round fringe of hair a little above ear level. The scalping of modern clerics in Rome was more modest. The bishop, at the tonsuring ceremony, merely snipped off a lock or two; thereafter we had to keep free of hair a small circle at the back of the head about the size of a half-crown. From time to time admonitions from the Rector on the notice board exhorted us to keep our tonsures well burnished; we would perform this service for each other with electric razors. The tonsure's function was not simply symbolic. A cleric who, *per impossibile*, entered a brothel or a theatre or a cinema, or some other forbidden establishment like a mixed bathing beach, could always be recognized no matter what his state of disguise or undress.

English clerics were allowed to grow their tonsure before returning to their homeland; but it could cause embarrassment and concern to the barbers of those who had to return home suddenly. 'Sorry to see the little trouble you've had with your scalp, Sir. Do you mind my asking if it is infectious?'

Before tonsure and Minor Orders we had to take special examinations. These were not very serious matters, but they were an indication that ordination was controlled not by the University but by the local diocesan authorities. It is for the bishop in each diocese to satisfy himself of the qualifications of the clergy he ordains. In Rome, of course, the bishop was the Pope, who was rather too busy to examine, or indeed to ordain, the hundreds of clergy promoted in his diocese each year. This, with other diocesan matters, was delegated to a bishop who was Vicar General of Rome; he ran the diocese from a gloomy palace near the Trevi fountain called the Vicariate. It was there we would go for our ordination examinations. The task seemed to be entrusted to slightly shopworn clerics, in the way in which medical examinations for insurance policies are sometimes carried out by doctors off the main medical track. Our only other ventures to the Vicariate would be to obtain relics for friends in England. If your parish priest, for instance, had just completed building a church of St Dorothy or St Timothy, and wanted to have a relic of his patron for the altar stone, he might write and ask you to get one for him. You would go with his request to the Vicariate; there, in a room full of antique filing cabinets, a monsignor would walk over to the letter D or T, open a drawer, and take out a tiny bit of hair or bone dust or, if the worst came to the worst, cloth. He would then fill out a certificate that this was the genuine bone, hair, or clothing of the saint in question. The relic would then be wrapped in the certificate and handed over the counter. No charge was made for the relic, of course — that would have been simony — but a suitable fee was exacted for the issue of the certificate. I caused some scandal when in my first year I read a paper to the College's Wiseman Society casting doubt on the authenticity of many of the relics preserved in Rome. The paper was based largely on articles in the *Dictionnaire d'Archéologie chrétienne et de Liturgie*, a Catholic work which was similarly sceptical of Veronica's veil, the Holy Stairs and the Spear of Longinus; but I think some of my colleagues now look back on that paper as my first step on the road to heresy.

The diaconate and subdiaconate were much more serious matters than the tonsure and the Minor Orders; the diaconate because it was a sacrament, the subdiaconate because it was the point at which the future priest submitted himself to the discipline of celibacy. There was no rule forbidding the clergy, as a whole, to marry; but once a person took the subdiaconate, so long as he remained a Catholic or had not received an extraordinary dispensation from the Pope, he was irrevocably committed to celibacy. Any attempt to marry was not only sinful; the marriage, if it took place, was not valid in the eyes of the Church. Almost all of us had some misgivings as to whether we should be able to carry out the obligations thus incurred; no one approached the subdiaconate without seeking a good deal of advice.

The persons to whom we turned first for advice were our confessors. One's confessor, after all, had heard one's sins for many years; he would know as well as anyone one's strengths and weaknesses of character, one's sexual propensities, one's capacity for self-reliance and self-control. That was so, at any rate, if one had a regular confessor; no one was obliged to do so and one could confess in the anonymity of St Peter's. But we were strongly encouraged to take one of the confessors provided by the College, and treat him as a permanent spiritual director. The College confessors were not members of the College staff; it was judged wrong for someone in disciplinary authority over a student to be also his confessor and pastoral counsellor.

My own confessor was Mgr Heard, a Vatican official who had a small apartment in the College. He was a Scotsman, the son of a headmaster of Fettes, who had brought him up in a manner old fashioned even in the first years of the century. He had gone to Balliol in 1903, and obtained a Third in Law and a rowing blue. Having been converted to Rome he became a priest, and after a brief period as a curate in East London spent his whole career in the Vatican legal hierarchy. When I knew him he was an auditor, or judge, of the Roman rota, of which he later became Dean. His principal job in this capacity was deciding marriage annulment cases: he had, for instance, annulled the first marriage of Evelyn Waugh, whom he once described to me as one of the best witnesses he had ever examined. As a member of the Congregation of Rites, his duty was to consider candidates for canonization. He told me he preferred to deal with annulments in the mornings, and canonizations in the afternoon; the canonizations were less depressing, because even the failed candidates had at least tried to be good. I was impressed by the trouble he and his colleagues took over canonizations. Once, when helping to clear out his room, I found seven volumes of argument devoted to two words of Maria Goretti, who was eventually canonized as a martyr to chastity. Her last words were *'Sì, sì'*. Were these reinforcing her previous words to her would-be seducer, namely *'Dio non vuole'*? Or were they a last-minute surrender to his proposition, too late to ward off the knife? Postulator and *promotor fidei* had argued the case before Heard and his colleagues for many an hour.

Heard was an impressive figure, and some of us treated him as an oracle. He lived a solitary and austere life, rarely eating in Hall since his health permitted him only the most meagre diet. He slept little and rose early to make himself available for confessions to those who might wish to confess, before Communion, any sins they may have committed during the night. He had decided and outspoken views on a variety of topics from dental surgery to the history of cheese. Later, when I was a priest, we became quite friendly; he lent and gave me many books and often asked me to his room for a nightcap. But as a young seminarist I was much in awe of him, and never queried his advice. Nervous as I was, on his recommendation I proceeded to the subdiaconate.

It was a decision which I had to take earlier than most of my classmates. Most seminarists in the English College were ordained shortly before Christmas in their final year, some six months before completing their theology course and taking their licentiate. They were ordained deacon in the previous summer, and subdeacon the preceding Easter. But each year two were ordained early before the summer vacation: the Senior Student and his deputy. These two were elected by the students, and in my year I was chosen deputy. So my ordination to the priesthood was scheduled for midsummer 1955, and my diaconate was moved forward to the preceding Easter and my subdiaconate to the last days of 1954.

We prepared for the Major Orders by a week of retreat in a religious house away from the College. My subdiaconate retreat was in the monastery of the Passionist Fathers on the Caelian Hill, overlooking the Colosseum and the city. I would look at the city lights at night and muse on the renunciation of the world and the flesh. A Spanish seminarian, also preparing for the subdiaconate, said to me: 'I have seen some of your English girls, and I don't think you have much to sacrifice. But a Spanish priest, now, he has to give up *real* women.'

Ordinations in Rome were carried out in wholesale batches: there might be as many as 200 ordinands from all the different national colleges. The ceremonies were held in various churches in the centre of Rome; a large sanctuary was essential since before ordination all the candidates for Major Orders had to prostrate themselves while the Litany of the Saints was sung. One of the most popular was the Church of the Twelve Apostles, near the Piazza Venezia; there I received one set of Minor Orders, and the diaconate. The ceremony might last five hours, starting with the conferring of tonsure at eight in the morning and continuing without a break to the end of the ordination of priests an hour after midday. Prelates of the curia took it in turn to officiate. I received the subdiaconate from Archbishop Traglia, the Pope's Vice Gerent for Rome. He was a popular ordainer because he was brisk, clear and decisive, with an efficient grip and a firm hand. That removed all fear that one's orders might be invalidated by inaudible mumbling of the formulae, or mismanagement of the crucial gestures.

The subdiaconate altered our lives at once. In the first place, we could now play a major role in the principal liturgies: at High Mass, priest, deacon and subdeacon perform together the main ceremonial acts except the actual consecration which is reserved for the priest alone. The subdeacon wears elaborate vestments: white amice, a hood pulled down over the shoulders; white alb from shoulders to ankles, bound by a woven girdle; and a wristband called a maniple, of a colour appropriate to the feast of the day. Deacons and subdeacons both wear a kind of tabard with sleeves, coloured for the feast; worn by a deacon it is named a dalmatic, by a subdeacon, a tunicle. These vestments resemble the garments in the Byzantine mosaics in Ravenna; they have a lineal descent from the court dress of the late Empire. At High Mass the subdeacon, in addition to assisting the priest, has the duty of singing the first lesson or Epistle, and has custody of the paten on which is laid the consecrated Host.

More importantly, the subdeacon is bound to the daily recitation of the breviary. This divine office consists of the eight canonical hours of Matins, Lauds, Prime, Terce, Sext, None, Vespers and Compline: services which in a monastery would be sung in church at the appropriate hour from Matins in the early hours of the morning to Compline at bedtime. A diocesan priest or seminarist instead of singing these services publicly recites them in solitary silence (though one's lips and tongue must move or one's obligation remains unfulfilled). The recitation of the office took about an hour a day. The services were built around the Psalter, with ecclesiastical anthems and prayers, and readings from other parts of the Scripture and from the Church Fathers. Most of the prayers and readings were organized as two annual cycles, one based on the life of Christ, the other on the Calendar of Saints. These prayers and readings varied, and most recurred only once yearly; so that with them there was no danger of monotony. But the entire Psalter was recited once a week, and some of the psalms became very tedious by repetition (particularly Psalm 118, the longest and most frequently used). None the less the Psalter must be one of the most magnificent collections of prayers in any religious tradition. It was, perhaps, a paradox that the core of the professional prayers of the Christian priesthood should be a Jewish prayerbook. But the psalms were commonly introduced by an antiphon which gave them a Christian interpretation; and it was part of Catholic doctrine that the Old Testament was the inspired word of God no less than the New. The most entertaining part of the breviary were the lessons in the second nocturn at Matins; these were (often legendary) lives of the saints whose feasts we were celebrating. Saints who were not important enough to have their own office written were celebrated by an office common to the class to which they belonged. For this purpose men were divided first into martyrs and non-martyrs, and then into bishops and non-bishops. Women were divided first into virgins and non-virgins, and after that into martyrs and non-martyrs. It did not strike me at the time that this was an odd way to classify the human race.

Shortly before I began reciting the office, Pope Pius XII issued a new Latin translation of the Psalter to replace the Vulgate. The new version was no doubt more faithful to the Hebrew and to modern scholarship; but it was bland and schoolmasterly beside the rugged phrases of St Jerome. This was the first of many emasculating liturgical reforms, carried out in several denominations, in the name of relevance and contemporary idiom.

New subdeacons were proud to walk up and down in the garden, reciting the office from handsome breviaries bound in limp leather with gold deckling and brightly coloured markers. Monsignor Heard once suggested to me that it was ostentatious to use such a volume in a public place like a bus or train. He lent me one cunningly disguised to look like a Baedeker. As the novelty wore off, the breviary could turn into a chore. A busy priest who has left the office to the end of the day finds little edification in keeping awake to gabble through to the end of Compline before midnight.

It was Cardinal Agagianian, a nobly bearded Armenian, Prefect of the Congregation of Rites, who raised me from the subdiaconate to the diaconate. The transformation from subdeacon to deacon was barely noticeable: some new formulae in the recitation of the office, the right to read the Gospel instead of the Epistle at High Mass, the wearing of a stole not round the neck, like a priest's, but from left shoulder to right thigh.

There was one privilege of the deacon, however, which made the office exciting for a devout aspirant to the priesthood. Unlike all others below the rank of priest, the deacon was allowed to touch the consecrated bread, to distribute Communion, and to carry the Host in its monstrance to its high place of enthronement at Benediction. To a believer in Jesus's sacramental presence this was awe-inspiring. It marked how close we had come to the priesthood and to its saving and mysterious power of consecrating bread and wine and turning them into the real body and blood of the Son of God.

The power to say Mass was indeed the centre of the priestly office. There were other sacraments which were reserved to bishops: in general only bishops could ordain or confirm. There were sacraments which laymen and women could administer: anyone, even a non-Christian, could validly baptize, and matrimony was a sacrament conferred on each other by bride and groom. The sacraments reserved to the priest were Eucharist, Penance, and Extreme Unction; and of these it was the Mass which was the most important. Sins could be forgiven to the perfectly contrite without the intervention of the priest, and the last anointing was not necessary for salvation. But the priest, and the priest alone, could bring about the mystery of transubstantiation and re-enact the death of Christ upon the Cross in the daily sacrificial renewal of the Mass. Moreover, to hear confessions or anoint the sick, the seminarist would have to wait until appointed to a parish, but he could begin to say Mass daily from the day of his ordination.

The philosophical difficulties I had felt about transubstantiation had not been solved. But they had been put into the background by an emotional commitment to the real presence and a hunger to be a protagonist in the ancient liturgy. In the very first year after ordination they revived when the time came, in the Gregorian course, to study the theoretical theology of the Eucharist, the doctrines of the accidents which adhered in no substance, and the sacrifice which was and was not identical with the one and only sacrifice of Christ. But the period of preparation for the priesthood coincided with the end of the two years of theological studies at the Gregorian which were intellectually the most satisfying of the eight years I spent there. And our attentions were fixed not on speculative theology but on the practical business of learning the correct performance of the liturgy.

Every word, movement, and gesture of the priest at Mass was carefully prescribed. The Roman Missal set out in black the words the priest must say and in red the actions he must perform. The red comments, called 'rubrics', prescribed whether he should stand or kneel, open or close his hands, pick up the bread or the chalice. Around these there had grown volumes of commentary, explaining at each point how loud the priest's voice must be, whether his head was to be bowed, and if bowed, whether slightly or profoundly; whether the body as well as the head should be bowed, whether the hands were to be open or shut; how, if open, the hands should strictly parallel each other, with the tips of the fingers at the width and level of the shoulders. It was no trivial task to commit to memory all these regulations. We spent months rehearsing the rubrics at 'dry Masses' under the drill of a senior priest. We were finally inspected, and passed or failed, by the Rector or Vice; it was like a driving test authorizing the removal of L-plates. After ordination, too, at our first real Mass, we had an assistant priest to make sure that we made no disastrous mistakes. After that the young priest was on his own.

Ordinands in Rome are in an unusual position. They are not normally ordained by the bishop of the diocese in which they are to serve. The Pope's deputy must be given permission to ordain them, by a 'dismissorial letter' from their own bishop. My own diocesan at that time was Archbishop Godfrey, who spent some years at Liverpool between being Apostolic Delegate and moving to the See of Westminster. He had been Rector of the English College in Rome when Alec had been a student, and the two had remained on friendly terms. At Alec's suggestion he agreed to take the unusual step of coming out to Rome to ordain the Senior Student and myself in the English College summer chapel at Palazzola. It was much pleasanter for the ordinands and their families to have a brief private ceremony in a cool country chapel, rather than take part in a mass ordination in the sweltering city.

Our ordination day was 10 July 1955. The ceremony was simpler than it would have been in Rome, but it was none the less moving. There were just two of us to prostrate ourselves for the Litany of the Saints and to receive the Archbishop's blessing. At the most solemn moment of the ordination the bishop and all the priests present lay their hands on the head of the ordinands: this is the sacramental transmission of orders. Then the candidates are invested in the priestly vestment, or chasuble. Their hands are anointed and bound in cloth, and touched to the chalice and paten which will be their tools in the daily workmanship of the Mass. Thus ordained, they join the Archbishop in the celebration of the Mass of the day — such concelebration, now common in the Church, was then a function unique to the ordination Mass. Finally, the newly ordained priests promise obedience to the bishop, and he imposes hands once again to confer the power to absolve sins.

New priests on the day of their ordination and first Mass are fêted like bride and groom at a wedding. Friends give one presents (a vestment, or a chalice, or an altar missal), and receive an ordination card, or memento of the day, with the name of the ordinand, the date, and a motto. For my text I chose a prayer of Blessed Ralph Sherwin, the protomartyr of the English College: 'God grant us all his grace and blessing until the end, that living in his fear, and dying in his favour, we may enjoy one another for ever.'

Almost always the families of Roman students travelled out for their ordination; my mother came with Alec and led the queue to the altar steps to kiss our freshly anointed hands. Archbishop, Rector, and all the staff knelt before the new priests to receive their blessing; for a day or two an air of magic and awe hung about them and set them apart from even their closest friends in a mist of glory.

If Catholic doctrine is true, every priest validly ordained derives his orders in an unbroken line of laying on of hands, through the bishop who ordains him, back to one of the twelve Apostles. This is a matter, of course, of faith not history; but there must be centuries-long, recorded chains of layings on of hands. It surprises me that priests never seem to trouble to trace their spiritual ancestry in this way, finding out who ordained their bishop, and who ordained him, and so on to Julius II or Celestine V or Hildebrand, or Gregory the Great, perhaps.

The day after ordination, the young priest says his first Mass. This, like ordination, is an event attended by family and friends and followed with feasting and jubilation. It is the climax of long years of preparation on the priest's part, and of sacrifice on his family's part. For the priest himself it is no less exciting than his ordination, but much more relaxed: he will never again be ordained, but this he will do almost every day of his life.

I have no clear memory of this celebration, but I do recall most vividly the exaltation of the first months during which I had the power to say Mass. Normally a slow and sluggish riser, I would leap early out of bed, fully awake and full of excitement at the thought of the momentous act I was privileged to perform. I rarely said the public Community Mass: most days I celebrated alone at a side altar with a junior member of the College to serve as acolyte and congregation. But that made no difference to the solemnity of the sacrifice or the validity of the consecration.

It was touching the body of Christ, the closeness of the priest to Jesus, which most enthralled me. I would gaze on the Host after the words of consecration, soft-eyed like a lover looking into the eyes of his beloved. Following St Bernard, and the *Imitation of Christ*, I thought of prayer as a loving colloquy with the human Jesus who must be every man's closest friend. In the privileged intimacy of the time between consecration and Communion I gave passionate rein to the romantic feelings of devout affection that welled up within. In thanksgiving in private after each Mass, I found that my emotional attachment to the Lord could find expression as well in Shakespeare's sonnets:

> *Being thy slave, what should I do but tend,*
> *Upon the houres, and times of your desire?*
> *I have no precious time at all to spend,*
> *Nor services to do till you require*

as in the hymns of the Bernardine tradition:

> *Jesu, dulcis memoria*
> *Dans vera cordis gaudia*
> *Sed super mel et omnia*
> *Eius dulcis presentia.*

During the summer at Palazzola, the mere saying of Mass each day was an immensely exciting event, one which I hated to miss for any reason. After the return to Rome, there was the added excitement that on chosen days I was free to go out in the early morning with my young server to celebrate at the historic shrines of the city. I could say Mass on the sepulchre of St Peter in the crypt of the great basilica; in candle-lit *memoriae* in second-century catacombs; in the Gesù, beneath the apogee of Baroque art in Pozzi's triumph of St Ignatius. Once, at the Palazzo Massimi, I said Mass for members of that ancient family in the bedroom where St Philip Neri was believed to have raised one of their ancestors from the dead. Those early days as a priest remain in my memory as days of fulfilment and tremulous happiness; something precious, and yet too fragile to last, like a romantic love-affair brought up short by the reality of an ill-assorted marriage.

Theology and Verification

The final year of theology, like that of philosophy, was taken up with preparation for the licentiate. Hitherto, emergencies excepted, the student had been allowed to leave the College premises only as a member of a *camerata*, or group of four; during these final months, theologians nearing graduation were allowed abroad alone and unaccompanied. As a mark of their entitlement to unescorted perambulation, they wore not the usual 'tails' or *soprana*, but a flimsy garment which hung down the back in concertina pleats from a stiff pad across the shoulders, a *ferraiuola*.

There were four years of theological studies to be revised, but an important and more creative task was the writing of a practical exercise or small thesis. I chose as my topic the logical status of propositions concerning God. The choice reflected my growing interest in contemporary English philosophy; even for a theological dissertation I chose a topic where the necessary reading was almost entirely philosophical. My idea was to apply to propositions of both natural and revealed theology the techniques of linguistic analysis; or rather, to record, with comment and criticism of my own, what was being done in this area in the English philosophical journals.

I did much of the reading for the dissertation not in the College or University, but in the British Council library in the Via Quattro Fontane, where I worked through recent issues of *Mind* and *Philosophy*. Looking back at the thesis now, I am struck both by the amount of linguistic philosophy I had already read while officially studying scholastic theology, and also by my almost total lack of discrimination. It was only after I got to Oxford that I learnt to tell good analytical work from bad. I wrote:

Contemporary English philosophy is dominated by the principle of verification, whether stated in its original form as imported from Vienna, or with subsequent modifications. The principle may be stated thus: 'The meaning of any proposition is given by its mode of verification.' So that the primary question to be asked of any proposition is not 'Is it true?' but 'How could we know whether it was true or false?' . . . With regard to religious propositions, then, we should be asked not 'Are they true?' but 'What would make us call them true or false?' The first question is not 'Is "God loves the world" true?' but 'What would make it true or false?'

The demand for 'verification' is no longer a demand that each proposition uttered should have a 'cash-value' in sense-experience. The earlier logical positivists decided that all non-tautologous statements were reducible to statements about sense-experience, and so they rigidly excluded from their philosophy, as being meaningless, all such statements as were not reducible. More recently, logical analysts have realized that a technique applicable to scientific statements is not necessarily applicable in all fields. Nowadays, propositions or systems of propositions are not measured against a pre-established criterion and found wanting. But they are expected to furnish some criterion (different, it may be, for each case) for measuring the truth or falsehood of their propositions. Thus, in our case, theology is not ruled out of court because its statements are not measurable by scientific criteria. Only theology is expected to state what is the criterion by which its statements are to be judged.

The theologian, I maintained, could not refuse the demand for an account of the meaning of the terms used in the description of God. One cannot maintain that they are something which has meaning only for God and not for human beings; one must have some understanding of the meaning of the words occurring in the Creeds, otherwise there would be nothing to distinguish one dogma from another, or to distinguish orthodox dogma from heresy. Belief would thus be reduced to the recitation of a magic formula at God's behest.

I went on to argue that not only must faith involve an understanding of the propositions believed, but that faith itself conferred that understanding:

There must be a sense in which dogmatic propositions 'mean something different' to the believer and the unbeliever. For it is undeniable that believer and unbeliever use exactly the same propositions. There is nothing to stop an atheist from reciting the Creed, and prefacing it with 'non credo' instead of 'credo'. Theologians tell us that faith puts us in contact with God's own knowledge; but when it comes to expressing that knowledge in words, the believer uses exactly the same statements to describe it as the atheist does to refute it. It seems to me, then, that one must say that the gift of faith enables one not only to accept God-propositions as true, but also to see them as meaningful. So that one and the same proposition does not mean the same to a Catholic as to an atheist.

This paragraph is full of muddles. What a proposition means must be independent of its truth value; one cannot take it to mean one thing if one believes it and another thing if one disbelieves it. Belief and disbelief are contrasting attitudes to one and the same proposition, and two sentences cannot express the same proposition if they have different meanings. After this muddled beginning I went on to inquire in what way God-propositions were meaningful. Were they meaningful merely by evoking emotional responses? No: theological propositions purported to be informative, not merely evocative. Five classes of statements had been the topics extensively discussed by analytic philosophers: the propositions of logic and mathematics; empirical statements; scientific hypotheses; principles of ethics; aesthetic judgements. I proceeded to compare theological statements with propositions in each of these classes.

Some statements about God might be analytic in the way that (so I then believed) statements of logic and mathematics are: but neither 'God exists' nor any revealed article of the Creed could be analytic; otherwise the Ontological Argument would be valid, and revelation would be no more than a lesson in logic. I accepted the then almost unanimous consensus against the validity of the Ontological Argument, but argued at some length (in particular against J. N. Findlay) that its failure did not mean that the notion of God was nonsensical. In calling God a necessary being, believers did not mean that 'God exists' was a necessary proposition. Even, therefore, if all necessary propositions were tautologies, mere rules for the use of language (a positivistic view which I then found tempting), it did not follow that there was anything incoherent in the concept of God.

But if the most important theological propositions are not analytic, I went on, they must in some sense of the word be empirical propositions; some sort of experience must be relevant to their truth and falsehood. But does not this present a difficulty?

What experience would verify the proposition 'God is good'? If God makes me healthy, wealthy and wise, I say He is good; if He makes me a leper on a dunghill, I must still say that He is good. There is no experience imaginable, it seems, no state of affairs conceivable which is not consistent with the proposition 'God is good'. Therefore it is impossible that I could have any experience of what the proposition 'God is not good' would mean. But if I cannot know the meaning of one term of a contradiction, how can I know the meaning of the other? If I cannot know what 'God is not good' means, then I cannot know the difference between the state of affairs described by the proposition 'God is not good' and the proposition 'God is good'; therefore, on the criterion given above, both statements are meaningless.

Some people claim to meet God in specific effects of His operation, seeing victories in battle, or rescue from misfortune, as confirmation of the divine goodness. But, according to most theologians, God's activity, if it is anywhere, is everywhere. But the specific effect theory of verification, I conceded, was not entirely false. Natural effects did not verify any God-proposition, but a miraculous effect might partly verify a proposition such as 'God is omnipotent' and 'God is good'. The Resurrection of Christ, whether or not provable, is eminently verifiable; and it helps to confer meaning on these propositions and others.

If theological propositions could not be put on a par with straight-forward reports of experience, nor were they really comparable with statements of scientific hypotheses:

> Scientific hypotheses are refutable by facts, while theological propositions are not. Theological propositions seem to be compatible with all possible factual statements. This all-compatibility of theological statements does seem to go perilously near to making them meaningless on any view of meaning whatever. For the minimal requirement for a significant statement seems to be that it should not be compatible with every other conceivable descriptive or factual statement . . . And so we can say nothing, either for or against, God's existence. For unless we know what a created world looks like, and what an uncreated world looks like, we never have any standard to which we can compare our own world, in order to see which of the two types it belongs to. To ask 'Does God exist?' is only a pseudo-question, like 'What does my desk look like when no one is looking at it?'

I considered and rejected various possible answers to this difficulty. It was no good saying that there *were* some factual states of affairs incompatible with God's goodness, e.g. the eternal damnation of all human beings; for the language describing such eschatological states was itself problematic. Nor was it sufficient to point out that all-compatibility was a property which God-propositions shared with propositions of logic and mathematics.

I more or less gave up the attempt to answer this familiar positivist difficulty about the meaningfulness of theological propositions, merely remarking:

> It is to the point to notice that the property of all-compatibility belongs to the verification principle itself (and also to all other metaphysical principles; but the verification principle is the only metaphysical principle now accepted in many philosophical circles).

But I continued to strive anxiously to bring theological propositions into accord with the verification principle. Taking a lead from Bergson's *Les Deux Sources de la Religion et de la Morale* I explored the possibility that propositions about God were verified by mystical experience. I concluded a long discussion of Bergson and some of his critics with the words: 'It seems then to be a perfectly plausible position to maintain that for the mystic a statement such as "God is loving" is verified, and therefore made meaningful, by his own experience.' It would not be correct to argue that in that case 'God' became a word for a particular type of experience and nothing more; one could say that only if one was prepared to say that all names of human beings were words for experiences and nothing more. 'It is no scandal if certainty of the existence of God turns out to be no greater than certainty that other people exist. Perhaps only Descartes thought it was.' But can the mystic communicate to others? Or will religious language, on this account, be meaningful for him but for no one else?

The answer to this is to be found in Bergson's remark that the reading of mystical writers awakens a distant echo in every reader's own mind:

> If we say that ultimately only religious experience . . . can give meaning to propositions about God, then it is true that it is useless to try to explain the meaning of such propositions to those who have had no religious experience whatsoever. But it remains possible that all have had some religious experience which has hitherto remained implicit . . . We can agree that to teach the meaning of religious experience to those who hardly possess it at all, is an extremely difficult task. The difficulty has always been realized, and has perhaps never been better stated than by Plato in his parable of the Cave.

From the point of view of natural theology, Christ could be looked on as the greatest of mystics; for him theological language had meaning in virtue of his own experience, and from him meaning could be communicated to others:

> We believe that when he who had seen the sunlight came into our cave, the darkness did not comprehend him, but took him and crucified him, as Plato had prophesied. (*Rep.* 517a4)

The way in which the mystic makes other people's implicit religious experience explicit is by analogical discourse. The traditional scholastic theories of analogy, I argued, were powerless to confer meaning on theological discourse if they were not reinforced with a consideration of religious experience. The mystic can see which of various analogies are more like the ineffable reality of God. Thus, he can tell the non-mystic that he should think of Him as a loving father rather than as a thundering Jove. His hearer can at least obey him, thinking of God as a loving father in the literal sense, but with a vague awareness of the inadequacy of his thought. He can repeat what the mystic says, knowing that it also has an analogical meaning. 'So we say the "Our Father", not knowing what it means, but knowing that Christ did.'

The experience of the mystics provides an ostensive definition of the word 'God'. An ostensive definition consists in telling someone the behaviour to be adopted in order to experience the object intended; thus, we point to tell people to look in the direction of our finger. And the mystics can give us directions on how to experience God—these are clear and precise, however austere and disagreeable they may be, like St John of the Cross's rules for entering the Dark Night:

> The mystics' experience gives them the power to draw ethical conclusions, which they can then pass on to others (e.g. the Sermon on the Mount). It also gives them the power to construct analogies to describe their experiences, just as musicians use analogies in programme notes. These analogies can be understood in two ways. First, the hearer may think of them as being literally true . . . accepting, on the word of the mystic, that such a picture is helpful but inadequate. Secondly he may consider the analogy in order to make explicit to himself a religious experience which he already has.

Atheists were quite correct when they said that statements about God were meaningless. But the verb 'to mean' needs a dative: the statements are meaningless *to them*; and the defect might be in them and not in the statements. All the atheist could do was to follow the ethical recommendations of the mystic and then see whether he is granted the experience which gives the words meaning. Thus Pascal, advising the atheist to take holy water; thus

Gerard Manley Hopkins writing to the atheist Bridges, agreeing that since he did not rightly believe in God, it was useless to tell him to pray for faith. 'But I have another counsel open to no objection, and yet I think it will be unexpected. I lay great stress on it. It is to give alms. I daresay indeed you do give alms, still I should say give more: I should be bold to say, give, up to the point of sensible inconvenience.'

There was hardly anything original in this licentiate dissertation; most of what it contained was commonplace among those in England or America who combined an uncritical admiration of linguistic empiricism with an interest in the philosophy of religion. On the other hand, it was very different from most other dissertations at the Gregorian University; and it derived almost nothing, for better or worse, from the theology taught there. The official supervisor of the dissertation was P. Paul Vignon who, in our final year, had given us a totally baffling series of lectures on the virtue of faith. He was charming and friendly, but he had no interest in the kind of analytical philosophy which I found attractive. Much more helpful, in an unofficial capacity, was Fr Copleston, then teaching in the philosophy faculty: I relied on him for advice about reading and borrowed from him the galley proofs of his then unpublished book *Contemporary Philosophy*. It must have been he who introduced me to Professor R. B. Braithwaite's pamphlet *An Empiricist's View of the Nature of Religious Belief*.

The dissertation bears the marks of Braithwaite's conviction that it was most important that one should be a good empiricist, whatever havoc this might wreak on the traditional interpretation of theology. This is particularly evident in the final chapter of the dissertation, concerned with specifically dogmatic propositions. There is a problem about dogmas defined by the Church, such as the hypostatic union, or the nature of justification. How can it be said that two theologians are believing the same dogma if, as is very often the case, they attach quite different interpretations to the dogma? Is it the words or the meaning which constitute the dogma to be believed? Or is there some minimal meaning about which all must agree?

It seems truest to say that what theologians agree on about a dogmatic definition is neither the words alone, nor a minimal meaning, but the literal sense of the words — that is, the sense in which an inquirer without any religious experience could understand the mystic's parables. Revealed statements are always symbolic: theologians must agree on the symbol, but may disagree on the reality which it symbolizes; i.e. in practice, on other symbols into which it is translatable, or on the aspect of religious experience to which it refers. It is rather as if two people agreed that Jane was like a flower, but one thought so because she drooped, and the other because she was pretty.

Theologians did have to agree about the behaviour demanded by the Church as a consequence of a dogmatic statement; even though we might not be sure what was meant by the justification of infants, we could expect trouble if we stopped baptizing babies. The ordinary believer, in reciting the Creed, was, importantly, agreeing to this direction of behaviour by the Church.

> Thus, we none of us know (except by some quasi-mystical experience) what it really means to say that Christ is present in the Eucharist; but we do know two things, univocally. (a) The proposition 'This is my body' is true in the sense in which Christ meant it (b) I must act as if it were literally true (genuflect before the Host, treat it with care etc.).

I concluded my treatment of dogmatic propositions thus:

> The defined meaning of a dogmatic proposition need not be more than this: 'This proposition, understood in its *prima facie* sense, is a helpful picture of God.' The situation is the same as that which we suggested obtained in the case of our Lord's parables. To find any meaning other than the *prima facie* one from a dogmatic proposition, one must have a supernatural religious experience. Dogmatic propositions are *constructed* out of the religious experience of Christ and the Apostles; but they are understood by means of each one's own faith . . . To understand the meaning, no less than to assent to the truth, of dogmatic statements, faith is necessary.

In the last pages of the essay I explicitly related my argument to Braithwaite's pamphlet. Braithwaite maintained that the criterion for the meaningfulness of the assertions of the Christian's faith was 'the intention of a Christian to follow the Christian way of life'. The meaning of the whole body of Christian assertions is given by 'their proclaiming intentions to follow an agapeistic way of life'. So it is the behaviour policy which gives the meaning to the religious propositions. How then does one religion differ from another, if their behaviour policies are the same? Apart from ritual practice, the key difference is that the behaviour policies are associated with the telling of different stories. The stories do not need to be believed in order to influence one's conduct; and since they do not have to be believed in there is no need to concern oneself with whether all parts of the story are consistent with each other.

> I cannot help feeling that Braithwaite's views on religious propositions are very nearly correct. It is true that the intention to live up to Christian morality is a fundamental part of any conversion to the Christian religion. And it is true that in our religious life, it is the imaginative and inaccurate stories — the imaginative pictures of God present to us, for example, in very much the same way as our human friends are present — which are the stimulus to prayer and every form of good work. It is also, as I have tried to show, true that it is only the literal 'story' sense of dogmatic propositions which is strictly defined and believed.

There were, however, a number of gaps in Braithwaite's account. He had left out, for instance, the fact that the believer was aware, at least implicitly, that the stories in their literal sense are not true; but that on the other hand our Lord, who first 'told the stories', knew (empirically) what they meant in their analogical sense.

> The believer accepts, on the word of our Lord and the Church, that these stories have an analogical sense even if he cannot understand what it can be; and that the literal sense of the story is a useful picture of God and of his relations with the world. The believer's own religious experience can gradually enable him to see the analogical meaning of the stories. The more he progresses in faith and charity, the less he will be dependent on the imaginative stimulus of the inaccurate literal picture, and the more he will rely on his own experience of the religious reality which is behind the analogical sense of the stories.

I have analysed this licentiate dissertation at length because it is the fullest record I possess of the state of my mind when I was ordained as a priest. I find it painful to re-read after twenty-five years: not only am I embarrassed at the philosophical naivety of so much of its content, but I am astonished at the thinness of the intellectual underpinning of a lifetime commitment to the service of the Church. Emotionally, as I have described, I was at this period totally committed to the priestly life; as devoted to the Church as the most adoring lover to his mistress. But the emotional investment provided no more adequate a basis for life of fidelity to the priestly ideal than infatuation does for a lasting marriage. The intellectual rationalization which the dissertation provides for the religious emotion looks, from this distance, merely like a licence to wallow in make-believe.

I completed the dissertation on the feast of the Finding of the Cross, 3 May. Some weeks after handing it in I received the mark: not the 10 or *summa cum laude* that I had grown to expect, but a 9. P. Vignon, who was the examiner as well as the supervisor, called me up to explain the mark. The industry and intelligence shown by the dissertation, he explained kindly, was sufficient to justify a 10; but the doctrine it contained was so dubious from a theological viewpoint that it had been decided to give it only a 9. If it were to be published as a dissertation approved *summa cum laude* by the Gregorian it might do harm to the reputation of the University. I told myself that the disappointing mark reflected not my inadequacies, but the bigotry of the authorities.

A few weeks later there came the final examination in theology, when I was questioned orally on four theses selected out of the 100 which the licentiate candidate had to master. I have little memory of the examination, but I know that I had no complaint to make of the way it was conducted. This time, again, the result was a 9, not a 10; and I had no excuse for not having matched my philosophical *summa cum laude* with a theological one.

- IX -

The Jerusalem Bible

At the Gregorian I began to appreciate many of the academic merits of Upholland. In particular I came to realize the liveliness of my uncle, Alexander Jones, as a Biblical scholar. I spent many hours as a teenager arguing with him and learning from him, whether walking up and down the leafy avenues of Upholland on summer evenings, or cycling along Lancashire lanes during the vacation. My classmates and I heard his lectures on Biblical inspiration in Syntax, and on the Gospel of St John in Rhetoric. He was a witty and imaginative teacher, who entertained but also puzzled students who could not always tell when he was being serious. He worked hard to make us love the Bible: he firmly believed that Catholics should give it no less attention and respect than Protestants did. But he was also anxious that it should be interpreted as liberally as was consistent with the Catholic doctrines of inspiration and inerrancy. He strove, not always successfully, to show that the official Catholic expressions of these doctrines were compatible with a non-fundamentalist exposition of the Scriptures.

His model as a scholar was Père Jean-Marie Lagrange, founder of the École Biblique in Jerusalem. Lagrange, a French Dominican, had been at one time suspected of heretical tendencies during the Modernist crisis; he had, however, made clear his submission to Roman teaching while resisting the ultra-conservative anti-Modernist trend characteristic of the Jesuit Biblical Institute in Rome itself. It was at the 'Bib' that Alec had received his own specialist training during a year at the Beda College after he left the Venerabile in 1934. He was unhappy there, finding the conservative spirit of the institution stifling. Lagrange became his hero, and after Lagrange's death in 1938 he looked up to his successors at the École Biblique, Roland De Vaux and Pierre Benoit. He greeted eagerly the quarterly arrival of the *Revue Biblique*, and his New Testament teaching was based on Lagrange's

four massive Gospel commentaries. What he particularly admired
in Lagrange was his ability to assimilate the findings of scholarship
and archaeology with the tradition of Catholic teaching. Alec lent
me the life of Lagrange for my edification. I was not altogether
warmed by the picture. One thing that was clear was that Lagrange
was a phenomenally hard-working scholar. One Christmas
morning a young novice in Jerusalem called on him in his study
to wish him a merry Christmas. 'Very civil of you, brother,' said
the scholar, 'but could you not have waited until recreation time?'

Alec had the gifts, had he been encouraged, to make an original
contribution to Biblical scholarship. But his task, as he saw
it, was to present the results of first-hand scholarship in a form
digestible to a wider public. Friends of his have blamed successive
Archbishops of Liverpool for not encouraging him to work at the
frontiers of learning; but there was something in his own character
which made *haute vulgarisation* more congenial to him than academic
life would have been. He was unnecessarily diffident about his own
academic ability; he felt he lacked the erudition to talk on equal
terms with English Biblical scholars, and after a few months spent
in the École Biblique in the early 1950s he knew that he lacked
the physical and intellectual stamina to work at the pace of the
Dominican scholars there.

His first book was a textbook on the history of Israel for Catholic
schools and seminaries, *The Kingdom of Promise*. It was written
in collaboration with a Jesuit of the Biblical Institute, Robert
Dyson S.J., but the collaboration was an uneven one, and
Alec wrote all but four chapters of the book. It is densely
packed with information; too densely, for most of its intended
readership—I speak as one who had to use it as a class
textbook—found it very hard going. His second book was
much more successful. It began life as a series of articles
on the Old Testament in the *Catholic Gazette*, the monthly
of the Catholic Missionary Society. The articles were written in
a light, sometimes knockabout style whose flavour can be caught
in the very first sentence of the first lecture: 'Adam's apple has
stuck in many a throat and wits have observed that it needs a pillar
of salt to digest the ''Whale'' story.' But the serious underlying
purpose was spelt out in the Foreword:

These pages are written for the average person. Few have time or taste
for the rich food of Biblical learning as it is presented in weighty
volumes and yet we all need the nourishment. This is an attempt to

offer a little of it in light form for delicate digestions. The style is therefore a shade unconventional. I hope it will not be thought facetious and flippant, or rather that nobody will infer that one thinks lightly upon these grave matters. The first might be excused, being an error of policy; the second would be intolerable as an offence against piety. Where the honour of the Word of God and the dignity of Catholic exegesis are concerned there may be room for simple style but not for superficial thought.

In the first version of one of the articles, he wrote that it was no part of Catholic doctrine to read Genesis as teaching that the entire human race was descended from a single pair. This made the diocesan censor uneasy and in summer 1949, when the article was in the press, Pius XII issued an encyclical, *Humani Generis*, in which the descent from a single pair ('monogenism') was singled out as one of the indispensable elements of the creation story. The encyclical appeared while Alec and my mother and I were on holiday just before I left for Rome; and energetic efforts had to be made to recall the relevant part of the proofs to add a footnote to bring it into accord with the Papal directive. The book, entitled *Unless Some Man Show Me*, in allusion to Acts 8, 27–31, was popular and sold well in hardback and paper editions on both sides of the Atlantic. It led also to many invitations to lecture, in the U.S.A. and Australia, as well as in Britain.

Alec's greatest work was editing the English version of the Jerusalem Bible. From about 1946 the Ecole Biblique had been engaged in producing a new annotated French version of the Bible, which appeared in forty-three fascicules under the general editorship of Père Chifflot. By 1956 the Bible was complete, and the whole was issued in a single volume, with abbreviated introductions. It presented, in a form accessible to the lay reader, the fine flower of Catholic Biblical scholarship; an English reviewer in the Dominican periodical *Life of the Spirit* said: 'We now have within our reach what must be called, quite soberly, the best Bible in the world.'

Alec was excited by the solid and liberal scholarship of the French Bible de Jérusalem. Even before the single-volume French edition had appeared he had begun to canvass the possibility of an English translation of the French commentary. But to what English version of the Scriptures should the notes be attached? At this time, though the Authorised version, like other Protestant translations, was forbidden by the Code of Canon Law, English Catholics had several vernacular Bibles available. There was the 'Douai version',

the Old Testament translated by English scholars at the recusant
seminary of Douai, the New Testament translated by the Douai
seminarians in exile at Rheims, the whole lightly revised from its
sixteenth-century original by Bishop Challoner in the eighteenth
century. As a piece of English literature the Douai version
had been trumped by the Authorised version of King James;
as an expression of Biblical scholarship both versions had been
outdated by many modern developments. Twentieth-century
Roman Catholic scholarship had offered the Westminster version:
learned, turgid, incomplete, and unknown to all but specialists.
One of the finest writers of English in the twentieth century, Mgr
Ronald Knox, toiled in solitary misery for some twenty years to
produce a version of the Bible which literate Catholics could be
proud of. He was a master of the language, adept at rendering
into English the ambiguities of the original. To take one example
among a thousand, the fifth verse of the Prologue of St John is
translated thus in the Authorised version: 'The light shined in
darkness and the darkness comprehended it not.' The Greek word
translated 'comprehended' is ambiguous in the original: does it
mean 'understood' or 'quenched'? Either version is defensible:
Knox, keeping both options open, translated 'the darkness could
not master it'. Knox's version, at this time, enjoyed such prestige
that it would have seemed absurd to offer a brand new Catholic
translation to compete with it. On the other hand the notes of the
Bible de Jérusalem could not simply be attached to any existing
version. So Alec decided that while the notes and introduction were
the main purpose of an English Jerusalem Bible, they would have
to be attached to a new, unpretentious and workmanlike English
text.

With such a project in mind Alec approached the well-known
English Catholic publishers Sheed and Ward. They were frightened
by the expense and risk of the venture, and turned it down. A
new and comparatively unknown publisher, Darton Longman and
Todd, agreed to the proposal, and Alec drew up a list of translators
for the Biblical texts, reserving to himself the major task of
translating the French introduction and notes. Since what was
planned was not a new version of the Bible, but a text on which
to hang the fruits of French Catholic scholarship, it was not
important that the translators should know the original Biblical
languages of Greek and Hebrew. (Officially, indeed, Catholic bible
translations had to be made from the approved Latin text of the
Vulgate; Knox, who knew Greek perfectly, had to pretend to be

translating the New Testament from the Latin.) Even those who did know the original languages would have to accept the verdict of the French translators on the interpretation of controverted passages, otherwise their versions would be unsuitable as pegs for the Jerusalem notes.

With all this in mind, a team of translators was chosen. The majority were English Catholic seminary professors. Tom Worden, Alec's pupil and eventual successor as Scripture professor at Upholland, was to do Genesis; Hubert Richards, the Biblical scholar at Ware, was given Exodus, Numbers, and Deuteronomy; Lionel Johnston at Ushaw, poor man, was entrusted with Leviticus. Leo Alston, a classicist at Upholland, was to do the Pastoral Epistles; Walter Shewring, a schoolmaster at Ampleforth, was to be the translator of Ezekiel, Zechariah, Joshua, and Revelation. J. R. R. Tolkien, then better known as a Catholic Old English scholar than as the author of the *Lord of the Rings*, was asked to do Judges and Jonah. He proved a difficult collaborator—I once visited him with Alec in an attempt to iron out some of the difficulties—and in the end he contributed only a version of Jonah, leaving Judges to Walter Shewring. As one or other collaborator defaulted, Alec took personal responsibility for more and more of the translations of the Bible texts. In the end, he translated the final version of Psalms, Proverbs, Ecclesiastes, Wisdom, Isaiah, Jeremiah, Baruch, Hosea, Joel, Amos, Obadiah, Micah, Habbakuk, Zephaniah, Haggai, Malachi, Matthew, Mark, and Luke. In many of the other books, such as Samuel, Kings, and Chronicles, his editorial activity was so extensive that he became in effect co-author of the translation. His task was an enormous one, stretching over ten years, far beyond the time he had estimated or the £1,000 which the publishers had offered him.

By a pleasing act of nepotism, I was included in his list of translators. The books assigned to me were First and Second Peter, and Galatians. Since my Greek was not too rusty, I was able to translate these with one eye on the original text, and one on the French version: thus I could render the original faithfully, adopting the French translator's preferences where there was doubt about the meaning of the original, but knowing where the French version incorporated Gallicisms which could be discarded in English. The versions which I submitted were found satisfactory, and I was given two more substantial commissions: the Epistle to the Romans and the Book of Job. It was an honour to be given the most controversial and the most poetical of the books of the Bible: I soon came to appreciate the ambiguities of the one and the splendours of the other.

In Romans, I discovered there was hardly a line which could be translated without taking sides on some issue which had caused ink to be spilt and blood to be shed at the time of the Reformation. Take the Greek word *'dikaiosynē'* and its cognates. The Authorised version translates this 'righteousness'; the Douai version 'justice'. In favour of 'justice' could be alleged that this is how the same word is uncontroversially translated in the writings of Plato, and that it allowed the related Greek verb *'dikaioo'* to be translated by the cognate English 'justify'. In favour of 'righteousness' could be alleged that it made clear that it was personal, rather than social, uprightness that was in question; against it was that it introduced irrelevant overtones of self-righteousness and smugness. But the merely linguistic considerations were overshadowed by sectarian ones. The word 'righteous' was associated with the Lutheran belief that sinful men, after salvation, did not really become just, but were merely declared righteous by a forgiving God. The word 'just' and still more the verb 'justify' were associated with the Tridentine counter-Reformation doctrine that after the Redemption, humans were not merely deemed but actually became just, once more, in the eyes of God. The declared aim of the Jerusalem Bible was to provide, for the general public, notes which were 'neither sectarian nor superficial'. In line after line of Romans, decisions had to be taken which looked like taking sides on Reformation quarrels. I decided, in the end, that it was better to err, if at all, on the opposite side of the sectarian barrier, and in the version which I handed over to the editor, I systematically translated *'dikaiosyne'* as 'righteousness', paying the price that the corresponding Greek verb had to be rendered, as in the Authorised version, by the unconnected English verb 'justify'.

My agonizing in the end turned out to be so much wasted time. The publishers, having seen the first draft of a number of translations, decided that the texts needed revising not only by the Biblical editor, but also by literary specialists. My own versions of the New Testament were handed over to a Benedictine poet, Sylvester Houédard O.S.B., who subjected every verse to a drastic revision. The version of Romans which appeared in print was some distance from the draft which I had submitted. The difference can be seen by comparing the two versions of Romans 2,17–21. In my version it read as follows:

You may bear the name of Jew, you may trust in the Law, and boast of God. With the help of the Law, you may know his will and tell what is right. You may pride yourself on being a guide to the blind, a light to those in darkness, a teacher to the ignorant and an instructor for the unlearned, because you possess in the Law the embodiment of knowledge and of truth. If so, then why do you not teach yourself as well as others? Why, when you preach against stealing, do you steal? Why, when you forbid adultery, do you commit adultery? Why, when you abhor idols, do you rob their temples? When you boast about the Law, and then disobey the Law, you bring God himself into contempt.

By the time this had been revised by both literary editor and Biblical editor, it turned into the following:

If you call yourself a Jew, if you really trust in the Law and are proud of your God, if you know God's will through the Law and can tell what is right, if you are convinced you can guide the blind and be a beacon to those in the dark, if you can teach the ignorant and instruct the unlearned because your Law embodies all knowledge and truth, then why not teach yourself as well as the others? You preach against stealing, yet you steal; you forbid adultery, yet you commit adultery; you despise idols, yet you rob their temples. By boasting about the Law and then disobeying it, you bring God into contempt.

At first I resented the changes made in my version, which turned it into a quite different translation. But as time went on, and I could look at the two with a more impartial eye, I saw that Houédard's version was an improvement on my own. Galatians, like Romans, was almost totally rewritten. With First and Second Peter, however, I can make a greater claim to be the author of the published version.

I had a better success with my only Old Testament task, which was the translation of the Book of Job. By this time I had taken the Gregorian course in Hebrew; but this involved little more than the ability to translate into Latin the first two chapters of Genesis. To pass the examination it was easier to learn the Vulgate text of those chapters by heart (we knew them pretty well from the liturgy anyway) and to learn a few key words, rather than actually to master the Hebrew tongue. So essentially I was translating the French version of Job in the Bible de Jérusalem, with an eye on a number of commentaries and an occasional reference to the Hebrew to check on difficult passages. Alec was then to go through my version to see that it was faithful to the Hebrew.

I thoroughly enjoyed the work; I was captivated by the poetry
of the book, which I had scarcely known earlier. I tried to find
an English medium which would correspond most closely to the
stress structure and parallelism of the Hebrew poetry; here it
seemed to me that something similar to Hopkins' sprung rhythm,
which had fascinated me in adolescence, was the appropriate
equivalent. The literary editor of the Old Testament, the novelist
Alan Neame, was much happier with my style than Houédard had
been, and told the general editor that my approach could serve
as a model for the other translators.

This time, therefore, my version reached the printed page almost
unscathed. Here is a sample of it, drawn from God's rebuke to
Job in Chapter 38:

Where were you when I laid the earth's foundations?'
    Tell me, since you are so well-informed!
Who decided the dimensions of it, do you know?
    Or who stretched the measuring line across it?
What supports its pillars at their bases?
    Who laid its cornerstone
when all the stars of the morning were singing with joy
    and the Sons of God in chorus were chanting praise?
Who pent up the sea behind closed doors
    when it leapt tumultuous out of the womb,
when I wrapped it in a robe of mist
    and made black clouds its swaddling bands;
when I marked the bounds it was not to cross
    and made it fast with a bolted gate?
Come thus far, I said, and no farther;
    here your proud waves shall break.

Have you ever in your life given orders to the morning
    or sent the dawn to its post,
telling it to grasp the earth by its edges
    and shake the wicked out of it,
when it changes the earth to sealing clay
    and dyes it as a man dyes clothes
stealing the light from wicked men
    and breaking the arm raised to strike?
Have you journeyed all the way to the sources of the sea
    or walked where the Abyss is deepest?
Have you been shown the gates of Death
    or met the janitors of Shadowland?
Have you an inkling of the extent of the earth?
    Tell me all about it if you have.

The idea was that the pairs of English lines, marked by the indentations, would match the Hebrew parallelism, and that each pair would have an equal number of strong stresses (commonly three or four) which would be emphasized when reading aloud, so as to mark the poetic structure of the Hebrew.

Because of the method chosen for translation, and the amateur status of some of the translators, the general editor had almost more work than if he had translated the Bible single-handed. The work took from 1956, when the first translators, like myself, sent in their typescripts, to October 1966 when the Bible first appeared. When the work began Alec was still Prefect of Studies at Upholland. In 1961, when Archbishop Heenan was in office in Liverpool, he was moved from Upholland to become chaplain of the School for the Blind at St Vincent's, West Derby. This post carried light duties, involving little more than an occasional sermon to the blind children and a daily Mass for the nuns who ran the school. It left more time for the work on the Jerusalem Bible, but Alec felt cut off from the academic community which had been his home for twenty-five years, and he suspected that the new Archbishop had been glad of a pretext to remove him from the seminary, regarding his influence there as unhealthy, perhaps because of his liberal style of Biblical interpretation. He spent each day alone in his study, surrounded by a dozen versions of the Bible stacked on an enormous semicircular bookrest which he had had specially constructed, and which formed a kind of pen on the desk, in the middle of which he huddled over a typewriter, wrapped in an ancient Roman cloak, or *zimarra*. My mother moved to the large chaplain's house at St Vincent's to keep house for him. The arrangement did not prove altogether satisfactory, and Alec's morale was poor during the years at West Derby.

Alec was dispirited by the need to fight on several fronts for his preferred versions of certain terms: against other translators; against literary editors; against the publishers; and in one or two cases against the hierarchy. There was a controversy over the correct use of 'will' and 'shall' that seemed to last for several years; but the biggest storms centred on the rendering of the divine name in the Old Testament. Alec insisted that the Hebrew word YHWH was a name and not a mere description of God; hence translators had no warrant to change it, and it must be transliterated faithfully into English. The archaic version 'Jehovah' resulted from a misreading of the vowels to be interpolated into the original text; only 'Yahweh' was an accurate transliteration, and so 'Yahweh'

must appear in the text wherever older Bibles used 'the Lord'.
So the creation of woman, for instance, reads in the Jerusalem
Bible:

> Yahweh God made the man fall into a deep sleep. And while he
> slept, he took one of his ribs and enclosed it in flesh.
> Yahweh God built the rib he had taken from the man into a woman,
> and brought her to the man . . .

Many of Alec's collaborators were unhappy with this, but he fought
and won the battle for the use of 'Yahweh'. It appears in the
published text, with a defensive note in the foreword:

> It is in the Psalms especially that the use of the divine name *Yahweh*
> (accented on the second syllable) may seem unacceptable — though
> indeed the still stranger form 'Yah' is in constant use in the acclamation
> Hallelu-Yah (Praise Yah!). It is not without hesitation that this accurate
> form has been used and no doubt those who may care to use this
> translation of the Psalms can substitute the traditional 'the Lord'. On
> the other hand, this would be to lose much of the flavour and meaning
> of the originals. For example, to say 'The Lord is God' is surely a
> tautology, as to say 'Yahweh is God' is not.

Gradually, the translation of the text came to assume as much
importance as the translation of the commentary. During the ten
years the Jerusalem Bible was being translated the Knox version
lost much of its initial popularity; in particular the Old Testament,
which Knox had claimed to render into timeless English, came
to seem very dated and mannered. By contrast, some of the
Jerusalem Bible translators, assisted by the literary editors,
produced versions which were clear and unfussy. It became a
possibility that the Jerusalem Bible might be licensed by the
Catholic hierarchy for public use in the liturgy.

Alec laboured on, through periods of encouragement and
discouragement. Almost by way of relaxation he would steal time
away from the Jerusalem Bible to write other books. *God's Living
Word* was the published version of a set of lectures given on a tour
of Australia. Commentaries on Mark and Matthew, the first
published in 1963, the second in 1965, grew almost spontaneously
out of his own work in translating the synoptic Gospels. Both books
offer a rather complicated solution to the problem of the order and
relation of the synoptic Gospels, and have frontispiece diagrams
exhibiting the content and structure of the texts in the form

of concentric circles. Alec had a firm conviction, which he never quite succeeded in communicating to his pupils, of the value of presenting an abstract structure in visual terms.

At last, in 1966, the Bible appeared. By that time I was laicized and married; Alec presented the sumptuous American version of the Bible to myself and my American wife, with the dedication 'To my dearest Nancy and Tony, these ten years of my life— with more love than I can say'. The Bible was an astonishing success. It was indeed licensed for liturgical use—with the proviso that in the liturgical texts 'the Lord' was substituted for 'Yahweh'. It has become, so far as I have been able to observe, the version of the Bible most commonly used in church in English-speaking Catholic services.

X

Student Priest in Rome, 1956–7

For most students at the English College the course ended with the licentiate in theology; a few each year went on to further studies, in Rome or elsewhere. It was decided that I should return to Rome to study for a doctorate in divinity after my vacation in summer 1955. I joined the small band of graduate student priests who were nicknamed 'The O.N.D.': O.N.D. being the initials of Opera Nazionale Dopolavoro, a grandiose term given in the Mussolini era to recreational clubs for superannuated workers. Members of the O.N.D. continued to live in the English College but under a more relaxed discipline. One's principal official occupation was the preparation of a doctoral thesis. One year's further residence was required, after which the thesis could be completed elsewhere, with the candidate returning to Rome to defend it in an oral examination and to complete the requirements for being awarded the *laurea* and declared a doctor.

Because of the example of Alec before me I had always assumed that I would, sooner or later, end up on the staff of a seminary, and that my contribution to the Church in England would take an academic rather than a pastoral form. But it was uncertain in what academic discipline my career would lie. To become a Scripture scholar would be to follow too closely in Alec's footsteps, and in any case my gifts were abstract and speculative rather than linguistic. Philosophical problems never ceased to absorb, and sometimes torment, me; but I recoiled at the idea of learning more scholastic philosophy in the Gregorian manner. Naturally, in the end I had to accept whatever assignment I was given by my diocesan, Archbishop Godfrey; obligingly he agreed that I could pursue topics on the borderline of philosophy and theology, but under the auspices of the theology faculty, where there were teachers that I respected. So I chose as my thesis the relationship between linguistic analysis and the language of religion, the theme which I had treated with embarrassing results in my licentiate dissertation. Bernard Lonergan was assigned as my supervisor.

Lonergan's interests, like my own, were as much philosophical as theological; and indeed his longest and best-known book was *Insight*, a work of philosophy rather than theology. In our meetings in 1956-7 he tried to make me see that scholastic philosophy should not be judged by the dehydrated version I had become acquainted with: the way to appreciate it was to come to grips with the massive works of St Thomas himself. But I did not fully learn this lesson until later when I came among Catholic philosophers in Oxford. I did not see as much of Lonergan, or derive as much benefit from his supervision, as I should have done. This was my own fault, as I wrote very little work for his scrutiny—not through idleness, but because I was devoting my main effort to a different project.

One of my main preoccupations in Rome had always been ecclesiastical history: in particular recusant history, the history of the Catholic community in England during the period when Catholics were subjected to penal laws. The English College had played a central role in that history, as one of the main suppliers of the clergy who had kept the community in existence during the centuries of persecution and intolerance. Its archives contained a substantial portion of the primary sources for the history of recusant England; and its own past deserved a better record than the slapdash official history produced in the 1920s by Cardinal Gasquet. I spent much of my spare time in these and other Roman archives and wrote a number of articles on the history of the College.

I was particularly interested in the Elizabethan period when the building in the Via Monserrato was gradually turned from a pilgrim hospice into a seminary for missionary priests. The lives of its first generation of martyrs had been well written up by others; but there was much to be chronicled about the stormy internal history of the College during the closing years of the sixteenth century, when it was often a microcosm of the strife between pro-Jesuit and anti-Jesuit factions in England. I wrote in *The Venerabile* a long series of articles about the student riots of the 1590s which ended with the triumph of the Jesuit party under the Rectorship of Robert Persons (once Bursar of Balliol and then Jesuit companion of St Edmund Campion on his mission to England in 1580) from 1597 to 1610. I also wrote a piece on Persons' life as Rector of the College, drawing on the day-to-day account books in the College, which recorded the extraction of his teeth, the coaches he hired, and even the guests he had to lunch. I offered this article to the Jesuit periodical *The Month*, but it was rejected as frivolous and biased against the Society. I wrote too a long account of the way in which the College grew out of the hospice amid the plots and plans for the reconversion of England by force in the 1570s.

I enjoyed working in the Vatican archives, in a disarmingly ramshackle reading room under the eye of the Cardinal Prefect on his high desk, slipping out into the garden alongside from time to time for a quick cigarette in the shamefaced company of internationally renowned scholars similarly addicted. And I was lucky enough, eventually, to be admitted into the secret archives of the Jesuits: difficult of access, but where a scholar once admitted was treated with enormous consideration and courtesy. From Roman sources, and from the archives at Westminster Cathedral, where I worked as a temporary curate in summer 1955, I gradually built up a great dossier of material for writing the history of the College in Elizabethan days; a project for the distant future, which is now unlikely to be realized.

One of the treasures of the English College archives was the *Liber Ruber*, the diary of the College from its inception, listing all the students from St Ralph Sherwin onwards, the martyrs among them proudly picked out by crosses in the margin. This book had been published in the 1930s as a volume of the Catholic Record Society. But a number of other College records still awaited publication. In particular there were the *Responsa Alumnorum*, a set of autobiographical statements written by students on entering the College, in answer to a questionnaire instituted, with the purpose of filtering out Government spies, by Fr Persons in 1597. The series was almost complete up to 1685, and though many of the entries recorded unexciting lives of schoolchildren, there were many which chronicled the religious vacillations of Anglican converts, the hair's-breadth escapes of recusants hunted by pursuivants, and the more universal hazards of Elizabethan travel. Moreover, the record was complete enough to provide genealogical and sociological information about recusant families, many of whom sent children to Rome in successive generations. The Rector of the English College agreed that I could edit these *Responsa* on behalf of the College, and for a number of years I transcribed the Latin texts, and compiled English summaries of their contents. The task was quite substantial, involving the decipherment of a large number of different scripts (with the aid of some previous transcripts) and the detection of many personal and place names beneath their Latin disguises. It was to the completion of this task that I devoted much of my working time during my year in the O.N.D., anxious to have the work ready for publication before I left Rome. The *Responsa* finally appeared, some years later, in some 700 pages as volumes 54 and 55 of the publications of the Catholic Record Society; the first volume was my first published book, appearing just before my Oxford D.Phil. thesis.

Though I could borrow time from my thesis, I did of course have to submit theological papers to the doctoral seminars I was attending at the Gregorian. One seminar was on the theology of St Augustine, under Fr Charles Boyer. It must have been the topic rather than the lecturer which attracted me, for he rightly enjoyed a reputation as a bad teacher. By some irony he was chosen to give the pedagogic course on how to deliver lectures. 'The first essential for a lecturer,' he would begin, in an inaudible mumble, 'is to be clearly and distinctly audible.' 'And the next,' he would say, glowering round at those who greeted this remark with a giggle, 'is to have a sense of humour.' Another course was on the theology of St John Chrysostom. I still possess the seventeen pages of Latin which I contributed to this under the title *'De Doctrina Sti Ioannis Chrysostomi de Gratia et Vocatione ad Fidem'*; it was later translated in a theological journal as 'Was St John Chrysostom a semi-Pelagian?' At the same time I wrote a piece which appeared in 1957 in the *Catholic Biblical Quarterly* on the Transfiguration and the Agony in the Garden, exhibiting the parallelism between the two narratives in the Gospels and, in Luke, their relationship to the Lord's Prayer.

One of the most interesting special courses I attended was one on Biblical inspiration and inerrancy at the Biblical Institute, next door to the Gregorian, under Fr Agostino Bea. I had long found incredible the traditional Catholic doctrine that the Bible, as the literal word of God, was totally free from error. Alec had accustomed me to draw a distinction between inspiration and revelation: every page of the Bible had the authority of inspiration by God, but that did not mean that it was a revelation from God to the writer. Dominicans at Jerusalem were now beginning to say — despite earlier Papal pronouncements, like Leo XIII's encyclical *Providentissimus Deus* — that there were errors in the Bible. In Rome itself, Fr Bea, although clearly aware of the difficulties of the doctrine of inerrancy, did not feel free to go as far as that, and his course, though interesting, was very cautious. It was something of a surprise to those of us who had studied under him when, as Cardinal Bea, he was one of the most liberal and ecumenical influences at the Second Vatican Council.

The Easter vacation I spent in the Holy Land with a colleague. In those days, before the Six-Day War, Jerusalem was divided between Israel and Jordan: Galilee was a part of Israel, and Bethlehem of Jordan. As neither country recognized each other, it was necessary to acquire two passports, so that neither side would be compromised by issuing a visa in a passport that already contained a visa issued by the other. The only point at which one could cross from one country to the other was the Mandelbaum Gate in Jerusalem; so one's itinerary had to be planned with care.

We landed at Beirut in the morning of Maundy Thursday, seeing no more of the Lebanon than could be glimpsed as the airport taxi drove us along Parisian-style boulevards. The aeroplane to Amman was full of Arab university students on the spree: they dressed one of their number in a robe and crown and then pelted him with apples, singing American songs. We watched out of the windows the unfolding mountain ranges; the plane seemed to climb all the way to Jerusalem across the River Jordan and above the desert of Judah. We arrived just in time to attend an hour's meditation and Scripture reading in the church of Gethsemani.

We rose at 5.30 on Good Friday to attend the Latin Liturgy of the Presanctified in the Church of the Holy Sepulchre; we were there before the doors opened, and were nearly crushed on entry. The different Christian rites celebrated their liturgies in a spirit of fierce competition: the Copts, at the back, chanting incessantly in their own chapel; the Latins, Greeks, and Armenians sharing the main part of the church, claiming their share of the timetable in processions led by fierce beadles in fezes, tapping the flags with their maces to clear a way through the throng. Between ceremonies we snatched a visit to the sepulchre itself, darting in after a group of Greek women backed out reverentially. The most dignified inhabitants of the basilica were the Arab Legion tourist policemen. 'Do you see your God in there?' asked one of them as we left the tomb shrine.

After breakfast we were shown round the Church of the Flagellation, and then across the road into a Muslim school on the site of the Roman fortress Antonia for the first of the Stations of the Cross. I noticed that the classroom had a map showing the Muslim empire of the tenth century: half Europe covered green, as

British schools used to show maps of the British Empire with half the world coloured red. We followed the Via Dolorosa, sometimes joining groups carrying crosses amid the blue berets of the United Nations troops. When the pressure of the crowd became too great we squeezed out and sat beside a fountain to read the text of the dialogue between Pilate and Jesus in St John's Gospel.

In the afternoon, with two Irish pilgrims, we attached ourselves to a busload of Canadians. We visited Gabaa, the site of Saul's impatient sacrifice; Silo, the home of the infant Samuel; Jacob's well beneath the shadow of Mount Garizim. There we found a Greek priest sitting on a broken column watching over his flock of white sheep and black goats. He lowered a candle fifty metres into Jacob's well and gave an unintelligible homily. I escaped to read the fourth chapter of St John alone under a fig tree. On our way home we blew a tyre at Kerioth, the hometown of Judas Iscariot.

The driver of our car, Ali, was keeping Ramadan strictly, and would not smoke or drink water during the day. Just as we reached the Crusader church at Emmaus, the sun went down and we observed the Muslims all around light up as if at a word of command. Supper was eaten in a great hurry as we wished to attend the ceremony of the burial of Christ in the Holy Sepulchre church. A large figure of Christ, a life-size doll with moving limbs, was taken down from the Cross, swathed, and carried in procession to an anointing stone where it was drenched in scent. The bishop had to fight his way through the crowd to lay it in the sepulchre. We listened to sermons in French, Arabic, and Spanish; when all was over the Copts were still singing, as they seemed to have been since six o'clock in the morning. As we went home to bed, we noticed some of the faithful already sleeping on mats to have a good place for the blessing of the holy fire on the morrow.

Next day we walked to the church of Gallicantu, the memorial of Peter's denial of Christ and the crowing of the cock. Here, as elsewhere in Jerusalem, I was impressed by the way in which tradition was backed up by archaeology: so unlike the largely legendary shrines of Rome. We read the account of Peter's denial in Mark, then on the Roman steps towards Cedron parts of the Last Supper discourse from St. John. We discovered that Mark reads better in the open air, John reads better in the study or the church.

After supper we watched the Ethiopian ceremony of searching for the body of Christ on the roof of the Holy Sepulchre basilica in a procession of green and gold umbrellas, with hissing sistra; then we watched the midnight ceremony in the Latin rite, including—the first time I had ever seen it—the blessing of the font.

On Easter Sunday morning we said our own Masses in Gethsemani, and then joined the festive procession at the High Mass in St Sepulchre. We learnt that some Canadian pilgrims in our hostel had an audience arranged that afternoon with King Hussein in Amman, and they kindly allowed us to drive after their bus. So we travelled via Jericho and the deserted road leading past the Good Samaritan Inn (then a military post) and through the moonscape of the desert, across the Allenby Bridge over the Jordan, past the camels of Abdullah's winter palace. We lost contact with the bus, and arrived in advance, in danger of being exposed as gate-crashers; during an embarrassing half an hour closeted with the Chef de Protocol we had to think carefully how to answer questions like 'Is there much snow in your country?' without actually telling lies. After the Canadians did arrive, we had a very long wait for the arrival of the King; he appeared nervous, though he replied perfectly fluently to a speech in atrocious English by the French Canadian group leader. I particularly recall the nervous gesture with which the King braced his shoulders on exit. Later, we learnt that at that very moment the general of the Arab Legion had resigned and fled to Syria; there were rumours of a coup, and a large and angry crowd in Amman was demonstrating against Hussein.

On the following day I paid a visit to the École Biblique and met, with some awe, the foremost Catholic Biblical scholars of the age: Père de Vaux, Père Boismard and others. They were principally occupied with the wedding of one of the convent servants to the servant at an adjacent convent of nuns. During the wedding, a giant Samaritan with a red turban arrived with a suitcase full of Biblical *scholia* copied from a synagogue in Sichem, which he tried to sell. I felt sorry for him as he went off dejected, having failed to make a sale, but was later told that he owned a soap factory in Nablus. I gave him a few shillings and in return received a 'key to the Samaritan alphabet'.

In the evening we went up the Mount of Olives, visited the shrines there and admired the view of the desert and the Dead Sea, and listened to the Russian nuns singing Vespers in their convent. As we descended to the city, we heard the mu'ezzin proclaiming the end of the Ramadan fast. We were at once invited into the house we were passing, to take a meal. Reclining on mattresses in almost pitch darkness we dipped our hands into dishes of french beans, sausages and other unidentifiable delicacies as they were offered. I ended by trying to eat, in the darkness, the hand-washing cloth, to the amusement of the many children in the circle. The children were frightened by the crosses on our rosaries: and the grandfather, a 75-year-old *muktar*, told us how much Allah must disapprove of the Western practice of contraception. We explained that the Pope did not much like it, either. We tried to spell out the Lord's Prayer into the pidgin English which was our common language; we found that we got stuck when it came to spelling out the notion 'forgive'. The householder, Mahmoud David el Tur, told us that his uncle was 136 years old, and worked as a gardener in the Gethsemani church.

Next day we were shown the pool of Siloam by a shepherd boy, Ali Ahmed Ali, who arranged to bring lights for us on the following day to swim through Ezekiah's tunnel. He took us to the Virgin's fountain. There I assisted a woman to fill her petrol can with water; by way of thanks she made me a proposal of marriage.

Rumours of riot and possible civil war continued, but we decided to drive to Jericho by the old road; fortunately, it turned out, as cars driving along the other road were stoned that afternoon. We inspected the Tell of old Jericho, and went to the site of Jesus's baptism on the Jordan; there we were told that four communists had been killed by the Muslim Brotherhood in Jericho an hour or two earlier. Determined to carry out the duties of a tourist, we took our swim in the Dead Sea while vultures perched on the telegraph wires above. Foreign radios blared the (false) news that the Government had fallen, and that Arab and Syrian troops were massed on the borders. 'King Hussein he live today; King Hussein he live tomorrow' said our driver, 'but on the third day . . . ' he completed the sentence by drawing his hand across his throat. Then he drove us back under a lowering sky to Jerusalem.

It had been our plan, the next day, to go to Bethlehem. We rose at 4.30 and set off, but were turned back by the police. So we decided to take up an invitation which had been made to us on Holy Saturday night by the Arab Legion policeman, a dark-skinned eighteen-year-old, who had escorted us to the Holy Sepulchre. His name was Naif Eb'd Bar'Aram Behit.

We walked to the prison where he was posted, and after seeing several officers, we were allowed to enter and look for him. We found him standing on the roof, armed, guarding the frontier. He asked us to photograph him, and we were about to take pictures when there were shouts of 'Stop!' and angry policemen appeared from all sides. 'What is the matter?' we asked. 'They are angry', said Naif, with the air of one giving a complete explanation. The three of us were arrested and marched off to await interview by the commandant of the barracks. It seemed that we had violated some regulation about photographing military targets. When the commandant appeared the three of us were interrogated separately and at length; but the proceedings, in impeccable English, were most amicable. We did not lose our cameras, and we were not even searched; which was as well, as we were carrying letters from friends in Israel. We were waved off the premises, but poor Naif was confined to barracks for the rest of the day.

At four next morning, the loudspeakers announced that curfew was to continue until further notice. We got up to see the sun rise from Gethsemani, but we were turned back by some devout Christians who were afraid we would be shot. All telephone communication was cut off, and in theory no one was allowed out of doors. I found that if one walked slowly, and was polite to anyone met in uniform, it was not dangerous to wander in the Christian quarter. I went into the Lithostrotos convent to take some photographs from the roof, and to buy slides of the magnificent pavement on which, it is said, Christ was mocked. But the city was clearly no longer a good place for visitors. So we applied for a permit to cross into Israel, and during the hour in the afternoon when curfew was lifted, we took our bags across the Mandelbaum Gate.

Once across the Mandelbaum Gate, past a gutted house with a tattered sign 'Welcome within thy gates O Sion!', we went to the Jesuit Biblical Institute. Most of the historic sites of the city were in the Jordanian sector; but a friendly archaeologist took us to the Dormition church, and through the barbed wire into the Cenacle, the traditional site of the Last Supper, right by the ceasefire line. He pointed out three Jerusalems: the Jordanian Jerusalem, the Israeli Jerusalem and — pointing to the minefields of no-man's-land — the quickest way to the Heavenly Jerusalem.

A bus took us to Nazareth, where the Franciscans made us welcome, as did the mosquitoes in their dormitory. After Mass at the Annunziata grotto we visited the excavations of the Dames de Nazareth; only the Jesuit who had excavated them believed them to be the genuine remains of the house in which the Blessed Virgin was reared; but the basilica nearby had a more established claim. In the afternoon we walked over to Tabor, the mount of the Transfiguration. The village of Daburiyeh, at its foot, where the lunatic child was healed, had just, we were told, had a mass conversion to Catholicism. From there an hour's gruelling path led up to the Crusader Gate and avenue of pines which leads to the Franciscan hospice. This was inhabited by three cheerful Franciscans and a sleepy dog called 'Milord' — because he had the eyes of an old Englishman, they said. The only other guest was an Estonian priest; he was, he told us, the only one: he had fought in the Russian army in Finland and was now translating the Bible into Estonian in Münster. We went with him across the summit of the mountain to the Greek monastery where the solitary monk gave us the toast *'Christos aneste'* in excellent red wine, to which we replied *'Alethos aneste'*. In the hospice we listened to the Italian news reporting the end of the Jordanian crisis and the flight of the communists into Israel.

The next day was Low Sunday; we walked past the ruins of the Crusader fortress and down to the Lake of Tiberias. We were able to picnic by the church which commemorates Christ's commission to Peter to feed his lambs and sheep; there we read John 21, and watched an Arab wedding party depart on a lorry overlaced with palm branches. As we walked uphill to the Hospice of the Beatitudes — a beautiful, modern octagonal building with a colonnade overlooking the lake — a shepherd posed for a photograph with practised grace, holding a sheep over his shoulder, in the stance of the good shepherd.

In Haifa the German nuns welcomed us to our first good night's sleep in Israel under their very efficient mosquito nets. We rose before sunrise to say Mass by the grotto of Elias, and watched the sun come up on the road to Mount Carmel. With a busload of Israeli children, who sang lively Hebrew songs about Noah, Pharaoh and David, we visited the excavations of Megiddo, and admired Solomon's very large stables, and not so large barracks.

Much of the voyage back, on a steamer to Bari, was spent in arguments with fellow-passengers on religious topics. We shared a cabin with a Polish Jew from London, who had celebrated the Pasch with his brother in Jerusalem, and returned very anti-Zionist. Jesus, he told me, had been a social reformer, fighting against an avaricious priesthood, who preached a bogus religious message to free persecuted Jews from slavery; he had no wish to found any new religion or break with Jewry. I told him how the Christian

Eucharist had begun as a Paschal meal, given a new significance by Jesus saying of the bread, 'This is my body.' 'He said WHAT?' the Pole exclaimed, wide-eyed. Clearly, I had rather spoiled his good opinion of the enlightened social reformer.

The last few months in Rome were an anti-climax after our Biblical wanderings. Fond as I was of the English College, I was now anxious to move on. Theology graduate students usually had two further years of full-time study; but I had persuaded Archbishop Godfrey that I should do only one, the minimum permitted, in Rome. Since my thesis was concerned with analytic philosophy, it would make more sense for me to do the second year at Oxford, internationally recognized at that time as the centre of the analytic movement in the English-speaking countries. So it was arranged that, while continuing to work for the Gregorian doctorate, and while still enrolled in Rome, I should live and work in Oxford for a year as a private student so as to get a first-hand knowledge of the linguistic philosophy which I had so far encountered mainly in books and periodicals.

XI

A Philosopher at Oxford, 1957–9

The initial purpose of my being sent to Oxford was to finish the Gregorian thesis on linguistic analysis and the language of religion. I enrolled as a recognized student, which conferred the right to use libraries, attend lectures, and have some guidance in my research. The Roman Catholic chaplain, Mgr Valentine Elwes, found a house on the Iffley road where a devout Catholic, a Dominican tertiary, had lodgings for half a dozen students, which he named Aquinas House. The garage had been converted into a chilly but tasteful chapel in which there was permission to reserve the Blessed Sacrament; I could say Mass there daily, with one of the student lodgers to take his turn at serving Mass. Mgr Elwes already had a curate chaplain resident at the Old Palace in St Aldate's; but from time to time I was asked to help out with chaplaincy work, sometimes preaching, sometimes hearing confessions, regularly running one or two Catholic student discussion groups.

About ten per cent of the total university population was Catholic, which was probably a reflection of the numbers of Catholics in the population as a whole, though at university a greater proportion took their religion seriously. Catholics were spread around the colleges; some were from recusant families, coming up from the main Jesuit or Benedictine public schools; others were converts or children of converts from a variety of backgrounds; others, like myself, were of Irish descent and products of the grammar schools of the Butler education act. The social mix was much the same as in Rome; the intellectual ability of the average undergraduate seemed little superior to that of the typical seminarian at the Venerabile. I was surprised to find that in Oxford, as in Rome, I seemed to belong to the academically most able group of students, and was able to hold my own in discussion on philosophical and theological topics.

Among the Catholic graduate and undergraduate students I found a great deal of intellectual curiosity about religion, and a dissatisfaction with the religious instruction which they had received in sermons and homilies in their own parishes. The chaplains took pains to see that there were available preachers and discussion leaders to meet the students on their own intellectual terms. It was the student Catholic generation so well described by David Lodge in *How Far Can You Go?*—loyal, devout, but beginning to question the authoritarian control of the clergy, and to resent in particular the sexual discipline of the Church which they compared enviously with the freedom of their non-Catholic contemporaries.

After a slow and lonely start, I made many friends among the young Catholics at Oxford. A group of us met for lunch each day in the coffee rooms attached to the Newman bookshop; over sandwiches and scotch eggs we would debate theological paradoxes and ecclesiastical politics. I soon learned that even the most highly educated undergraduate often had totally incorrect ideas about the official doctrines of the Church. On the other hand, mixing with priests from many different Catholic colleges and universities, I came to realize that the high ultramontane line of the Gregorian differed from the interpretation of Catholic doctrine taught in other universities. At Louvain and at Paris, they seemed to order many things differently. In Britain, there was no independent centre of Catholic thought and we used to argue whether English Catholicism would be intellectually better or worse off if there had been a Catholic university in this country along the lines of Newman's ideal.

I shared some of the dissatisfaction of the young Catholic laity at Oxford with the official policies of the Church hierarchy. But coming to Oxford at first strengthened rather than weakened my faith as a Catholic. It was quite a liberation to discover that anti-authoritarian views of the Roman Church could go with keen intellectual commitment to the Faith and a devout and charitable life. And I soon found that clever people who attacked the Church could display as much ignorance, bias, and sophistry as I had ever encountered in its defence.

I was sometimes invited to preach, or give the conference, as it was called, at the main Sunday Mass in the chaplaincy. One such occasion was on a Lenten Sunday in my second term in Oxford. I find that of all the sermons I preached as a priest, this is the only one whose full text has survived. It began with a survey of the history of the Eucharist, from a domestic celebration of the first century, through a liturgy with a sermon by St John Chrysostom, through a medieval performance of the Mass as a sanctified mime, into the counter-Reformation emphasis on the reservation of the Blessed Sacrament and other non-sacrificial Eucharistic devotions to 'the prisoner in the tabernacle'. Our own age, I said, was seeking for a new form of Eucharistic devotion, to preserve a just mean between the different aspects of sacrifice and sacrament:

Union with Christ in the Eucharist should find its expression in three main ways: in prayer, in sacrifice, and in love for one another. We English Catholics are unfortunate in having so few good vocal prayers in our own language. It is all the more important that when one does meet a good prayer one should treasure it. Everyone should have his own anthology of prayers, especially of Biblical prayers . . .

One may find good prayers in unexpected places. At the elevation of the chalice, for example, one could do worse than think of the last speech of Marlowe's Faustus as he awaits damnation. 'See where Christ's blood streams in the firmament; one drop would save my soul — half a drop, ah my Christ.' If one has ever committed mortal sin, one can say to oneself: 'I might at this moment be damned, like Faustus; it is due only to God's mercy that I am not, and that Christ's blood still has power to save me' . . . But the best form of private prayer is the traditional one: the leisured and meditative reading of the Gospel. Only reading and re-reading the Gospel can make Christ come alive for us as a real person; only by meditation on his words and actions can one come to answer the question: what would he have done, if he were in my position here and now? And this is the only question that ever matters.

Union with Christ in the Eucharist must be expressed in sacrifice too. One cannot be united with the victim on the altar without in some way doing to death one's own desires; whether it be by the constant fight to break a habit of sin, or the spontaneous forgoing of innocent pleasure as a sign of love. The making of Lenten resolutions must be not just a pastime for Ash Wednesday. By now, most of us will have broken our resolutions more than once. But a Lenten resolution is not something like a gramophone record which once broken might as well be thrown away. The constant effort to renew a broken resolution teaches humility as well as self-control.

Our love for Christ in the Eucharist must overflow towards our fellow-men. First of all, to those who share with us the common table of Christ's family. It is unthinkable that there should be enmity, or jealousies, or serious differences between those who communicate at the same altar. To receive Communion with genuine ill-will in one's heart towards any of one's fellow communicants would be blasphemous

mockery. But if we really value our union with Christ, we will not
rest until we have done all that we can to bring him to those who are
cut off, for one reason or another, from communion in the bread of
life. The conversion of England should not be an impossible ideal.
If every adult Catholic in this country brought one of his friends into
the church every ten years, then the whole country would be converted
by 1988. The attitude of other undergraduates to the Catholic Church
is going to be very largely influenced by your behaviour. For many
of them, you may be the only Catholics they have met outside the pages
of medieval history. It isn't Alexander VI with his bastards and his
poisons who keeps people out of the Church: it is John Smith with
his bad temper and biting tongue . . .

It is not easy to believe in Christ's presence on the altar. It is often
harder to believe in his presence in the Christians who receive him.
Too often Christ's presence in us passes unperceived by ourselves and
by others.

The pastoral assistance which I lent to the chaplaincy was not,
of course, the reason for my being in Oxford. I was to deepen my
acquaintance with the philosophy of linguistic analysis, and
complete my doctoral thesis. Another academic task was soon
imposed. As a recognized student working for a foreign doctorate,
I was ineligible for any grant, but it was discovered that the
Liverpool Local Authority would give a grant if I was
simultaneously enrolled for an Oxford doctorate. As the minimum
residence requirement for this was two years, I would have to stay
an extra year at Oxford. The diocesan authorities financing me
thought two years at no cost was a better bargain than one year
at full cost, and as I liked Oxford I was happy to stay longer. But
the plan did mean a tight timetable. I had to complete the
Gregorian thesis in the academic year 1957-8, and then write
enough of the Oxford D.Phil. thesis in 1958-9 to be able to complete
it in the parish, or the seminary, or wherever I was next posted.
The task would have been easier if the material for the two theses
could have overlapped; but that was forbidden by the regulations
of the two universities. In any case I was not long in Oxford before
I discovered that, on the whole, it was philosophers of the second
rank who had written on the philosophy of religion; and when those
of the first rank, like Russell and Wittgenstein, had turned their
attention to the philosophy of religion they had not produced their
best work. Someone who wanted to contribute to the understanding
of religious topics from an analytic viewpoint would not be
best employed in analysing what had been said by linguistic

philosophers about religion. The real task would be more daunting: he had to immerse himself in learning from the analytical tradition, and then return afresh, on his own, to the religious doctrines and the theological speculations. So the topic which I chose for my Oxford doctorate was a purely philosophical one, remote on the surface from any theological concerns: my title was 'The Intentionality of Psychological Verbs'.

It was not, of course, until my second year that I started any serious work on this topic; the Gregorian thesis had to be completed first. I attended lectures and seminars in the philosophy sub-faculty, and was an assiduous attender at the Socratic Club, founded by C. S. Lewis for discussion of topics on the borders of philosophy and theology. It was a good time for a philosophy student to be at Oxford, in the heyday of linguistic philosophy; philosophers were confident that they had discovered new philosophical methods which superannuated much of the metaphysics of the past. Wittgenstein was not long dead: the gradual publication of his works enabled his genius to be appreciated not only by the small circle of his Cambridge pupils, but by the philosophical world at large. Linguistic philosophy was in its 'ordinary language' phase; and after Wittgenstein's death Oxford came to be regarded as the centre of this movement. It had the largest philosophy department in the world. John Austin and Gilbert Ryle, Professors of Moral Philosophy and of Metaphysics respectively, were both inspiring figures. Austin, a sharp and witty lecturer, and Ryle, a brilliant writer, were both devoted teachers and worked hard to foster young talent. From all over the English-speaking world philosophers gathered to sit at their feet, and at the feet of other Oxford figures then holding junior posts, such as R. M. Hare and Peter Strawson. With George Hughes, from New Zealand, another clerical philosopher, I attended the seminars of F. Waismann. It was exciting to be studying under a survivor of the dreaded Vienna circle. We knew little of the tragedies of his personal life; only later did we discover that we were his last generation of students.

Naturally enough, the Catholic philosophers at Oxford influenced me most. I talked with them until the small hours about the problems of philosophy. In later years, as a tutor myself beset with the enthusiasms of young graduate students, I learnt to appreciate more fully the generosity with which they made themselves available. From Elizabeth Anscombe, then a lecturer at Somerville, I learnt gradually, and sometimes painfully, to understand what Wittgenstein meant, and why it was important.

Her seminars on the private language argument were the most
formative educational experience of my life. Eventually convinced,
by slow stages, of the insights of Wittgenstein, I found my whole
mind-set altered, so that every philosophical problem looked
different seen from the perspective I then acquired, and have ever
since kept. From her husband Peter Geach, when he was at home
in St John Street from his teaching in Birmingham, I learnt that an
understanding of Wittgenstein and Frege could go along with a
great admiration for Aquinas. He carried a pocket edition of the
Summa Theologiae, which he would produce to quote passages to
puncture trendy theological persiflage produced by unwary clerics
at Newman meetings or Socratic seminars. Michael Dummett,
less often, took part in theologico-philosophical discussions in
chaplaincy circles; his interests in formal logic seemed, at that time,
to keep him some distance from issues in philosophy or religion;
and though I quickly realized his gifts I formed the sad, and totally
wrong, impression that he would never publish anything of any
substantial length.

   I learnt at least as much from unofficial discussions and argument
with philosophers as I did from official courses and supervision.
When I arrived as a recognized student I was assigned to the Rev.
Ian Ramsey, then Nolloth Professor of the Philosophy of Religion,
later to be Bishop of Durham. Ramsey was a genial, friendly,
helpful, unassuming man, who had written extensively on topics
of religious language; but I soon became impatient of him as a
supervisor. While his works paraded the style and jargon of
linguistic philosophy, he had not really entered into the
fundamental insights of a philosopher like Wittgenstein; and, on
the other hand, the logical empiricism which he espoused left very
little room for a real belief in any of the fundamental dogmas of
religion. When I was transferred to probationary status as a
doctoral student I asked Ryle to arrange a change of supervisor,
alleging that I would prefer a supervisor who was less in sympathy
with religion, so that I would be subjected to more searching
criticism. Ryle assigned me to Antony Quinton, as an atheist in
good standing; it was a lucky choice for me, since Quinton, in
addition to being one of the most entertaining dons in Oxford,
was an omnivorous reader who could save his pupils hours of
wasted library searches by providing, in a vivid nutshell, the main
points of every book or article on the topics within his field.

   Just as I had to come from the Thomist Gregorian to secular
Oxford to be really introduced to the works of St Thomas, so too,

in spite of my three years of 'Aristotelian' philosophy, it was only at Oxford that I began seriously to read Aristotle. This was at the seminars of G. E. L. Owen, at which we read the text of the *Physics*. He became and remained for me a pattern of how to be erudite without being stuffy: I was honoured when he replied to a paper on Aquinas and Wittgenstein which I read to the Socratic Club and which later, appearing in the *Downside Review*, was my first philosophical publication.

Like other graduate students before and since, I discovered that Oxford, while an excellent place to collect and sift ideas, is not a good place for the quiet writing of a thesis. The deadline for my Gregorian thesis was in April 1958; I left Oxford at the end of the preceding Hilary Term with little more than a quarter of it in shape. I went to stay as a guest at Upholland; there, within the framework of the seminary timetable of the last weeks of Lent, and without distractions, social, pastoral or academic, I wrote the 200-odd pages in some twenty days. I found it hard to keep up the necessary daily output of 4,000 words. A friendly priest offered me some pills his doctor had prescribed as a way of increasing the work-rate in a crisis. They turned out to be benzedrine, which had not yet acquired the reputation which made it notorious in the sixties. I found that it did indeed enable one to work deep into the night. By the time I stopped taking the pills, and experienced the mammoth hangover which they left behind, the thesis was safely on its way to Rome. It had been bound in haste for me, to meet the deadline, by the devout hands of the nuns in the Carmelite convent adjoining the seminary. So far as I can tell, re-reading the thesis in later years, the drug, whatever havoc it caused in my own constitution, had no visible effect on the style of writing or the cogency of the arguments. Not that I now consider all the arguments of the thesis valid, but only that they seem no worse than ones which I defended when cold sober.

The thesis was a historical, not a speculative, one; it examined what had been written by British linguistic philosophers about the language of religion; it made no attempt to apply the techniques of linguistic analysis in an original manner to the field of theology. The title was 'The Philosophy of Linguistic Analysis and the Language of Religion'; by the philosophy of linguistic analysis I meant the philosophy, predominant in the universities of Great Britain since the end of the Second World War, deriving partly from the analytic philosophy of Moore and Russell, partly from the Vienna circle of logical positivism, and above all from the later

work of Wittgenstein while at Cambridge. In the first part of the
thesis I sketched the pedigree of the current analytic philosophy,
devoting one chapter to the logical atomism of Russell and of
Wittgenstein's *Tractatus Logico-Philosophicus*; and two to the Viennese
logical positivism imported to England by the youthful A. J. Ayer.
In a fourth chapter, on 'Post-positivist philosophy in England',
I drew on recent writings of Warnock, Strawson, and Waismann,
and Wittgenstein's posthumous *Philosophical Investigations:*

> The Oxford analysts would not care to commit themselves explicitly
> to Wittgenstein's view that an appeal to everyday language can cure
> all our philosophical problems; they would prefer to say more modestly
> that it can clarify our formulation of them. But they have given
> themselves with enthusiasm to the Wittgensteinian task of exhibiting
> the difference between different types of discourse. For they believe
> that one of the most helpful ways of clarifying a puzzling philosophical
> situation is to undo mistaken assimilations between different types of
> language; to bring out the different truth-tests and decision procedures,
> the different 'logics' of different types of utterance.

I instanced Austin's classifications of speech acts, Hart's theory
of ascriptive utterances and the work of Anscombe on expressions
of intention, and of Hare on imperative sentences. The recognition
of the variety and autonomy of different types of discourse, I
maintained, had led to a rejection of the phenomenalism which
had been one of the obstacles to the acceptance of religious
metaphysics. The field in which the programme of ordinary
language philosophy had been carried out with the greatest
perseverance and *éclat*, I suggested, was the philosophy of mind,
especially by Wittgenstein himself, and to a lesser extent by Ryle.
Wittgenstein denied that psychological words derived their meaning
from reference to private mental processes. This was not to be taken
as a denial of the obvious fact that mental processes take place;
Wittgenstein was no behaviourist, but his philosophy, if successful,
was destructive of the rival philosophies of Cartesianism and
empiricism.

I concluded the first part by an affirmation of the substantial differences that there were between post-war British analytical philosophy
and the classical logical positivism which many on the Continent, and
in particular in Rome, were still inclined to identify with it. The
eight chapters which made up the second part were devoted to a
survey of the attempts made to discuss particular religious topics by
philosophers with some allegiance to the analytic movement.

I began by discussing the verificationist Christianity which had attracted me when I wrote my licentiate dissertation in Rome. I rehearsed the position of Braithwaite's Christian empiricism, but from a much greater distance. I was more impressed by the criticisms made of it by writers like Ewing and Mascall than by the sympathetic restatement of it by Hare ('Taking up an attitude of worship to an object considered as a person is not quite like adopting a purely factual belief; nor is it simply subscribing to certain principles of conduct; but it involves both of these things'). At the end, all we learn from attempts to synthesize a Christian empiricism is that theology and positivism will not mix. But since the verification principle has by now collapsed under its own weight, why try to reconcile theology with it?

In the succeeding chapter, I discussed the notion that God is a necessary being. This venerable concept had been attacked, among others, by Professor J. N. Findlay, who argued that Kant had shown that it could not be necessary that anything, of any description whatsoever, existed, and therefore the notion of necessary being was incoherent. What was necessary, if anything, were propositions, not things; and necessity in propositions, on a really modern view of the matter, merely reflected the conventions of our language. To be an adequate object of worship, Findlay argued, a god had to be a necessary being; but 'modern views make it self-evidently absurd (if they don't make it ungrammatical) to speak of such a Being and attribute existence to him'. The most decisive intervention in the debate came from A. N. Prior, who could be said to have started the whole topic of discussion in a 1948 dialogue in the *Australasian Journal of Philosophy* entitled 'Can Religion Be Discussed?' In a paper of 1953 called 'Is Necessary Existence Possible?' Prior observed that the line of argument to show that 'necessary being' was a senseless notion started from the proposition that existence is not a predicate: what is not rightly thought of as attaching to a subject cannot be thought of as attaching to a subject necessarily. Prior accepted the customary analysis of existential propositions deriving from Frege and Moore; 'lions exist' asserts that the concept of lionhood is exemplified, and 'unicorns do not exist' asserts that the concept of unicornhood is not exemplified. Now one can distinguish between the necessary and contingent non-exemplification of concepts; so why should there not be properties of concepts which *necessitate* their exemplification? The kind of necessitation involved here is not logical necessity: logical necessity is to be defined in terms of it, a logically necessary proposition being one whose truth is pre-logically necessitated by its logical form. This recognition of another sort of necessity alongside and prior to logical necessity marked a complete break, I maintained, with positivism.

One of the longest sections of the thesis treated the controversy over theology and falsification. Professor Flew had put to the theist the challenge: what sort of evidence would count against propositions such as 'God created the world', 'God loves us as a father loves his children'? If no evidence can be suggested, then these putative assertions are not really assertions at all; for if there is nothing which an assertion denies there is nothing which it asserts either. I described the reaction of a number of Christian writers — Corbishley, Hare, Donagan, Mitchell, Crombie, Lewis, Ewing — to Flew's challenge; and I concluded:

> Once again, the sceptic is presenting the believer with the dilemma: either your statements about God are tautologies, in which case they tell us nothing about the world; or they are empirical hypotheses, in which case they are very implausible ones . . . The philosophical gambit which consists in seeking to clarify the meaning of a sentence by asking what states of affairs it excludes, or what would count as evidence for its contradictory, has its uses, particularly in distinguishing between genuine and spurious scientific hypotheses. But it also has its limitations. In particular, it can rarely be helpfully applied to the statements made by philosophers. For all worthwhile philosophical statements express an insight; and the opposite of an insight is not a contradictory sentence, but a muddle . . . In the sense in which a scientific hypothesis can be falsified, no historical statement at all can be falsified. There is no need, then, for the theist to choose between saying that his assertions about God are falsifiable, and saying that they are vacuous. For the dilemma with which he is presented rests on false premises and supposes a criterion of meaning whereby neither philosophical nor historical statements could be said to be meaningful.

Shorter and later chapters dealt with recent treatments of the ancient problem of reconciling omnipotence and freedom, and the appeal to religious experience as a way of combining allegiance to Christianity with the native British preference for empiricism and the Protestant emphasis on the private conviction of justification. I took Wittgenstein's argument against private ostensive definition as being decisive against the appeal to religious experience as verifying and therefore rendering meaningful the statements which we make about God. In any case, I argued, from the theological viewpoint, if God is transcendent then he cannot be the object of any human experience analogous to sense-experience. 'If God was the sort of being that could be "met with" in some empirical "encounter" then it would be nonsense to say that He was infinite and outside the spatio-temporal scheme of material things.'

Two chapters dealt with attempts to give an account of the religious 'language-game' as a whole by placing it in the context of religious life and worship: I considered at particular length papers by Bernard Williams and Alasdair MacIntyre on the varieties of religious discourse, and papers by Ian Crombie and Austin Farrer relating recent work in the philosophy of language to the scholastic tradition of treating statements about God as analogical.

In the final chapter I tried to relate Wittgenstein's private language argument to the traditional doctrine of the immortality of the human soul. If Wittgenstein is right, psychological words like 'pain' do not derive their meaning from a private internal experience. This does not mean that we have to accept the kind of behaviourism propounded by Ryle, according to which psychological predicates are correct hypothetical ascriptions of physical behaviour. But we must not go to the other extreme, with philosophers such as J. R. Lucas, and claim that an immortal soul can be discerned by introspection. The human soul must be conceived, in Aristotelian fashion, in the form of the body.

A Latin summary of the thesis had to be presented to the examiner. I quote, as an illustration, from the summary of this final chapter:

Gilbertus Ryle, Professor Oxoniensis, in libro The Concept of Mind, *quem contra psychologiam cartesianam scripsit, ex ideiis Wittgensteinianis non bene intellectis ductus est ad conclusiones valde miras. Negavit prorsus existentiam actuum mentalium; omnes propositiones quae videntur referre ad tales actus sunt revera propositiones obliquae vel hypotheticae de actibus corporis visibilibus . . . Positio Ryleii videtur clare inconciliabilis cum doctrinis de immortalitate et spiritualitate animae; haud mirum ergo si philosophi analytici christiani in eum invecti sunt. Sed pro dolor non pauci philosophi ex ecclesia Anglicana fundaverunt argumenta sua supra notiones erroneas de anima. J. R. Lucas, v.g. e coll. Corporis Christi Oxon. putavit quod ad defendendam notionem animae spiritualis necesse est defendere etiam notionem tou ego cartesiani. Eius argumentum contra Ryle paucis verbis est hoc: scio per introspectionem me habere aliquod ego invisibile, intangibile, spirituale; ergo habeo animam immortalem. Hoc argumentum nullo modo convincit eos qui (ut nosmet ipsi) nulla tali facultate introspiciendi gaudent.*

The thesis ended on a confident note. Wittgenstein's criticism of Cartesianism and empiricism would open up an era beneficial to a revival of Thomist theology; if the contributions of analytical philosophers to the philosophy of religion had been comparatively jejune thus far, that was because they were hampered by the Barthian upbringing which many of them had received.

I travelled out to Rome in June to defend the thesis. The examination for the Gregorian doctorate was in three parts. There was the oral defence of the thesis, there was a written examination on its broad theological context, and there was a third item called the *'lectio coram'*. The *lectio coram* was a most enlightened form of high-level assessment. It was a lecture given before a jury of professors: the topic was assigned at 9 a.m. and the lecture was to be given at 5 p.m. In the meantime one was allowed to make full use of notes, libraries, and works of reference. The topic was chosen from a field selected by the candidate well in advance, corresponding to roughly one year's undergraduate work. Thus the *lectio* tested one's knowledge of a chosen field of specialization, without, like most examinations, putting too much weight on sheer memory, but testing, as a dissertation does not, the ability to co-ordinate thoughts at speed. Unlike most examinations which give one entry to a career, it tested precisely what the career involved, namely the preparation of theological lectures under the constraints of a schedule.

The dissertation was well received in Rome: it did not arouse the suspicions which had been caused by my licentiate exercise. Indeed, Lonergan congratulated me on entering so fully into the mind of my philosophers without having imbibed their errors. It was awarded a *summa cum laude*, and the marks in the other examinations were similar, so that my overall grade for the *laurea* was a *summa*.

To obtain the doctorate, however, two other things were required. The thesis, or at least a substantial portion of it, must be published; and one must make a profession of faith and take an oath against Modernism. I was reluctant to publish the thesis: though much of it seems to me to this day to be philosophically sound, it was too much of a survey of other people's work to attract a publisher, and I did not want to be at the expense of publishing it privately. I was willing enough to make the profession of faith but I did not want to take the anti-Modernist oath. For that oath, unlike the profession of faith, included a number of items which were not defined dogmas of the Church and were not obligatory on all Catholics to believe. The oath, for instance, committed one to asserting that it was possible to prove the existence of God. Now the First Vatican Council had defined that natural reason could know the existence of God; but it left open whether this was by proof, or in some other way. As I regarded the proofs of the existence of God as invalid, I was reluctant to take the oath. I had taken it before, to receive Orders, with some qualms. I decided now that I was no longer willing to take it, so that, despite passing the examination, I was never officially listed as a doctor.

The lack of valid proofs of the existence of God began to worry me for other reasons too. At a time when I regarded positivism as the great threat to the rationality of religious belief, my main concern was the meaningfulness, rather than the truth, of religious assertions. At a time when I thought of mystical encounter as the high road to the knowledge of God, I was happy enough to distinguish between the possibility of knowing God by reason (which the Vatican Council had proclaimed) and the possibility of offering a logically valid proof of God (of which I was and remained very doubtful). But my initiation into the philosophy of Wittgenstein at Oxford, while it removed the bogey of positivism, equally took away my confidence in religious experience as providing justification for the assertions of natural theology. I began to think — as I do to this day — that belief in God can be rationally justified only if the traditional proofs of the existence of God are valid. Faith will not do instead of proof; for faith is believing something on the word of God; and one cannot take God's word for it that He exists. Belief in God's existence must be logically prior to belief in revelation.

There was another aspect of Wittgenstein's philosophy which made it more difficult to believe in God. Wittgenstein put forward in his works very persuasive considerations to the effect that it is only to human beings, bodily creatures like ourselves, that one can attribute the kind of mental life we have. Perhaps this does not rule out the possibility of a divine, bodiless, intelligent being; but it makes it enormously difficult to see how such a being is conceivable. It makes it even more difficult to conceive of the survival of a human disembodied soul.

During my second year in Oxford these and other difficulties began to worry me seriously. Old doubts that had gone to sleep came back to life. I was again unhappy about the doctrine of transubstantiation, and sought for Wittgensteinian solutions to its incomprehensibility. ('Can one say that after the consecration it

is not bread and wine in the sense in which money is not—just—
paper?')

Why did I take transubstantiation so seriously? Isn't the
important thing, even from the Catholic point of view, the real
presence of Jesus in the Sacrament? If one is willing to accept that,
then the point at which the doctrine of transubstantiation goes
beyond the real presence (namely, in denying that the Sacrament
is bread and wine) seems comparatively trivial. If the belief raises
philosophical difficulties, why not just give it up: will it really take
away from one's priestly ministry?

The difficulty was rather this. There is no doubt that
transubstantiation was a defined dogma of the Catholic Church,
however minor it might be. And it was an essential part of having
the virtue of faith, without which neither charity nor salvation was
possible, that one should believe *all* the defined doctrines; one could
not pick and choose. To fail to believe even one was not only sinful
in itself, it called in question one's belief in all the other doctrines:
for one could not be believing them with the correct motive, namely
that they were revealed by God through Christ and his Church.
That is why, for a Catholic, a doubt about any doctrine is, in a
manner, a doubt about every doctrine.

The whole account of faith given by the Church troubled me.
Faith was to be something irrevocable: any doubt must be resisted
as a temptation to sin. But to accept something as an article of
faith one had to accept a number of historical facts: as that the
article had been defined by the Church, that the authority claimed
by the Church had been conferred on it by Jesus in well-known
passages of the Gospels, that the Pope was the successor of St Peter
and spoke with the authority given to him. Now these historical
assertions were vulnerable to the progress of history and exegesis,
and many of them were hotly controverted by scholars of standing.
How could one give them the kind of irrevocable commitment to
which we were exhorted? And if these 'preambles of faith' could
not be the objects of irrevocable assent, how could the faith which
rested on them be irrevocable?

Practical as well as theoretical issues of Catholic discipline gave
trouble. One was the practice of giving and taking Mass stipends;
the other was the main topic of debate in Catholic moral theology
in the sixties, contraception.

A priest, when he offers Mass, is allowed to offer it 'for a
particular intention.' In a way which even the most orthodox
theologian would admit to be obscure, he is supposed to be able

to direct the benefits of a particular Mass in a particular way. He can offer it for the welfare of some person living or dead, or as a petition to bring about some state of affairs, like the cure of a sickness, or the end of a war. Since ordination, I had accepted this practice, without claiming to understand it; the first Masses I offered when I became a priest were for the members of my family then living, and for the repose of the soul of my dead father. But it is further the custom that if a lay person wishes a priest to offer Mass for a particular intention, he should offer the priest a stipend for doing so. Canon lawyers explained, in a way that was again mysterious, that though acceptance of a stipend was not simony (the exchange of money for a spiritual benefit) it did set up contractual obligations. I still have the account book in which I entered all stipends received and the due offering of the Mass in accordance with the intention. Like other students of the English College I had a duty to offer some Masses for benefactors long dead, whose ancient munificence had done something to provide for our upkeep. Thus I said Mass for Owen Lewis, an Elizabethan bishop from Wales, and for 'King James III of England' and several of his Jacobite courtiers. But most of the Masses said by student priests in Rome were offered in return for stipends from distant and anonymous sources, especially in America. In an American parish stipends of various sizes would be offered. The larger stipends — say five dollars and upwards — would be pocketed by the local clergy and the Masses said on the spot; the less profitable offerings, the dollar stipends, would be sent to the impoverished seminarists in Rome to whom a dollar was a substantial sum. The Church of St Columbanus in Rome was the great clearing house for dollar stipends, and the great source of pocket money for student priests. To avoid the complicated book-keeping which would be necessary if the intention of each benefactor was spelt out, we used to offer the Masses *'ad intentionem dantis'* — for the intention of the giver. The practice was so universal in Rome that I do not remember having more than momentary qualms about it. But in Oxford I began to ask myself the question: since the donor's name was not preserved, nor the actual dollar bill he had handed over, was there an identifiable donor, known even to God? The more I thought about it, the more obnoxious the whole practice began to seem. To think this was not necessarily to depart from orthodoxy: but I decided to stop taking stipends; after all, I had quite enough money to live on from my student grant, and no need to enrich myself in this dubious way.

Contraception was a different matter, in several ways. The wrongness of contraception had been taught as explicitly and definitively by the Church as any moral doctrine. Yet, like most of the Church's critics, I could see little force in the natural law arguments against it. But now that I was hearing confessions and giving pastoral advice I must constantly repeat and enforce the Church's doctrine. Doubt about this point of faith was different from most other doubts. If the other doctrines that I doubted turned out false, then in general no one was a loser but myself; but in a case like this it was others who were paying the penalty if the advice was wrong. It was most disagreeable giving advice on a matter where one was oneself inclined to be dubious; yet, so far as I could see, there was no alternative for a priest but to do so.

My last year in Oxford was academically rewarding, and I made many friends. But I made little progress on my second doctoral thesis, and my doctrinal worries grew. I left Oxford in summer 1959 in a disturbed and sombre state of mind.

XII

Curate in Liverpool, 1959–63

Early in 1959, my last year in Oxford, I wrote to my Archbishop to find out what plans I should make: had he an appointment in mind for me in Liverpool? Archbishop Godfrey, who had ordained me, had now moved on to become Cardinal in Westminster, and the new Archbishop of Liverpool was John Carmel Heenan. Heenan, while he was running the Catholic Missionary Society, had come to the English College in Rome to give one of our twice-yearly retreats: we had been impressed by his energy and the wealth of practical advice he had given us on the administrative, not to say managerial, aspects of the priesthood. Since then he had been Bishop of Leeds, where he gained a reputation as an uncompromising reformer, a great rebuker of idleness among the clergy, who had nicknamed his diocese 'The Cruel See'. In Liverpool he tackled a number of problems which his predecessors had shelved: plans for a mammoth cathedral were scrapped and a new, modest, one built after a competition for the design. Heenan wrote in February in answer to my letter:

> After your concentrated studies I think you should have a good long rest. You must let the Vicar General know when you have had enough holiday. I certainly would not want you to think of an appointment before September. If you need longer then we could wait until October.
>
> I have given a great deal of thought to your future and I think that from every point of view it will be best if you have a year or two in a busy city mission. You will have a great deal to offer in years to come and I am sure that if you have some pastoral work as a foundation you will be better able to use your knowledge later on. Your time at Oxford will have been a benefit not only to you but to the Catholics at Oxford. But I am sure that in the immediate future you will benefit spiritually by working in a parish. No amount of study of pastoral

work—or even the occasional supplies—can substitute for the experience of active work in a poor parish.

So far my pastoral experience had, indeed, been limited. In my first vacation as a priest I had been in sole charge of a small parish at Ponders End, in North London, during the holiday of the parish priest. My inexperience endeared me to the parishioners, who made me a handsome presentation when I departed; but the regular priest was not altogether pleased with everything he found on his return. I had thought the water in the baptismal font, for instance, rather scummy, and emptied it out and replaced it with clean sweet water; I then learnt that the scum was the holy oils supposed to remain in the water from one Holy Saturday until the next. While working on the recusant archives I had helped the clergy of Westminster Cathedral, and had learnt that long hours in the confessional could be gruelling and depressing. From time to time I had helped out in my home parish in Grassendale; I had solemnized the marriages of a number of couples among my Oxford friends. Now, from September 1959, I was to be a full-time curate at the parish of Sacred Heart, Hall Lane, Liverpool.

During the 'long holiday' of which the Archbishop spoke, I spent part of the time, as I had the year before, at an Oxford-Borstal camp. A group of college chaplains in Oxford had set up an arrangement whereby for two weeks in the summer a score of Oxford undergraduates from their chaplaincies would camp in Yorkshire with an equal number of boys from Borstal. The plan was to give the Borstal boys a holiday in the company of non-criminal companions, who could give them some experience of Christian fellowship. I do not know whether the scheme, in the end, fulfilled the expectations of those who planned it. Certainly, the Borstal boys seem to have enjoyed themselves, and usually behaved very well; certainly, too, it provided challenging pastoral experience for the undergraduates. Each pair shared a tent with two potentially hostile Borstal boys, and accompanied them on a two-day hike in groups of four, which was the climax of the trip; it was not a trivial task to restrain them from wrongdoing without forfeiting their comradeship. At the end of the camp the Oxford campers would return to the Borstals for a day or two to share the prison regime. I went along as chaplain to the Catholic campers; I was made particularly welcome as the proportion of Catholics among Borstal boys was much higher than that among Oxford undergraduates.

Sacred Heart parish, where I was now to be posted, was indeed a busy city mission. The massive but undistinguished Victorian church lay in the centre of Liverpool 8, a district which was not then as notorious as it has since become for urban decay and civil disorder, but which was already depressed and depressing. The most serious problem then was not unemployment but inadequate housing. The parish was divided into four sections, one to each of the priests; as the junior curate I was given the most rundown quarter. Half of my parishioners lived in unsound and often squalid houses; the other half, who lived in the blocks of flats built to replace the older houses as part of slum clearance, were often equally discontented; communal entrances and staircases, already ramshackle, would soon be noisome, and would eventually become downright dangerous. Everyone had lost families or neighbours who had been rehoused in outlying suburbs like Kirby. Though some of the migrants returned weekly to do their shopping in the cheaper city-centre shops, we began to feel that the parish was losing its base as more and more solid parishioners left or lost their families. About 3,500 must have remained, in 1959.

We four priests did not share, indoors, in the squalor with which we were surrounded. Far from it. Shortly before I arrived, the ample but antiquated presbytery had been completely renovated, at a cost of £25,000. As hardly any of our parishioners can have lived in a house worth more than £2,000, this fact was a source of embarrassment, and, to me at least, uneasy conscience. We ate good, and often expensive, food which was not, however, always very appetizing, since we were catered for by the parish priest's sister, who was an indifferent cook. She had one or two maids to assist her with the house cleaning. Curates were not allowed to keep alcohol in their rooms; but the parish priest was generous with cocktails, and there was wine on the table several times a week. Considered absolutely, our lives were not very luxurious; no more comfortable than those of the bachelor Oxford dons of the period, certainly. But they contrasted uncomfortably with the lives of our parishioners.

The discomfort was increased by the fact that our main personal contacts with our parishioners took the form of asking them for money. The collection plate was handed out, once, twice, sometimes thrice on Sundays; but there was not only this 'indoor collection'—one of the clergy's major duties was the outdoor collection held every Friday evening. Each Friday from four until ten we would visit fifty or so houses in our area, to greet the

parishioners and to collect their offerings, spending between five
and ten minutes with each household. Beside collecting money,
we could inquire how the children were progressing, check whether
the teenagers had been to Mass last week, answer questions about
Catholic teaching, have a cup of tea and learn about grandmother's
arthritis. The system meant that we could see each household about
once a month, and keep a reasonably accurate record of their
progress in our notebooks. It also brought in a substantial part
of the parish income. It was quite exhausting, and one of the
happiest moments in a curate's week was when he could wash off
the marks of the dirty copper and silver from his hands and settle
down to a late supper in front of the television.

The money collected in the parish did not all go to parish
expenses and the support of the clergy. Our own stipends indeed,
being nominal sums of about £200 a year, were a very small charge
on the parish. Much of the takings were taxed by the diocese for
the support of the Catholic schools being built in new areas in
accordance with the Butler legislation on education. One of the
major sources of such funds was the parish Bingo. Mercifully, at
Sacred Heart, the conduct of Bingo was in the hands of lay helpers.
But the parish football pool called for clerical co-operation: it was
a regular Saturday afternoon task to listen to the results, check
the entries for the winner, and seal up the prize money in buff
envelopes for distribution to the lucky ones.

Our principal task in theory, and a major one in practice, was
of course the administration of the sacraments and the preaching
of the Gospel. On Sundays there would be one or two Masses for
each of us to say in the morning; we would help distribute
Communion at our colleagues' Masses; and we would take it in
turns to preach. Sunday lunch was always a good one, for which
we had worked up a good appetite, helping with Masses and
counting the collections; each of us, one Sunday a month, would
have to leave early to do the afternoon baptisms. Christening babies
is one of the more agreeable clerical duties: I never failed to be
entertained by the baby's surprised gurgle as you put the salt on
its tongue. As a young priest I was at first rather worried about
the actual pouring of the water: if you splashed too much water
on the newborn, the godparents would be annoyed; if you didn't
make the water actually run down the baby's head, the sacrament
would not be valid.

Each day of the week there were Masses to be said, but usually
for small congregations of thirty to forty, not for the hundreds

who would come on Sundays and 'holidays of obligation'. In a parish, unlike at Oxford, it was difficult to avoid taking Mass stipends: a priest who refused to take them would offend his parishioners, and would be hard put to find money to buy clothes and books and other necessaries not provided as part of parish commons. But there was, fortunately, none of the anonymity of the Rome dollar stipend market: each Sunday the names of those for whom Mass was to be offered, and at whose request, were read and listened to with careful attention by the congregation.

The hearing of confessions took place principally on Saturdays, morning and evening. We priests would take up our position, sitting in small rooms in a corridor which ran beside the aisle communicating with the church through curtained grilles before which the parishioners would kneel in anonymity to confess their sins. Most people who have never heard confessions imagine that it must be an enthralling experience to listen to people confiding their most shameful secrets. In fact, the hearing of confessions consists of hours of tedium occasionally relieved by embarrassment. Interestingly wicked people never go to confession at all; most of those who go do not realize what their real sins are. So most confessions are repetitions of short catalogues of unimportant and humdrum sins. The moments of embarrassment most frequently occur in connection with the confession of sexual sins. The priest is obliged to satisfy himself that every mortal sin has been confessed specifically: it will not do, for instance, for the sinner to accuse himself of being unchaste, he must specify whether he was guilty of adultery, fornication etc. Consequently, if a penitent says 'I did something dirty', the confessor must embark on a series of questions designed to elicit the nature of the sin. It was not easy to do this without appearing prurient, or without falling foul of the strict rules prohibiting 'solicitation', i.e. any form of abuse of the confessional for sexual purposes. From time to time, in the confessional, the priest would realize that he was faced with someone in real trouble or depression or despair. A good confessor in such circumstances has an opportunity to make a real difference in people's lives: advice given in confession is often taken with unusual seriousness even by the most lukewarm Catholic. But the anonymity and brevity of the priest's contact with his penitent make it very difficult for him to tailor his advice to the penitent's need.

Information received in this way is, of course, strictly confidential, and 'breaking the seal of the confessional' is a very serious sin for a priest; the calendar contains the names of canonized saints who were martyred rather than reveal the secrets of their penitents. In my experience this obligation is taken by priests with complete seriousness. Living among the clergy in close contact, I had ample opportunity to observe, in my own case and in that of others, clerical obligations which were honoured more in the breach than the observance; but I have never, at any time, heard a remark which could be taken as an explicit or implicit breach of the confidentiality of the confessional. I cannot say the same of the confidential secrets of other professions with which I have been in contact.

Much of our parochial work was connected with the marriages of our parishioners. The wedding itself was a fairly brief ceremony on a Saturday morning or afternoon, even if both partners were Catholics and it was followed by a Nuptial Mass. But there was a lot of paperwork involved beforehand, such as checking registers to see that the parties were baptized, and not already married, and filling out forms for diocesan records. A mixed marriage, one between a parishioner and someone who was not a Catholic, involved a great deal more work. A dispensation had to be applied for, from the bishop or from Rome; different kinds of dispensation were necessary, depending on the status of the non-Catholic. (Was she baptized? Had he been married before?) The non-Catholic party had to come weekly for a series of instructions on Catholic doctrine, and the Catholic party had to agree to promise to bring up the children of the marriage as Catholics. Any mistake by a curate in any of the paperwork could lead to the dispensation being refused.

In addition to the full-scale marriage ceremonies, held in the church with the registrar in attendance, there were also more hole-in-the-corner affairs: the remarriage, or ecclesiastical convalidation, of couples who had been married in a registry office in violation of the laws of the Church and without benefit of the Church's blessing. In most city parishes many couples might fall into this category: they were 'not married in the eyes of God' until they had put things right with ecclesiastical law. In clergy jargon they were called *'Ne Tems'* because they were married in breach of the Papal decree *Ne Temere* which made the presence of ecclesiastical witnesses an essential condition for the validity of a Catholic wedding. Persuading *Ne Tems* to get their marriages convalidated was an important pastoral duty. There was also a certain amount of what might broadly be called 'divorce work'; not that the Church allowed divorce, but the provisions of the Canon Law were so complicated that many marriages were, unknown to the parties, null; and spouses dissatisfied with their partners might seek one's help to find a nullifying element in their original marriage.

Part of the job of a priest in a poor parish overlaps with that of the social worker. There is much simple and elementary good to be done, whose value in no way depends on the truth of Catholic sacramental claims: lonely people to be visited, old people to be helped with the forms they have to fill up, neighbours to be shown ways in which they can help. This kind of thing was in some ways the most satisfying part of my life as a curate, since it made no demands on a weak and overburdened faith.

Sacred Heart had no hospital in the parish, so that we did not have the daily and nightly calls to attend on emergencies that are such a regular feature of the lives of many priests. But there were the bedridden to be visited, have Communion taken to them when they were chronically ill, and be anointed when death seemed near. And there were the dead to be buried, and the bereaved to be consoled. One of the most taxing parts of the curate's life was the quick changes of mood which it called for: on one and the same morning one had to do one's best to identify with the mourners who were burying their dead, and the rejoicing bride and bridegroom at a wedding. I admired priests who could shift from one emotional gear into another, without either coldness or hypocrisy. I found it very hard to do so myself.

While there were many things to admire about them, I found my fellow clergy difficult. The parish priest was a canon, a former seminary professor of theology whose mind, when it turned to academic topics, could be very acute. But theology had long been succeeded by horse-racing as his major interest outside his daily duties. The other curates nicknamed him 'Patwig': the code name he used on the telephone to place his off-course bets. From time to time he would go on a drinking spree, which meant that one or other of us might have to stand in for him to take a service or preach a sermon. A state of quiet war with the parish priest seemed almost to be the normal condition of presbytery life; the senior curate would sometimes pick childish quarrels with him and refuse to communicate directly, sending notes or messages via us junior curates. I remained, most of the time, in uneasy alliance with both parties.

Priests were not encouraged to make any close social contacts with their parishioners. We were expected to drop in at the Young Men's Club and drink the sweet dark beer provided for the rather aged clientele. Teenagers attended the Youth Club, which the junior curates supervised: one came to dread the nights of overloud music and the occasional fights to be sorted out. And there were semi-social and semi-religious groups like the Children of Mary, with whom it was the junior curate's task to drink tea and go on the occasional outing. But it would not have been easy to make friends in the parish, even if that had been encouraged. Only one person in the whole parish, in the time I was there, had gone to a university, and a graduate like myself was rather an odd fish. So I was glad of brief escapes to meet old Oxford friends. Weekends are the busiest times for parochial clergy. We were each given one weekday a week off; on most of these I would go to visit my mother.

Partly, I think, in order to give me an intellectual task, the Archbishop also appointed me archivist to the Archdiocese. The archives were kept in the diocesan administrative building (the 'Curial Offices') which were ten minutes' walk downhill. I spent my spare weekday mornings sorting and cataloguing assorted papers there, dealing with the history of the diocese since its foundation in the 1850s. Most of the official records—of marriages, decisions of diocesan tribunals and the like—were very systematically preserved; but there was a mass of assorted papers and miscellaneous correspondence, which I tried to reduce to order. Heenan had heard that the Nazis in Germany had ransacked the archives of dioceses to find papers which could be published to discredit the Church. He was anxious to prevent anything of that kind happening here; he asked me to go through and weed out stories of clerical misdeeds which could have been used for propaganda purposes. I did not like to refuse point blank, but as an archivist I found it went against the grain to destroy, on such a partisan basis, material of historical interest. So I compromised by simply sorting, into a special section, documents of an embarrassing nature; what has happened to them since I ceased to be archivist I do not know. Thus I spent many mornings working through the soot-covered records of the misdemeanours of long-dead clerics, sad tales of the rash entanglements and stern official separations between Victorian clergymen and their Children of Mary. A statistician, I think, would have been impressed by how little material there was; but some of it would no doubt have been grist to the mill of any anti-clerical party which seized power as the Archbishop feared.

Sometimes the duties of an archivist were more interesting and fruitful. One day, for instance, I was told by a colleague in the

Curia that historical material lay uncatalogued in one of the country parishes in Lancashire. I drove to the parish and asked if I could look at it. The priest was out, but the housekeeper showed me, with a torch, into the attic where the stuff was kept. It turned out to be not archives, but printed books: the first two I spotted were both *incunabula*, and it was clear even from a very quick look that this was a valuable library, collected when the parish had been a recusant mission in the eighteenth century. I telephoned the priest later to ask if I could call again to catalogue the books. 'Bring a bloody lorry and take the whole bloody lot away!' I heard an Irish voice say. I accepted the invitation. With a friend from the Bodleian Library I worked through the books; we found that a dozen of them were not in Bodley, another dozen were not in the British Museum. These volumes were sold to those institutions; some I bought myself, having had a valuation made; others, the great majority, were sold at auction by a London bookseller. The priest was rather surprised when, at the end of it all, I sent him a cheque for some £500 for his parish funds.

All this time there was my Oxford thesis still to be completed. It was not easy to find long periods for study and writing at Sacred Heart, but it was not much more distracting than Oxford had been. I completed it in 1961, and was orally examined in Oxford by David Pears and Patrick Gardiner. They thought well of the thesis, and I was awarded the doctorate. It did not need much alteration to be made ready for the publisher. I did, however, need the permission of my Archbishop to publish it. He was anxious that I should submit it to the diocesan censor. I argued that as a work of pure philosophy, not theology, it did not fall under the censorship requirements of Canon Law; moreover that a censor's *nihil obstat* was a kiss of death for a book published for the secular market. He agreed in the end to let me publish it uncensored. I sent him a copy on publication; so far as I am aware it contains nothing which contradicts Catholic teaching. It was published under the title *Action, Emotion and Will* and was well received by philosophical reviewers. When, later, I came to look for academic jobs, it must have been largely due to that book that I was successful.

The years at Sacred Heart were among the most depressing of my life. At the day-to-day parish chores I worked as hard as the average curate, and I got on reasonably well with colleagues and parishioners. But I was lonely and felt very starved of congenial company, in spite of the kindness I received. Even those parish tasks which, in themselves, I would have found enjoyable and

fulfilling — like saying Mass and administering the sacraments —
were cankered by the doubts I harboured about the validity of the
Catholic claims. If those claims were unfounded, then I was helping
to preserve and enforce a fraudulent system, preaching doctrines
to people which they should not be asked to believe, binding
burdens on them they should not be asked to bear. If, on the other
hand, they were well founded, then my own doubts, and the
carelessness of clerical discipline which resulted from them, were
grievous sins; sins which would not, indeed, vitiate my ministry —
it is an age-long doctrine of the Church that the unworthiness of
the minister does not invalidate the conferring of the sacraments —
but which put me in danger of Hell, and cheated my parishioners
of the holiness and spiritual guidance they were entitled to expect.
I could not, must not, continue as I was. Either I must give up
Catholicism, or I must throw myself into it with greater energy.
But which?

I came to think that the right thing for me to do, perhaps, was
to seek laicization: neither to abandon Catholicism altogether, nor
to continue as a priest, but to seek a dispensation which would
allow me to return to the lay state. But the prospect was not an
attractive one. It would involve disappointment and suffering to
many of those closest to me, like my mother and Alec and friends
who were proud of me as an apparently successful priest. It could
provide no guarantee that the doubts against faith would cease
to torment me, even though it would mean that in the worst case
I was deceiving only myself and not other people. In the
ecclesiastical discipline of the 1960s, laicization would not include
permission to marry. And in the loneliness at Sacred Heart I had
come to realize how difficult I was going to find it to lead a celibate
life.

Even to share one's doubts with others was difficult; and to do
so except to someone whose own faith was well assured could be
to put an occasion of sin in their way. But I did tell some of my
Catholic friends in Oxford. I was, and am, grateful to them that
they did not take the snap-out-of-it-and-take-a-cold-bath attitude
which many confessors take but treated my difficulties as serious
intellectual problems about which they corresponded with me in
detail. I remember an exchange of daily postcards which went on
for months about the proofs for the existence of God. Also I
confided in Alec, who was sympathetic, being no stranger himself
to doubt and difficulty; but it was clear that he was enormously
saddened and worried by my consideration of being laicized. An

attempt to warn my mother what I was thinking of was maladroit and distressing.

While I was still tergiversating, my deliberations were cut short by a spell in hospital. I gave a lift to a hitchhiker who turned out to have infective hepatitis; twenty days later I began to vomit and turn yellow myself. I spent three weeks in Fazakerley isolation hospital, much cosseted by friendly Catholic nurses. The bout of hepatitis did me one good turn. Hitherto, I had been a heavy smoker; I had long wanted to give up, but quite lacked the willpower. During my period in isolation in hospital I was forbidden to smoke; on leaving, I found myself to be sufficiently denicotinized to be able to forswear cigarettes altogether. Giving up smoking is perhaps the only decision in my life which I have never for a single moment regretted. While convalescing at home I was informed by the Archbishop that he wished me to change parishes: I was to move from Hall Lane to St Peter and Paul's, Great Crosby.

This was in many ways a more congenial environment than Sacred Heart. Crosby is an interesting place for a Catholic. At the one end is Liverpool dockland, at Seaforth; at the other end is the village of Little Crosby, still feudally centred on the residence of the squire, the Blundell family having remained in the same spot, and with the same religion, since the twelfth century. St Peter and Paul's was in the middle of Crosby; a parish of teachers, doctors, office workers and the like. The air, both physical and intellectual, was easier to breathe. Most important of all, the parish priest was a man I could unfeignedly admire: Mgr Turner, who had been Rector of Upholland in my schooldays. His unselfish holiness continued to inspire me. But his health was poor, and his austere virtues were not appreciated by the parishioners; he remained too senior and awesome a figure for me really to confide in.

The presbytery at Crosby, though quite comfortable, was not at all as expensively equipped as that at Sacred Heart; and there was not the painful contrast between the standard of living of clergy and laity that had troubled me in Liverpool 8. Nor was there an outdoor collection to be taken: pastoral visits to parishioners were genuinely pastoral — but, it must be admitted, they were also less frequent. The translation to Crosby was a great relief, and I postponed thoughts of laicization. I began to devote myself more and more to tasks which were clearly valuable, whether or not Catholic doctrines were true.

As I mentioned earlier, one of the great social problems of this period was the lack of adequate housing which the poor could afford. This was a problem which was particularly acutely felt by Catholics nationwide. A few years earlier Maisie Ward, the publisher, had founded an organization called the Catholic Housing Aid Society, designed to make it easier for the Catholic poor to purchase their own homes. With the aid of a friend, who had married Maisie's cousin, the heiress of Crosby Hall, I founded a Liverpool branch of the Society. Essentially it was a money-lending society, enabling poor Catholics to bridge the gap between the money they could save and the minimum deposit demanded by building societies for mortgages. We collected money from charitable donors, guaranteed Catholic mortgagors who were doubtfully creditworthy in the eyes of banks and building societies, found houses of the right price for them to buy, and offered topping-up loans. Archbishop Heenan took a friendly interest in our activites, and assisted us with a float of £1,000 from a charity he had set up out of the royalties on his books.

In the academic year 1961–2 I was also invited by Antony Lloyd, the Professor of Philosophy at Liverpool University, to take up a temporary lectureship to fill an unexpected vacancy. The philosophy department was a small one; Lloyd's predecessor, Alan Dorward, who wished to have time for canal-cruising, was said to have introduced a regulation that no honours students could be accepted who were unable to read the classics of philosophy in the original languages. This reduced the school to the few who had mastered Greek, Latin, French and German by the beginning of their course. In 1961 there were just three of us. My main task was to teach elementary formal logic to a couple of dozen first-year students in the university's very distinguished School of Architecture. Neither they nor I could quite understand why they had to learn logic; but most of them got through the prescribed exercises. More rewarding was teaching the history of philosophy to a small class of third-year students. It was pleasant to have a toe-hold in the academic world.

I was also asked by the Archbishop to give religious instruction to the sixth form in the grammar school opposite St Peter and Paul's run by the Christian Brothers. This was not a success: the Brothers clearly resented the imputation that they were not sufficiently qualified to teach religion without clerical assistance; and the boys obviously felt that they already had more than enough instruction on Catholic doctrine. They tried to while away the time as agreeably as possible by embarrassing their new teacher with questions such as 'What is the Pope's attitude to sex-change?'

In 1962 the Catholic Church was set in a ferment by Pope John XXII's inauguration of the Second Vatican Council, the first general council of the Church since the First Vatican Council of 1870 which, by defining the infallibility of the Pope, had been thought to render future ecumenical councils superfluous. The bishops of the world assembled in Rome to take part in its deliberations; some of them took theologians with them to advise on the draft decrees proposed to the Council; others, particularly the more impoverished ones, consulted theologians at home. I was surprised to be consulted by one of the English bishops, Pearson, the auxiliary of Lancaster, who wished to make a speech on the proposed decrees *De Ecclesia* and *De Oecumenismo*. He wished to plead for a fuller role for the non-Catholic Christian churches. I wrote for him a Latin speech, of which the following was the translation I provided:

It seems a pity that both the schema *De Ecclesia* and the schema *De Oecumenismo* should speak in several places as if our dissident brethren were not members of the Church. This has been in the past controverted, and has not hitherto been settled, since the interpretation of Pope Pius XII's encyclical *Mystici Corporis* too is controverted. If it is desired to settle this controversy in the negative sense, this should be done clearly. But it seems undesirable to do so. According to the Council of Florence, by baptism we become members of Christ and parts of the body of the Church.

Even the Council of Trent, when it condemned the heresies of the Reformation, did not suggest that the reformers were outside the Church. It lamented the heresies and other disturbances 'by which the Church of God is troubled and torn into many different parts'. It seems therefore open to a Catholic to say that members of other Christian churches are members of the one Church of God; heretical and schismatical members, no doubt, but still members. The plenitude of membership is enjoyed only by Catholics in a state of grace; from this plenitude there defect (a) bona fide heretics and schismatics; (b) Catholics in sin. The latter are more seriously defective than the former; since the former, if they die, enter the Kingdom of God, the Church without stain; the latter do not. Besides baptism our dissident brethren have faith, hope and charity; all retain the Christian name and carry out Christ's command to renew his supper. Many of them have other sacraments. The decree as it is proposed will seem to them arrogant; it should be replaced by a decree to be divided into two parts. The first should state what all Christians agree: that there exists on earth a gathering of the baptized who follow Christ (Christendom);

that this is miserably divided: that these rents in the Church are due to the sins of all; that the Council joins all Christians in praying that the schism will end by the means that Christ desires. Then, in the second part, state what we believe to be the means that Christ intended, viz. reconciliation with the Pope and the acceptance of the doctrines of e.g. Trent.

I know that Bishop Pearson spoke on the topic, only recently I learnt that he found my brief quite useful. In this early stage of the Council it was not easy, at first, to come by information about what went on there. I wrote a letter of Christmas greetings to Heard, now a Cardinal, hoping for some gossip in reply. His letter was concerned but uninformative.

My dear Kenny,
I was extremely pleased to hear from you. I did not know what had come over you as no one seemed to have any news of you. I put your silence down to (a) a bad attack of jaundice of which I had heard and which all too often leaves a colossal hump behind it or else (b) that in spite of the iterated warning of your confessor you were continuing to burn the candle at both ends and that the two ends were getting rather close together. However, thank God, your letters betray no signs of hump or undue fatigue. All the same, as it is a well known fact that all the Liverpool clergy are rolling in money, I am rather surprised that you have not been out. Now however I think the best thing would be to wait until the Council is over. The rector has done a wonderful job in rigging up an apartment for the Bishops, but I doubt if there would be any room for one of the 'inferior clergy'. Being boxed up in the Council for four hours a day I don't have any news. I am now doing a refresher course in theology so as to know rather more about it when the Council reopens.

At the beginning of the academic year 1962–3 my appointment at Liverpool University was not renewed. But I was invited, in the winter of 1962, to give a series of lectures at Manchester University. Arthur Prior, one of the authors whose work I had studied for my Gregorian doctorate, had come from New Zealand to be professor there, and I had made his acquaintance shortly before leaving Oxford. We became fast friends during my depressed years in Liverpool; as a former theologian and Presbyterian elder, Arthur could sympathize with the predicament which, when I got to know him and his wife well, I confided to them. As lectures I gave the chapters of *Action, Emotion and Will*, which were then with the printers. The philosophy department provided a very lively discussion; sometimes visitors from the Leeds department attended and joined in.

During my years as a curate I continued to think and write about theological topics and philosophical topics on the borderlines of theology. Every month diocesan clergy would meet in local conferences at their deaneries, to discuss a theological topic assigned by the Archbishop. I was assigned to treat the topic of development of doctrine. Catholics were taught that revelation had ceased with the death of the last Apostle, and that the Faith was unchanging. How was this to be reconciled with the manifest variation in the theological beliefs recorded during the long history of the Church? I set out the difficulties with gusto: the changing attitude of Catholic Christians to the imminent return of Christ, to the creation of the world in seven days, to the Pope's temporal sovereignty and deposing power, to the lawfulness of usury. Cardinal Newman had written a celebrated account of development: all it offered, I complained, was metaphor in place of explanation. But when it came to the positive part of my account, I had nothing to propose. It was easy to say that the doctrine of the Church could change only in accidental matters, not in essential ones. For it looked as if only after the event could we tell which elements at a given time were essential. If so, something now regarded as essential, e.g. the wrongness of contraception, might turn out with hindsight to have been accidental. I concluded:

> If a doctrine is defined, then it must be definable. And if definable, it must be contained — whether we would ever have guessed this for ourselves or not — in Scripture and tradition. For revelation ceased with the death of the last Apostle. If we accept these criteria, then no difficulty can be brought against the doctrine of the immutability of faith. The only trouble is, that our criteria render the doctrine impregnable only at the cost of making it vacuous. First we say — in order to avoid Modernism — that the Church teaches only those doctrines that are contained in Scripture and tradition. Then we ask: which doctrines are contained in Scripture and tradition? In order to avoid both the inadequacy of private judgement and the difficulties from Church history, we reply: those doctrines are contained in Scripture and tradition which the Church teaches. We have come round in a circle.

But not all my theological researches were concerned to point out the incredibility or vacuousness of individual Catholic doctrines. I made one discovery which made one of the mysteries of faith seem

easier to believe. Every reader of Gibbon knows that the Council
of Nicea defined, against Arius, that the Son of God was
consubstantial with the Father; not just *homoiousion*, of *like* nature,
but *homoousion*, of the *same* nature or substance. I inquired what
was meant by this word *homoousion*, which had caused centuries
of trouble. For a long time I thought I knew, until a friend asked
me: are we humans only *homoiousioi* with each other, or also
homoousioi? My reaction was to say we are only of like nature;
outside the Godhead there is no case of two different persons having
the *very same* nature; that is what the mystery of the Trinity is all
about. But on reading through the Fathers who gave the word its
theological currency I found that this answer (which was the answer
I got from every theologian I asked) was quite wrong: the
Trinitarian Fathers took it for granted that any two human beings
shared the same nature and were consubstantial with each other.
So the puzzlement which we had felt about the consubstantiality
of the Son with the Father was partly misplaced. Partly, only; for
of course the puzzle remains: if you and I are consubstantial with
each other and add up to two men, why do not the Son and Father,
consubstantial with each other, add up to two Gods? So perhaps
the mysteriousness of the Trinity was only shifted, not enlightened,
by my discovery.

During these years I did some reviewing for theological journals.
Like most young reviewers, I was a trenchant critic; and there
was certainly no lack of books for review which were ripe for the
hatchet. For an obscure Catholic bulletin on the philosophy of
science I reviewed Teilhard de Chardin's *Phenomenon of Man*,
anticipating by some months Sir Peter Medawar's magisterial
exposure in *Mind* of the essentially fraudulent nature of the book.
For *Blackfriars* I did a survey of recent moral theology, which began:

> It is hard to imagine why Karl Hörmann's *Introduction to Moral Theology*
> has been translated into English. The author states that the book was
> written for lay people. In fact, it is the kind of book which is most
> at home in the pocket of the seminarist at examination time. The
> publishers claim that it is 'a guide to principles and practice in modern
> life'. In fact, many of the infrequent practical examples are hot from
> Aristotle or the thirteenth century. Every page is leprous with jargon.
> We read of 'the positive method', of 'substantial union', of 'ontological
> goodness', of 'the sense-appetite'; words such as 'convenience',
> 'determine', 'incomprehensible' and 'elevated' are used in senses quite
> alien to their English usage. Frequently the examples take us back to
> that quaint and vivid world where men set fire to their neighbours'

houses and kill their friends while hunting, where captains throw overboard their merchandise to lighten the ship, and where maidens miss Mass to avoid being put to the blush by their banns. 'Modern life' is catered for mainly by brief asides on psychoanalytic theories and by a final chapter on cruelty to animals. Nuclear warfare is treated at the same length as water-divining; the ethics of advertising and race relations not at all.

I have no doubt that the books I attacked were bad, and that what I said in criticism of them was true: but was it really fair to attack bad Catholic moral theology when I was doubting more and more whether there could be such a thing as good Catholic moral theology?

My last theological essay as a priest was a contribution to a symposium held at Downside in 1963 on 'Theology and the University'. I was invited to speak on the relationship between theology and philosophy. Having summarized recent work in the philosophy of religion, I turned to the relevance of recent philosophy to a particular theological problem, transubstantiation. I pointed out how in one way recent philosophical work had made the doctrine less difficult to accept. If the kind of phenomenalism once espoused by Ayer were correct, then the notion of transubstantiation is flatly self-contradictory. But Austin, and others, had successfully disposed of phenomenalism of that kind. If we reject phenomenalism we are free to distinguish between a substance and its appearances, but it is still wrong to think of substance as an imperceptible part of a material object. Transubstantiation is often explained in this way; but, I argued, if we accept an Aristotelian account of substance there is no need to do so.

> According to scholastic theory, substance is not an imperceptible part of a particular individual. It is not a part of an individual; it is that individual. And it is imperceptible to the senses only in the following sense: I do not see *what kind of a thing* something is with my eyes as I see *what colour it is* with my eyes. For all that, substances may be perceived.

So when the Council of Trent says that the substance of bread and wine turns into the substance of Christ's body and blood, it simply means that the bread and wine turns into the body and blood. But why does the notion of *turning into* crop up at all? There is no mention of it in Scripture. It was introduced by Aquinas as the only possible explanation of the presence of Christ's body under the appearances of bread and wine after the consecration: Christ is *there* because something which was there has turned into him. But, Aquinas insists, and after him the Council of Constance, the accidents which remain, the whiteness and roundness, do not inhere in Christ; if they did, then Christ himself would be white and round. But this leaves us with a problem, with which I ended:

> The principle that the accidents inhere in no substance, however, leaves one problem with which I shall conclude. Among the accidental categories of Aristotle is the category of place. '. . . is on the altar', for instance, is an accidental predicate. But if the accidents which once belonged to the bread do not inhere after consecration in the substance of Christ's body, then it appears that it by no means follows from the presence of the host on the altar that Christ is present on the altar. Thus the doctrine of transubstantiation appears in the end to fail to secure that for which alone it was originally introduced, namely the real presence of Christ's body under the sacramental species. I do not know of any satisfactory answer to this problem. If I did I would give it. Since I do not, I must leave it, as the writers of textbooks say, as an exercise for the reader.

By the time this was published I had at last faced up to the consequences of my dwindled belief in transubstantiation, and was no longer a priest.

XIII

Banning the Bomb, 1962-3

I had come from Oxford to Liverpool firmly convinced of the immorality of the Western policy of nuclear deterrence. Such a conviction was, at the time, rare among Catholic clergy. The dropping of the bombs on Hiroshima and Nagasaki had shocked some of my priest friends, but in the years of the Cold War the majority of clergy had come to accept as legitimate the possession, and perhaps even the use, of nuclear weapons. Certainly, attachment to the cause of nuclear disarmament was something regarded as eccentric and dangerous, characteristic of unreliable figures like the Dominicans.

I was much influenced by Miss G. E. M. Anscombe's pamphlet *Mr Truman's Degree*: a *pièce d'occasion* opposing the proposal to honour the U.S. President in Oxford, on the grounds that he was responsible for murder on a grand scale. The pamphlet set out in a clear and vivid manner the traditional Catholic teaching on the wrongness of deliberately killing non-combatants in war. Despite the pamphlet President Truman was given his degree after an overwhelming vote in Congregation; that had been some years before I went to Oxford, but the pamphlet still circulated and many of us in the younger generation found it very convincing.

At the Gregorian University only one hour in seven years had been devoted to the ethics of warfare. Now I was brought to reflect on the just war tradition: the tradition according to which while war could be justly waged, and sometimes should be, there were strict limits on what was permissible in warfare, which ruled out the killing of prisoners and the area-bombing of civilian populations. The just war tradition seemed to me, and still seems, the best approach to the question of how far war is acceptable as an instrument for securing justice in international relations. There was nothing specifically Christian in those premises of the just war tradition which entailed the immorality of the nuclear policies of

West and East. Hence, my increasing doubts about the credibility
of the Catholic system as a whole did nothing to weaken
the argument. Here was a point on which, it seemed to me,
the application of traditional Catholic teaching reached the
same conclusion as the reflections of secular morality. I was
able, therefore, to throw myself with enthusiasm into the task
of trying to convince other Catholics where their doctrines should
lead them.

I did not join the Campaign for Nuclear Disarmament: there
were too many pacifists and Marxists in the local branches of the
campaign for me to feel comfortable as an official member. But
I did from time to time address meetings under the auspices of
C.N.D. The argument which I presented was a simple one. I quote
from the notes I made for my speech at one such meeting:

The central tradition of Christian teaching has always held that it is
justifiable to go to war. I say 'the central tradition' because I do not
deny or belittle the existence of Christian pacifists in every age. But
in general Christian teachers have not interpreted Christ's teaching
as ruling out war absolutely. They have, however, laid down stringent
conditions governing the taking of life in war. If a war is itself unjust —
if it is a war of aggression — then all taking of life by the aggressor
is unjust. But suppose that a war is just. Even so, the soldier, or the
government, has not an unlimited right to take life on the enemy side.
  Traditionally, it has always been held — by all the larger Christian
denominations — that he is allowed to kill only those actually engaged
in aggression against his country. Now who are those 'engaged in
aggression'? Until recent times, it was fairly easy to answer that
question: they were soldiers in uniform. Everyone else was a non-
combatant: non-combatants were technically known as 'innocents'.
The main principle of Christian morality concerning war was that
deliberately to kill innocents was murder. The sacking of cities, and
the killing of women and children, was always regarded as one of the
worst possible human actions. No purpose, however good, could justify
such an action; for the end does not justify the means. In the present
century, however, this traditional teaching has sometimes been
obscured. For one thing, it is obvious that in a modern war, the number
of those engaged in aggression is larger than the number of servicemen
in uniform. Those who are making munitions and transporting them
to the front are waging war no less than the army. This has led to
the muddled conclusion that it is now legitimate to kill anyone in war,
including full-time mothers and infants in arms. On the contrary, the
destruction of cities is as immoral as it always was. The invention of
nuclear weapons has made it vastly easier to destroy cities and kill

non-combatants; it has not made it a scrap more moral. The use of nuclear weapons as they were used at Hiroshima and Nagasaki is wicked. It is immoral, no matter what advantage may be gained by it. For the end does not justify the means.

This kind of argument was directed against those of my fellow-clergy who were prepared to defend the atom-bombing of Japan, or the area-bombing of German cities, on the grounds that it shortened the war and hastened an Allied victory. But there were those, and perhaps they were the majority of the minority who were concerned to reflect on the matter at all, who agreed entirely about the wickedness of the actual use of atomic or nuclear weapons on cities, but argued that the possession of nuclear weapons as a deterrent was justified, since it was possible to imagine lawful uses for them.

Catholic theologians were, in general, very loath to condemn the nuclear deterrent, and reluctant even to make explicit the condemnation of the use of nuclear weapons which most of them, if pressed, would agree was demanded by Catholic teaching. This was because they feared any weakening of the West's stand against atheistic communism which was seen as the Church's worst enemy. Thus, when a questioner asked, in the Liverpool diocesan paper, *The Catholic Pictorial*, whether a nuclear war, carried on against an unjust aggressor, could be justified, the paper's resident theologian, Fr Ripley, replied that Catholic theologians were divided on the matter. Some, he said, hold that the use of atom and hydrogen bombs could not be justified; others claim that the nation could use nuclear weapons to defend itself against the danger of communist domination. The Church, he said, had not decided between these two views. I wrote to the paper to protest:

By nuclear war most people mean a war involving the use of H-bombs or A-bombs against cities. Some of your readers may therefore conclude from Fr Ripley's reply that such a war may lawfully be waged. That is not so. The intentional killing in war of those not engaged in making war is murder. The use of large-scale nuclear weapons against cities involves the intentional killing of those not engaged in making war. Therefore it is murder. This is not a question which the Church has left open. In his Easter sermon of 1958 Cardinal Godfrey spoke as follows: 'Nobody can subscribe to the thesis that it would ever be morally lawful to use indiscriminate nuclear weapons on centres of population which are predominantly civilian.' It follows that to use nuclear weapons as they were used at Hiroshima and Nagasaki is always immoral.

It makes no difference whether those on whom the bombs are dropped are Japanese or Russians, Christians or Communists . . . Theologians in this country are indeed divided about the lawfulness of possessing nuclear weapons. But all agree that to use them — in the only way in which they are ever likely to be used — is out of the question.

That was in April 1962. I was perhaps sanguine in saying that theologians were united in saying that they could not be used lawfully. On the whole they tended to sidestep the issue. But Catholic politicians were naturally not so reluctant. At that time Mr Norman St John-Stevas had a column each week in the *Catholic Pictorial*, and a few weeks after my letter he attacked there the traditional teaching about the just war; it was worked out, he said, for medieval knights, and was out of date in the nuclear age. 'Take the sharp distinction which is made between "guilty" combatants and "innocent" non-combatants. Does this make any sense nowadays when war is total and the whole community is involved in waging it? An unwilling conscript may in fact be much more "innocent" than an ardent munition worker.'

I wrote back, arguing that this paragraph contained four mistakes. The justification for killing soldiers is not that they are wicked: it is because it is the only way to stop them waging the unjust war in which they are professionally engaged. Nor is the reason why we are not allowed to kill non-combatants the fact that they are morally innocent. Moreover, it is quite wrong to think that traditional Catholic teaching makes it immoral to kill munition workers; and it is untrue that the whole community is involved in waging war: even in wartime about half the population of any nation consists of children, the sick, the aged, and full-time mothers.

At the same time another Catholic M.P., John Biggs-Davison, was arguing in the pages of the *Catholic Herald* in favour of a British nuclear deterrent. We needed such an independent deterrent, he said, because we could not expect the U.S.A. to risk nuclear annihilation for the sake of Kuwait and Brunei. I wrote to the paper inquiring whether this meant that in Biggs-Davison's view Britain itself should be prepared to risk nuclear annihilation for the sake of Kuwait and Brunei. In reply, Biggs-Davison did not answer the question but said that if both sides to a potential conflict were prepared to retaliate with nuclear weapons, there would be no nuclear war. My reply concluded:

Mr Biggs-Davison cannot have it both ways. To use threats of nuclear devastation either involves a risk of nuclear annihilation or it does not. If it does not, then the American deterrent is sufficient to protect any conceivable British interest; we can surely expect the U.S. to support our legitimate interests if they have nothing to lose by doing so. If it does, then a British government which is prepared to take this risk for the sake of Kuwait and Brunei is criminally irresponsible.

Catholic theologians at this time argued that provided that a legitimate use for nuclear weapons could be imagined, their possession too was legitimate. Those of us on the other side said that what was relevant to judging the policies of our governments was not what they might do with nuclear weapons, but what they said they did intend to do.

The September issue of the *Catholic Gazette* in 1962 contained three questions about the bomb. The first: 'Can the use of the hydrogen bomb ever be justified, since it would cause far more evil than it could avert?' In reply, the theologian Edward K. Taylor said: 'The enslavement of whole nations, the destruction of faith and the corruption of morals, which would probably follow on domination by a ruthless atheistic power, would far outweigh the material destruction and moral evils resulting from the use of the bomb.' However, he went on to say that there were differences of opinion among theologians about the use of the bomb. Might it not be lawfully used, for instance, against a fleet at sea? 'We conclude therefore that in our present state of knowledge it is difficult to justify the use of the bomb, but one must hesitate to say that its use must be always and obviously immoral.'

The second question was: 'What justification can there be for possessing a weapon if it is unlawful to use it?' 'Theologians who would hesitate to justify the use of the weapon,' the questioner was told, 'have no difficulty in justifying the possession of it as a deterrent. Their point may be illustrated thus: one has seen hanging in the hall of a suburban house a murderous shillelagh or club; the gentle housewife who opens the door would never have the courage to use it, but she thinks it might make an intruder think twice before attempting violent entry. Nations may possess weapons they do not intend to use in order to deter a ruthless and unscrupulous enemy.' The final question was: 'Why had the official voice of the Church not given clear guidance in this matter?' The answer began 'It has', but then went on to admit, 'There has been no precise statement concerning the morality of the possession or use of the hydrogen bomb. Perhaps this is because the Popes think it wiser to keep silent. The Church is not always bound to speak out in the face of evil.'

This set of replies seemed to me to sidestep the main issue in such a way as to avoid contradicting the traditional just war teaching, while leaving the reader unjustifiably acquiescent in the deterrent policy. I sent the Editor a long letter of complaint, saying that the replies ignored the point that to use nuclear weapons as atomic weapons were used at Hiroshima was wicked:

> This is much the most important thing to be said about nuclear warfare. I am sure that Fr Taylor agrees with it: it astonishes me that he did not say it. Instead of discussing the likely use of hydrogen bombs, which is their use against cities, he discusses their use against a fleet at sea, which is very unlikely. It is as if a moralist, questioned about the use of contraceptives, was to reply that it was possible to imagine lawful uses for them — without mentioning that to use them *as contraceptives* was sinful . . . Materialists, says Fr Taylor, believe that the use of nuclear weapons could cause more evil than it would avert. But for a Christian, he suggests, the undesirable results of unilateral disarmament 'would far outweigh the material destruction and moral evils resulting from the use of the bomb'. Some of your readers, I fear, may understand this as meaning that while a mere materialist might shrink from laying waste a Russian city, a true Catholic ought to do so cheerfully in the good cause . . . The important question for a Catholic to settle is whether his government does or does not intend ever to use nuclear weapons on civilian targets. For if it does, he may not support nor take part in carrying out its nuclear defence projects. In our own case, we may concur in our governments' policy of deterrence only if we have good reason to believe that they intend never, in any circumstances, to use nuclear weapons murderously.
>
> Many people do believe that in the event of war our governments will be deterred, either by morality or self-interest, from using large-scale nuclear weapons against cities. Such a belief appears seriously mistaken. Our governments are unlikely to be deterred by moral considerations. The governments of the United Kingdom and of the United States of America in the last war used bombs in murderous fashion. Truman and Churchill, who authorized the commission of murder, are both still held in honour among our peoples. Nor are our governments likely to be held back by considerations of self-interest. Not, at least, if they believe, like Fr Taylor, that if it comes to the point the use of the bomb will do more good than harm. It seems, therefore, that we have no good reason to believe our governments innocent of murderous intent.

Moreover, the governments which possess large-scale nuclear weapons—our own included—have often in the past made it clear that they have no intention of restricting their use in war to military targets. The prospect held out to the enemy has always been, in the words of President Eisenhower, 'the virtual annihilation of his country'.

The Editor was, unsurprisingly, unwilling to publish the letter: quite apart from its content, it contained fifteen paragraphs as long as those quoted. He sent on the letter to Fr Taylor, who replied, agreeing that it was out of the question to use the hydrogen bomb to destroy a city:

If there are any of our readers who deduce from my remarks that a Catholic could cheerfully agree to the destruction of a city, they have not read my replies carefully. On question two you raise the point of the intentions of our Government. I did not. This might be a very good further question to ask.

I wrote back a letter which began:

I am so glad that you agree with me that it is out of the question to justify the use of large-scale nuclear weapons against cities. You must, however, know many Catholics, both clerical and lay, who are quite prepared to justify such a use, in spite of the traditional teaching of the Church concerning the killing of non-combatants. The most distinguished such Catholic is President Kennedy.

To the Editor I wrote:

It seems to me that anyone who read Fr Taylor's replies, however carefully, would be left with the impression that he could in good conscience acquiesce in the defence policy of the present British government. But this is not so. Fr Taylor agrees with me that it is out of the question to justify the use of large-scale nuclear weapons against cities. British defence policy is based on a strategy of using, in the event of war, such weapons against cities. Therefore no one may in good conscience acquiesce in it. It seems therefore that you have an obligation to correct any false impression on this point which your readers may have received. I understand, however, your reluctance to publish so long a letter, and am willing to shorten it to any reasonable length.

The Editor's response was terse: 'If you would put your comments into a letter of 350-450 words, keeping out references to issues which might also be political, I will print it.'

I abbreviated my letter to the required length, but it was obviously impossible to comply with the second part of the request. The Editor refused to print more than the first four paragraphs of my shortened letter. I sent the whole letter to the *Tablet*, with a plaintive covering note drawing attention to 'the difficulty of finding a hearing in certain Catholic quarters for the application of Christian principles to the judgement of the defence policy of this country'. My letter was neither acknowledged nor printed by the *Tablet*. I was clearly earning a reputation with the Catholic editors of the country as a nuisance with a bee in his bonnet. Moreover, I was violating the principle that 'priests should keep out of politics'—though I was unable to see how I was any more engaged in politics than those I was writing against.

The *Clergy Review*, however, a scholarly monthly, then edited by Fr Charles Davis, was willing to publish serious discussions of issues such as the morality of nuclear weapons; and bishops did not mind what the clergy published in journals which were read only by other clergy. So I write an article in the autumn of 1962 setting out the points I had been unable to get published elsewhere. I included a defensive paragraph about the charge of meddling in politics:

> Reasons are sometimes put forward why priests should not express a moral judgement about nuclear policy. To do so, we are told, is to interfere in politics, which is outside the sphere of religion. But those who say this rightly do not hesitate to preach and write against Communism, which is a political system. Injustice does not cease to be injustice, and murder does not cease to be murder, merely because it is championed by statesmen or canvassed by political parties. Public morality is as much within the sphere of religion as private morality . . . Everyone knows that Catholics have odd views about contraception and therapeutic abortion; but about war we are regarded by the man in the street as being substantially sound. People sometimes hesitate to consult a Catholic gynaecologist, but nobody minds giving a Catholic soldier a commission.

But in fact, I argued, Catholics must differ from most of their fellow-countrymen about the waging of war; because they accept divine laws, including the prohibition on killing the innocent, they could not accept the widespread belief that the way to decide whether any particular action was good or bad was to ask whether it would do more good than harm. Most of the article was taken up with documenting, from official statements and political speeches, that the deterrent policy of the West did indeed involve a murderous intent. I quoted the British Defence White Paper of 1958, and Eisenhower's State of the Union message of the same year; the report of Mr Watkinson of the N.A.T.O. ministers meeting in Athens in 1962, and recent speeches by leading American politicians.

The article was entitled 'Counterforce and Countervalue' and it was principally devoted to a discussion of the announcement made by U.S. Secretary of Defense MacNamara on 16 June 1962, that in the event of major war American strategy would be aimed at the destruction of enemy military forces (counterforce), not of the civilian population (countervalue), so as to 'give a possible opponent the strongest imaginable incentive to refrain from striking our own cities'. I argued that the emphasis still placed on second-strike capability as a deterrent to enemy attack on American cities meant that the restriction of American aim to military targets would be only a temporary measure, and the ultimate willingness to massacre remained. The article concluded with a much more explicit commitment to nuclear disarmament than anything I had published in the popular Catholic papers. If the use of large-scale nuclear weapons is immoral, as all Catholic theologians when pressed agreed, then their possession as a deterrent, I argued, must also be so.

> If nuclear weapons could be maintained and operated by one man alone, then that man might possess them as a deterrent and keep to himself the fact that he intended never to use them. But nuclear weapons are not like a revolver that can be kept locked in a drawer. The maintenance of the deterrent demands that the enemy shall believe that the deterring power is both able and willing to use the deterrent. But no democratic power can convince its enemies that it is able and willing to use its deterrent unless it has military units willing to operate the deterrent if ordered and parliamentary sanction to order its operation if necessary. Now what deters is not the threat of the lawful use of nuclear weapons, but the threat of their murderous use . . . The conclusion seems unavoidable that no Catholic may play a part in the maintenance of the N.A.T.O. deterrent, nor support any policy which involves this strategy. Nor is this all. We must not only not consent to murder, we are obliged to do all we reasonably can to prevent its commission . . .

Those who have followed my argument will see that I recommend
nuclear disarmament not as a policy but as a moral imperative. We
must give up our nuclear deterrent not because by so doing we shall
achieve some desirable aim, but because to retain it is wicked. What
will then follow is not in our hands. The prospect of standing
defenceless before Communist Russia is indeed a sombre one. But that
does not justify us in covenanting with the N.A.T.O. powers to commit
murder. *Neque ab Oriente, neque ab Occidente: Deus judex est.*

Between the writing and the publication of 'Counterforce and
Countervalue', the Cuban missile crisis occurred, in October 1962,
in which the world came closer to a nuclear war than ever before
or since. On the Sunday during the crisis it was my turn to preach
the evening sermon, in the course of which I denounced both
Kennedy and Khrushchev as 'wicked men who prefer to risk the
destruction of the world than to accept any diminution of national
prestige or interest'. The sermon gave offence to many
parishioners, to whom Kennedy was a Catholic hero defending
the free world against atheistic communism. I received some angry
letters, including one with a picture of the bomb the parishioner
would like to put beneath me and my pulpit. I touched up the
proofs of 'Counterforce and Countervalue' with a few references
to the crisis.

At the time of the Cuban crisis in October nothing more was heard
of the distinction between counterforce and countervalue. President
Kennedy simply threatened full retaliation on Russia in the event of
nuclear weapons being aimed at American soil from Russia . . . Neither
those who praised his action nor those who blamed it have suggested
that he was merely bluffing: and Mr Khrushchev took the threat with
full seriousness.

'Counterforce and Countervalue' appeared in December 1962. By
this time Archbishop Heenan had become concerned about my
writing and lecturing on nuclear issues. (There was, so far as I
recall, only one other secular priest, Canon Drinkwater, who was
taking a public unilateralist stance at the time.) In answer to a
letter asking permission to talk to a C.N.D. meeting Heenan wrote
on 22 December a confidential letter:

My dear Tony,
    I would not want to forbid you to address a public meeting on
nuclear disarmament but if you do so you will have to make it clear

that you speak only for yourself. This is difficult for a priest because it is always assumed — wrongly — that on moral issues there can be no diversity of opinion within the Church.

I hope that something will be said in Rome about nuclear weapons before the Council ends. I may tell you, in confidence, that I said as much in a brief speech on the very opening day of the Council. I understand that a number of bishops intend to make a formal move for a discussion on the subject. But of this I have no first hand knowledge.

The whole question is far more complex than the protagonists on either side seem prepared to admit. It is my purely personal view that it is possible to keep such weapons as a deterrent without any intention of using them while, at the same time, not disclosing to a prospective enemy the intention of abstaining from their use. If a particular hierarchy had the duty to make a pronouncement I should press our own hierarchy to speak. But this seems to me to call for a pronouncement from the supreme magisterium of the Church. I have had letters from unilateralists demanding guidance but I really do not think they want guidance so much as confirmation of their own view. I do not think that the issue is as clear as it appears to them.

I suspect — but in this I may be wrong — that they are less horrified at the thought of breaking God's law than of the havoc which the use of nuclear weapons could cause. Only very holy people are appalled by sin but quite ordinary people — even unbelievers — feel horror at the thought of widespread loss of life.

I sincerely hope that the Council will not disperse without considering this grave problem. I can assure you that I shall do all in my power to see that the question is considered before the end of the Council.

With an affectionate blessing,
        devotedly,
                † John Carmel

The letter was kind and thoughtful, but I found it hard to believe that the kind of bluff which the Archbishop thought legitimate was either possible or in fact the attitude of the Government. I thought it also odd to make such a distinction between something's being against God's law, and the reason *why* it was against God's law: it was, after all, supposed to be the *natural* law, discoverable by reason, and not some arbitrary additional precept. I wrote back:

My Lord Archbishop,
    I am very grateful for your kindness in writing me so long a letter about nuclear disarmament. I realize that it is difficult for a priest to speak publicly about morality without appearing to be putting forward

the official teaching of the Church. For this reason I do not intend to say to the C.N.D. meeting anything which is a matter of personal opinion.

I have argued in periodicals such as the *Clergy Review* and *Blackfriars* that it is not permissible for a Catholic to support the deterrent policy of the N.A.T.O. governments because that policy involves a conditional willingness to use nuclear weapons to destroy Russian cities. It does not seem to me to be possible for a government to deceive the Russians into thinking that it is prepared thus to use its weapons without at the same time deceiving its own servants and citizens.

In sermons, however, and in the popular press, such as the *Catholic Pictorial*, I have in general restricted myself to stating the general principle that it is wrong to use indiscriminate nuclear weapons against cities, as they were used against Hiroshima. In addressing the C.N.D. meeting, similarly, I do not intend to go beyond what we were taught at the Gregorian as being the common teaching of theologians.

It seems to me worthwhile for a priest to say this on a public platform, since the majority of Catholics whom I have met do not know that the Church condemns the deliberate killing of non-combatants in war. Perhaps this is because saturation bombing in the last war was met with no concerted Catholic protest. Moreover, many Catholics, learning that theologians are divided on the lawfulness of the retention of nuclear weapons as a deterrent, imagine that they are divided about the lawfulness of their use against cities.

It is very good news that there is hope that the Council will discuss the topic of nuclear warfare before it breaks up. But I do not know that this will solve the practical problems of conscience which affect individual Catholics in those countries whose governments are pursuing policies of nuclear deterrence. An ecumenical council is, I imagine, unlikely to pronounce on the lawfulness of the policy of a particular government. But it seems to depend on the lawfulness of such particular policies whether or not a Catholic in the U.S.A., the U.K. or France may take part in his government's policy. A general statement of principle from Rome, unsupported by a public and explicit application of principle by the local hierarchies, seems unlikely to prevent Catholics from lending support, if it comes to the point, to illegal warfare; just as *Mit brennender Sorge* did not prevent Catholics from fighting the unjust wars of Hitler.

My article 'Counterforce and Countervalue' was welcomed by Catholic unilateralists, and was several times reprinted, first in *PAX Bulletin*, in February 1963. This was not a pacifist journal, but many of its readers and contributors were pacifists, and I did not always see eye to eye with the company I kept in its pages. I was only prepared to allow my article to be published on condition that the same issue carried the following letter from me:

I was recently distressed to see circulating, apparently under the auspices of *PAX*, a pamphlet entitled *Thou Shalt Not Kill* by the Rev. Johannes Ude. This pamphlet put forward pacifism as being Christian doctrine. 'Christianity and war,' it states 'are irreconcilable. To be a Christian cannot be reconciled with being a soldier . . . The renunciation of arms, that is to say the complete rejection of the use of brute force, and therefore the renunciation of worldly power, is an essential part of the Christian way of life and of Christian standards.'

The doctrine thus put forward is in contradiction to the unanimous teaching of Catholic Saints and Doctors for many centuries. In the first years of the Church there was uncertainty and hesitation among Christians about the lawfulness of war, as there was uncertainty and hesitation about many doctrines which are now defined parts of the deposit of faith. But since the Peace of the Church, Catholic writers, almost without exception, have taught that it may be lawful, and sometimes obligatory, for a Christian to bear arms in war. The possibility of a just war was taught by St Ambrose, St Augustine, St Gregory, St Bernard, St Thomas Aquinas, St Alphonsus and by every school of Catholic theology since such schools began. It was defended by theologians against the Manichees and the Quakers, and against Wycliffe and Erasmus.

No infallible decree of Pope or Council, so far as I know, has ever condemned pacifism. But if ever any moral truth was part of the doctrine inculcated by the ordinary *magisterium* of the Church it is the possibility of a just war. The doctrine — like that of the permissibility of taking oaths — may appear difficult to reconcile with well-known texts of Scripture. But those texts were as familiar to the Doctors who gave us the doctrine of the just war as they are to us.

At this time the governments of the West are pursuing a military policy which is immoral by the standards *which all Catholics accept*. It is a difficult task to persuade Catholics to apply their moral standards to the policies which are being pursued in their name. The task is only made harder by the propagation among Catholics of pacifist literature. A pamphlet such as *Thou Shalt Not Kill* will merely confirm many Catholics in their comfortable and disastrous belief that only pacifists object to nuclear deterrence.

Some time before the appearance of my article a number of lay Catholics, under the editorship of Walter Stein of the University of Leeds, had brought out a volume of essays entitled *Nuclear Weapons and Christian Conscience*. This had taken a line very similar to my own; indeed it included essays by those who had influenced my own first thinking on the topic. I now had a letter from Stein saying that the hardback edition of the book had sold out, and a paperback edition was being prepared; would I allow my piece to be included in it as an appendix to the original? 'Censorship problems may rule this out for you; but I very much hope that the fact that the article has been passed for the *C.R.* might provide a loophole.' I cannot remember what problems, if any, there were, but the paperback was reissued, with its appendix, in 1981 at the time of the revival of the disarmament movement: the editors must have thought that my subsequent defection from the Church had not affected the force of its arguments. I do indeed stand by what is said there, though some of the arguments from specifically Catholic premises I can now regard as only *ad hominem* arguments; nor can I any longer comfort myself with the thought of a divine Judge standing beside the righteous who have disarmed themselves before the Russian threat.

Archbishop Heenan's expectation that the issue of the bomb would be discussed at the Vatican Council was not fulfilled. It was rumoured that the discussion was prevented for fear of alienating the U.S.A. But at Easter time those who wanted an official pronouncement by the Church on the topic did have their prayers answered. Pope John XXIII issued an encyclical, on 11 April, Maundy Thursday, with the title *Pacem in Terris* (Peace on Earth). The encyclical was not devoted exclusively to issues of war and peace — on the contrary, most of it was taken up with a discussion of human rights, such as freedom of speech, freedom of worship, and the right to free association and free movement. But there was one central passage which was studied with care by all those who looked to the Vatican for guidance on the issue of disarmament. In the English translation published by the C.T.S. the crucial text read as follows:

> . . . It is with deep sorrow that We note the enormous stocks of armaments that have been and still are being made in more economically developed countries, with a vast outlay of intellectual and economic resources . . .
>
> The production of arms is allegedly justified on the grounds that in present-day conditions peace cannot be preserved without an equal balance of armaments. And so, if one country increases its armaments, others feel the need to do the same; and if one country is equipped with nuclear weapons, other countries must produce their own, equally destructive.

It was hard to imagine, Pope John said, that anyone would deliberately start a nuclear war, but the conflagration might be set off by some uncontrollable and unexpected chance. The mere continuance of nuclear testing might have fatal consequences for life on earth.

> Justice, then, right reason and humanity urgently demand that the arms race should cease; that the stockpiles which exist in various countries should be reduced equally and simultaneously by the parties concerned; that nuclear weapons should be banned; and that a general agreement should be reached about progressive disarmament and an effective method of control.

Men were becoming more and more convinced that disputes should be solved not by arms but by negotiation; because of the cruel destruction and immense suffering which modern weapons would bring to the human family 'it is hardly possible to imagine that in the atomic era war could be used as an instrument of justice'.

During the following week I was invited by the Editor of the *Catholic Pictorial* to summarize the encyclical for the paper's readers. He sent me a copy of some comments on the encyclical which had been written by Norman St John-Stevas for his regular weekly column, which would appear in the same issue as mine:

> The Pope forthrightly rejects war and the use of nuclear weapons as a means of settling disputes between men . . . But the Pope is not a unilateralist: he lays down no one method of achieving the objective of world disarmament. How constructive is the Holy Father's thought on this subject compared with the specious oversimplifications of the unilateralists! Many Catholics in the past have been in a state of confusion on this issue, as I pointed out in this column some months ago, but now they have no excuse for being muddled.

I decided that my article would make clear that the encyclical could, with equal justice, be interpreted in the opposite sense. I divided the article into two parts: the first, a brisk summary; the second more expansive. In the second part I made the following comment:

> There are some Catholics in this country who say that against enemies so evil as the Communists, nuclear warfare is justified. It is to be hoped that they will stop saying this, now that the Pope has said that nuclear warfare cannot be an instrument of justice.
>
> Pope John has said that stockpiles of nuclear weapons should be reduced 'equally and simultaneously'. Those who want us to keep our nuclear weapons will seize on this as an excuse for refusing to disarm until the Russians do so too. But the Pope has made it clear that the

arms race is wrong. We must stop it, so far as in us lies. This seems
to mean that we must disarm. With the Russians, if possible; if not,
on our own.

Of course, Pope John has not made any pronouncement about the
military policies of any particular nation. That is a matter for the
bishops of the nation concerned. Pope John's letter leaves many points
open.

Here is one question for you to consider.

Suppose Cammell Laird's get the contract to build a Polaris
submarine at Birkenhead. Polaris submarines carry nuclear weapons
equal in destructive power to all the bombs used in the whole of the
last war.

After what the Pope has said about the arms race, would a Catholic
be justified in accepting work in a shipyard building a Polaris
submarine?

I do not know whether these words made any impression on
potential shipbuilders. I quickly learnt what impression they made
on the bishops. A week after the publication of that issue of the
Pictorial I received the following letter from its Editor:

> Dear Father Kenny,
>
> I've just been informed that the Archbishop was really annoyed by
> your comment on unilateralism in the *Pictorial*. I suppose you already
> know but just in case I thought I'd drop you a line.
>
> So far as my secular ears were allowed to burn the trouble was that
> two Bishops, one of whom was Grasar and I think the other Beck,
> complained that we were disturbing the good consciences of some of
> their people.
>
> My further information was that you had been told, or will be told
> (I don't know which) not to write for us. If this is so I'm sorry — in
> so much as I was to blame I hope you'll forgive me.
>
> Perhaps we can comfort ourselves with the thought that the more
> Polaris submarines that are built on Cammell Laird's or elsewhere
> the closer we all reach to hearing the Real Truth from the only One
> who knows.

The following day the Archbishop wrote me the threatened letter
forbidding me to write for the *Pictorial*. It was, as ever, very kindly
phrased:

> My dear Father Tony,
>
> Yesterday I told Monsignor Taylor to be very cautious in publishing
> in the *Catholic Pictorial* your views on unilateral disarmament. It has

occurred to me today that I ought to let you know this in case you have any contribution refused by the *Pictorial*.

Two bishops in whose diocese the *Pictorial* circulates have complained to me about your comments on the Pope's encyclical. I think you probably do not realise how different it is writing for the kind of semi-literate public which reads the *Pictorial* and, for example, the *Tablet* or *Clergy Review*. Educated readers will dismiss the view of a priest if they do not agree with him. The simple Catholic is likely to accept whatever a priest writes in a Catholic paper as part of the teaching of the Church.

I am quite sure that it was inexperience and not dishonesty which led you to make comments as if they were part of the Pope's teaching. The Pope does not say '. . . that we must disarm. With the Russians if possible; if not, on our own.' Nor does the Pope say that the military policies of a nation are 'a matter for the bishops of the nation concerned'.

You do not, of course, say that the Pope says these things. But you lead the simple Catholic to think that he does so.

Needless to say, what bothered the two bishops was your saying that a Catholic could not in conscience work for Cammell Laird if it were given a contract to build a Polaris submarine. In the security of our presbyteries it is easy for us to tell fathers of families to give up their livelihood. But such advice can be given only after very great thought.

I assure you that I do not criticise you for the views you hold. They are the same views as those of Archbishop Roberts and Canon Drinkwater. You have as much right as they to hold them. But I hope you won't let them become an obsession. I hope still more that you will not publish anything which proclaims as certain doctrine what is still a matter of opinion.

I am writing this letter simply because I would not want you to hear from the *Catholic Pictorial* before you heard from me.

With an affectionate blessing,

I am, devotedly yours,

† John Carmel

I replied:

My Lord Archbishop,

Thank you for your kind letter of yesterday. I am sorry that my article in the *Pictorial* displeased you. I am particularly grieved that you should think it presented an appearance of dishonesty.

I assure you that I had no intention of passing off my own views as the Pope's. In what I wrote I was careful to keep analysis and comment separate, and I am glad that the Editor marked this

distinction by a change of type. I regret, however, that he headlined
my comment with the sentence 'We must disarm, with or without
Russia'. This was the only headline I did not write myself. In my text
I was careful to present this sentence as a disputable conclusion from
a statement of the Pope's ('this seems to mean'). I do not think that
anybody who read the text I wrote would have any reason to be misled.

Needless to say I did not intend to attribute to the Pope the statement
that the military policies of a nation are 'a matter for the bishops of
the nation concerned'. But that statement seems to be in accord with
the general principle stated in the encyclical: 'The Church has the right
and the duty not only to safeguard the principles of ethics and religion,
but also to intervene authoritatively with her children in the temporal
sphere, where there is a question of judging about the application of
these principles in concrete cases.' The context suggests that by 'the
Church' the Pope here does not mean merely 'the Holy See'; in the
preceding sentence he has spoken of decisions which rest 'primarily
with those who live and work in the specific sectors of human society
in which these problems arise'.

The question about Polaris submarines was meant seriously as a
question, not rhetorically as a statement. Naturally I am in no doubt,
and intended the reader to be left in no doubt, what *my* answer to the
question would be. It seems to me clearly wrong to contribute to
continuing the arms race by building Polaris submarines; and this
independently of the question whether there may not be lawful uses
for more accurate nuclear weapons, and of the question whether
already existing stocks of weapons are best disposed of unilaterally or
multilaterally. But whether I am right or wrong about this, it seems
to me important that even the simplest Catholic should at least *ask*
himself whether the natural law against killing the innocent, and Pope
John's words about the arms race, have any relevance to his own life
and work.

Nonetheless, I should have analysed the encyclical without
comment, had I not been shown, before writing, the comments of
Mr Norman St John-Stevas which were due to appear in the same
issue as my article. These comments appeared to me so one-sided
that I felt obliged to point out that conclusions opposite to those
of Mr St John-Stevas could with equal right be drawn from the
encyclical.

It appears to me that if any reader would be justified in concluding
from my article that the Pope had explicitly recommended unilateral
nuclear disarmament then he would be equally justified in concluding
from Mr St John-Stevas' comments that the Pope had spoken of 'the
specious oversimplifications of the unilateralists' and that he had
endorsed the attack which Mr St John-Stevas made in the *Pictorial* some
months ago on the principle that even in a just war one must not
deliberately kill the innocent.

Nevertheless, if your Grace feels that by what I wrote I have misled the readers of the *Pictorial* about the encyclical, I am ready to write a letter for publication distinguishing, as clearly as I am able, between the actual statements of Pope John, and the conclusions which I suggest could be drawn from them. Naturally, before sending any such letter to the Editor, I would submit it to you for approval.

I appreciate your Grace's kindness in informing me personally of your instructions to the *Pictorial*, and thank your Grace for your blessing.

> Your obedient servant,
> Anthony Kenny

P.S. Perhaps I should mention that before receiving your Grace's letter I wrote an article on the encyclical for the *Tablet*. I do not know whether they will publish it.

The Archbishop's reply was brief, and clearly intended to be friendly:

My dear Father Tony,

Many thanks for your letter. I don't think there is any reason why you should write a letter to the *Pictorial* by way of explanation. I want to insist that my concern is only because many of the readers of the *Pictorial* are uneducated. They cannot make distinctions between facts and comments on fact. Please do not think that I was accusing you of being dishonest — *quite* the contrary if you read my letter carefully.

I told the editor when he informed me of the appointment of St John-Stevas that I was not very pleased. Recently there was some talk of his going to the *Catholic Herald*. I strongly urged him to do so. I really do not think that the *Pictorial* is the kind of paper he should write for. Only the simplest statements can be grasped by the average reader. But you must remember that there is a big difference between what Norman St John-Stevas writes and what a priest writes. To these simple people I have in mind we of the clergy are all infallible.

I don't at all mind what you write in the *Tablet*. Its readers are well able to look after themselves . . .

P.S. I do not in any way condemn your views. I *think* you oversimplify this grave problem but I don't know. It is because I am in doubt that I have made no statement.

The Editor of the *Tablet* did not seem as sure as Archbishop Heenan did that his readers would be undisturbed by what I wrote. He kept it for several weeks without publishing it. Meanwhile, Pope John fell ill, into what turned out to be his final illness. In response to a query the Editor, Douglas Woodruff, wrote on 31 May:

Dear Father Kenny,

As requested, I return your article with apologies for having kept it without a decision for several weeks. As you can appreciate the state of the Pope's health has been a main cause these last two weeks. If he should die it would not be the moment to start exposing his ambiguities and taking to pieces his sentences. Apart from this complication it did not seem to me the kind of article that loses its topicality from one month to another. In the Secretariat of State they often complain at the way English Catholics approach encyclicals with an extreme literalness, looking for imperative commands which have not been intended and for which the Italians are not looking, and I know that one sentence in *Pacem in Terris* about just wars is being, they think, wrongly exploited by anti-nuclear protagonists.

Yours very faithfully,
Douglas Woodruff

The article which the *Tablet* returned was entitled 'Six Problems Arising From *Pacem in Terris*'. Less than a quarter of the article was about disarmament:

The passages on disarmament in *Pacem in Terris* have been taken by each interpreter, from Kennedy and Khrushchev downwards, as confirming his own previous opinion. In particular, arguments have been drawn from the text both for and against unilateralism. On the one hand, Pope John said that stocks of nuclear weapons should be reduced 'equally and simultaneously'; but equal and simultaneous reduction of stockpiles is not unilateral disarmament; therefore Pope John did not recommend unilateralism. On the other hand, Pope John said that the arms race was unjust; one must have no part in what is unjust, no matter what one's enemies may do; therefore Pope John recommended unilateralism. In fact, of course, neither of these arguments is convincing. Most unilateralists, including the policy-makers of C.N.D., hold out the simultaneous reduction of stockpiles by the U.S.A. and the U.S.S.R. as the most desirable end to the arms race. Everyone, no matter what his opinion about unilateralism, must hope that the Pope's encyclical and his dying appeals for peace will lead the statesmen of the great powers to make efforts more sincere than any they have made in the past to reach agreement about a test-ban and controlled disarmament. But the crucial question is this. What are we to do if such attempts to reach agreement fail, as all past such attempts have failed? There are then only two alternatives: either to disarm unilaterally, or to continue with the arms race. Which policy will be more in accordance with the spirit of Pope John's appeals?

The unilateralist says: if we cannot disarm with Russia, we must disarm without Russia; otherwise there will be no end to the arms race.

The multilateralist says: if Russia will not disarm, we cannot disarm;
for it is too dangerous to give up our weapons alone.

But we cannot be content, in that case, not to disarm. It is useless
merely to keep those weapons we now have, for they will grow obsolete
while the Russians develop newer and deadlier weapons systems. So
the multilateralist, in the end, is driven to call for a perpetuation of
the situation which Pope John deplored. 'If one country increases its
armaments,' he wrote, 'others feel the need to do the same; and if
one country is equipped with nuclear weapons, other countries must
produce their own, equally destructive.'

It was precisely this state of affairs which he said was condemned
by 'justice, right reason, and humanity'.

My article was eventually published by the *Catholic Herald*, but by
the time the article appeared Pope John was dead. 'The text of
his letter,' I wrote, 'needs more patient study than it could receive
during his lifetime.' But as the conclave elected Pope Paul VI,
the attention of the Catholic world moved elsewhere.

The article was the last thing I published as a Catholic priest.

The controversy over nuclear weapons acted in some ways as a
catalyst with regard to my decision to seek laicization. As doubts
about the Church's infallibility had become more and more
obsessive, I had become more and more certain that I would have
to leave the priesthood, and perhaps the Church, sooner or later.
But I found the leap of disbelief as hard to take as others have
found the leap of faith: to walk out of the institution around which
my own life and that of all those closest to me had centred for so
many years. I kept postponing the day of decision. Perhaps — but
this became an ever more faintly whispered perhaps — the doubts
would clear up, like mists on an autumn morning. At all events
I should prepare carefully for the actual taking of the decision:
this meant I must meditate and pray as earnestly as I could, and
somehow it seemed harder and harder to produce prayer of the
appropriate quality. Meanwhile, I continued as best I could with
the routine duties of the priesthood. Was it not hypocritical to
preach the doctrines of a Church whose mission I was internally
doubting? How could I advise penitents in confession to obey the
rulings of a Church whose wisdom and authority I was myself
questioning? I comforted myself with the thought that those who
listened to my sermons, or who came to me in confession, did not
come because they wanted to know what Anthony Kenny thought
on matters of faith and morals; they came to me to get the teaching

of the Church. I was only in the same position as a judge who has to administer justice according to the laws—which he may think need reform—and not according to his own opinion about what is right and fair. But this reasoning did not altogether satisfy me. I had taken refuge in tasks which were appropriate to the priesthood and which yet were worth doing even if the Church's claims were as false as I was every day more inclined to believe they were. Thus I threw myself into the work of the Catholic Housing Aid Society; I wrote articles and reviews exposing thinking which was muddled and erroneous by the standards both of Catholic tradition and secular philosophy, and, above all, I involved myself in the campaign against nuclear weapons.

XIV

Return to the Lay State, 1963

The outcome of the controversy in the Catholic journals showed how impossible was the position of someone like myself. It was true that both Catholic and secular moral reasoning showed the wickedness of nuclear weapons; it was true that when I quoted Catholic authorities in my writings on the topic, I was using, at the worst, perfectly valid *ad hominem* arguments to a Catholic audience. But Archbishop Heenan was right in hinting that it was not a horror of sin, as defined by the Catholic Church, which drove me to write against the bomb. According to Catholic doctrine, many of my own daily actions, contrary to the rules of clerical behaviour, were deserving of Hell no less than the policies of mass destruction implicit in the theory of deterrence. Writing on *Pacem in Terris* I was forced, by retaining the position of a spokesman in the Catholic Church, to pretend that it was a document deserving respectful scrutiny, when I could see that it was muddled, ambiguous, and unworthy of the importance of the subject it dealt with and the authority of the office held by its author. I could not remain a priest any longer; I had, I came to conclude, already continued as one longer than decency really allowed. I had been afraid of my own motives in seeking laicization; the lines from *Murder in the Cathedral* often echoed in my mind:

> *The last temptation is the greatest treason*
> *To do the right deed for the wrong reason*

At last I came to see that it was a worse treason to postpone the right deed for fear that one was doing it for the wrong reason.

In the summer of 1963 I decided definitely to seek laicization; even then, between the decision and its execution, I delayed, as someone who has reached a definite decision that his marriage is intolerable may put off from day to day the actual seeking of a divorce. There were loose ends to tie up, close friends to be warned, jobs that would have to be passed on to others. It was not until the middle of August that I acted. On Monday the 19th I told Alec that I was going to ask for an interview with the Archbishop on 26 August, the following Monday. On Friday the 23rd I took my mother out for the day and broke the news to her that I had now made a final decision to carry out the plan I had hinted to her in the previous years more than once.

I saw the Archbishop on the 26th and told him that I could not continue as a priest because I no longer believed in Catholic doctrines; I did not even have faith in God, but could continue praying only in the way that someone stranded on a mountainside might cry out for help without knowing that there was anyone within earshot. I did not want simply to walk out of the Church without a by-your-leave; I thought it likely that in the long run I would not remain a Catholic any more than remain a priest, but I would like to depart in stages, being laicized first and then, if I continued to think as I did, cutting my connection with the Church altogether. In this way I could discover whether my present all-absorbing doubts were something permanent, or an illusion generated by the strains of the priesthood.

The Archbishop was friendly and understanding in manner, offering neither exhortation nor rebuke. But he suggested that rather than be laicized immediately, I should go and 'live in a Catholic academic atmosphere' for a time. I could choose where to go: Louvain, Notre Dame; the Archdiocese would pay, and expense would be no problem; I would be my own master, and would not need to report to anyone, or do any clerical work. I said that for the purpose he had in mind I thought Rome would be better: I had more admiration for Lonergan as a Catholic thinker than for anyone I knew at Louvain or Notre Dame. Rome, he said, would be very convenient: the second session of the Vatican Council was beginning, and bishops needed theological advisers; no one thought it odd at this time if they sent their clerics off to live in hotels in Rome. He would send a cheque and I should take my leave of the parish and go as soon as I liked.

When I got home, I regretted having agreed. As I wrote later that day to a friend:

> I have just delivered by hand a letter saying (a) thanks v. much (b) don't think I'll change my mind (c) in any case, clever English Catholics more likely to change my mind than Continental ones

(d) would much prefer quick release (e) however since his plan contains nothing which goes against my conscience, but only against my preferences will accept if he insists (f) anyway would rather live on my own money than ecclesiastical.

The next day brought two letters from the Archbishop. The first, written before the receipt of mine, contained a cheque for the journey to Rome, with a promise of more when needed. It said:

> My Mass tomorrow will be for you. *I* don't think you are a man in a hole shouting in case someone is nearby. That, as you said, would make good sense. I wonder if you are shouting properly. In any case, I shall do some shouting for you — and so will your mother.

The second letter said:

> Thinking entirely of your own good I am going to insist that you go to Rome at least for a few weeks. Release from the priesthood can be granted only by the Holy See and, I think, personally by the Holy Father. Application for secularisation must be made by the priest either in his own handwriting through his bishop or by going to Rome and making the request in person.
>
> The reason for this cautious attitude of the Church is that the decree of secularisation is irrevocable and there must be no danger that a priest has been overpersuaded. Even when the decree is granted it must be accepted by the priest himself (*not* on his behalf by his bishop) and if not accepted within a few days it lapses.
>
> All these rules are made because in the experience of the Holy See the priest who takes this step often regrets it in middle age. The obligation of celibacy is also much more difficult to keep when a priest has become a layman . . .

The letter came with the gift of a book which, he said, he had found helpful in crises of his own. 'I know you have prayed but you must continue to pray. The strain is great but not intolerable. You are still young and you can afford to wait a few weeks before taking a final decision.'

I agreed to do this. I went to St Peter and Paul's for the last time and collected my belongings. The official version was that I was to go home to St Vincent's Lodge for a rest and then to go to Rome on a confidential mission for the Archbishop there. It was a great relief that I no longer had to say Mass: 26 August was the last Mass I ever said. Whatever else happened, that was one hypocrisy the less.

On my way to Rome I called in at a Catholic philosophers' conference at Spode House and in confidence broke the news of what I was doing to close friends there. I arrived in Rome in the evening of Monday, 2 September. I had planned to get a room in a hotel for two or three days, and then find a bedsitter for a month or two. Finding a hotel turned out very difficult: there was a conference of 5,000 doctors in Rome who seemed to have occupied all the beds left vacant by those attending the Vatican Council. I found a room in the thirty-first hotel I tried: a large room with four beds in a dive near Pompey's Theatre. I was woken up at midnight by the proprietor who asked me to vacate it since he had now found eight women who wished to hire it. I refused to budge, but I did not get much more sleep that night. Next day, after several hours of futile tramping round hotels and apartments, I found a small pensione off the Via Nomentana, amid pines and chestnuts, where the proprietress took pity on me and offered me a room for a month at just over a pound a day. I settled in and cheered up; but, as I wrote back to England: 'This expedition to Rome seems even more futile from this end than it did from England.'

I had brought with me the text of the questions of the *Summa Theologiae* of St Thomas which I had agreed to translate and comment on for the forthcoming *Blackfriars* edition. It was a task sufficiently ecclesiastical to keep faith with the Archbishop but sufficiently intellectual to keep me from boredom and despair. I would work on it in my room morning and evening, and visit churches in the afternoon, partly to pray and partly to see again the beauty and history of Rome.

One day I visited St Peter's for a general audience with the Pope, joining a Danish tourists' bus from the pensione. I wrote to my mother to describe it:

> We arrived in pouring rain just in time to join the scramble. The Pope sat behind the Papal altar; he wasn't visible from many parts of the basilica; in any case the nave is useless since it is fenced off to provide seats for the Bishops in the Council. After a good deal of exploration I found a post behind a crowd of Germans standing on benches in their stockings, from which the Pope was just visible, and past which, it turned out, he was due to come out. He has an attractive voice, with characteristic soft 'r's; looks very tiny in the *sedia gestatoria*; if John XXIII was a cuddly bear, he is a white mouse. He gave a short speech in Italian and then more or less verbatim repeated it in French, English, German and Spanish. Oddly enough, whereas Pius XII's audience

speech was an extremely non-sectarian affair ('Young men, you have travelled far and seen much . . .') Pope Paul's was very ultramontane, about the Pope being the successor of St Peter and the rock on which the Church was built.

I was embarrassed at this audience by meeting several priests who had been my contemporaries as students. It all seemed a far cry from the time when I had cheerfully gate-crashed the diplomatic box at canonizations. I had no very good explanation of my presence in Rome to give them.

Indeed, my position became more and more absurd. Bernard Lonergan, the Jesuit with whom I was supposed to discuss my intellectual difficulties, was away when I arrived; when he did return we had one or two inconclusive meetings. His gifts were academic rather than pastoral; it was in any case ridiculous to hope that one or two conversations with a very clever Jesuit would wipe away doubts that had grown up over years of philosophical reflection in a different tradition. Between my visiting Archbishop Heenan in Liverpool and seeing him again in Rome, he ceased to be my Ordinary, being translated to the See of Westminster, vacant by the death of Cardinal Godfrey. It had taken me months to pluck up courage to go and tell my story to Heenan; now everything would have to be done over again with the next Archbishop, or with the Vicar Capitular who ruled the diocese during the interregnum. I wrote to my mother in the middle of September: 'I expect that the Archbishop will arrive at the weekend. I expect he'll invite me to the English College for a chat. I shall tell him that I'm in good spirits but still think no purpose will be served by my staying long here.'

When I had scrupled to take the Archbishop's money he had told me that it came from a 'fund which can be used only for priests needing a rest: to that help you are entitled'. I took the money and resolved to return it after I was laicized. Friends in England offered to lend more, and I replied:

> . . . I am very grateful for your offer of a loan when I'm laicized. One thing which I feel beholden to my clerical education for is that I haven't any of the inhibitions about money which lots of people have: I've sometimes offended friends in the past by offering them money when I had some and they hadn't, and it seemed to me the most natural thing in the world. On another hand another result of seminary and presbytery life is that it makes one very improvident with money — since one always knew that the roof over one's head and the next meal never depended on the money that was in one's pocket.

Eventually Archbishop Heenan arrived at the English College to attend the Council, and a few days later he sent for me to see him there. I realized that the meeting was a decisive one for my future, so I made a note of it immediately afterwards, as verbatim as I could make it:

H.   Tell me how you are.
K.   I'm in good spirits, but nothing has changed in my mind.
H.   Nothing has changed?
K.   No. I still want to be laicized. I did not expect anything to change as a result of coming to Rome, and that was why I wrote you that letter, to try to make that clear.

I asked the Archbishop to explain the process of laicization; he repeated what he had said in his letter, about the irrevocability of the step.

H.   There is of course a complication that now, though I can give you advice, I can't arrange your application — once I accepted Westminster I ceased to have any authority over Liverpool — think what chaos Bishops could cause if this were not so — but this is all a matter of the mechanics of the thing. Tell me how you really are. I gather it is the faith, even more than the priesthood, that worries you.
K.   Yes, it is because of the faith that I want to give up the priesthood; I feel, on the other hand, that I have a better chance of keeping the faith as a layman. But perhaps I had better go back a long way, since I don't think I made my position very clear on that morning when I came to see you.

I then explained how as a student I had been dissatisfied with the accounts given in the textbooks of how we know that there is a God, and that faith began to seem to be a sacrifice of integrity rather than a virtue. I had papered over this difficulty with an existentialist type of approach, on the basis of which I had been ordained. I told how my theological practical exercise had been regarded as theologically unsound, and might damage the Gregorian's reputation if published.

K.   I laughed at this at the time, but at Oxford I came to think that they were quite right and that what I wrote was heretical; and I have not yet found anything to put in its place. Catholic philosophers in Oxford with whom I spoke were very helpful — but though they solved some problems for me, they left the

majority unsolved, until it came to seem hypocritical any longer
to go on being a priest. When I say that I stand a better chance
of keeping my faith as a layman, I mean that I may see clearer
when the daily pressure of my whole way of life depending on
something I'm doubtful about is removed.

H.   Yes, I can see that teaching religion in such a situation must be
     unbearable.

I went on to say that none of my Oxford friends had persuaded
me to seek laicization.

K.   I expected that you would be inclined to blame Oxford for my
     predicament; and in a way it is partly as a result of my being
     at Oxford that I feel as I now do; but only in the way I explained;
     it was not that I was filled there with positivistic ideas.

H.   No, I didn't think that.

K.   It would be natural for you to think that, or that I had become
     swell-headed there . . .

H.   . . . No, I have never thought you swell-headed. I had been
     inclined to blame Oxford, though 'blame' is not the right word,
     in a different way. I thought you had gone there too late, and
     were therefore more vulnerable to its ethos, more likely to be
     impressed by it, coming from a seminary instead of from a public
     school. I mean socially, even.

K.   I was impressed by the Oxford ethos, certainly. I found the people
     there much more . . .

H.   Civilized?

K.   No, more serious. Of course there were lots of frivolous
     undergraduates, as well, but I mean that I was impressed by the
     seriousness of the dons I got to know; they worked much harder
     at their subject than we had ever been used to in Rome — I dare
     say the Greg. profs worked hard enough, but we didn't ever see
     them — and also that their thoughts affected their lives, the way
     they thought in philosophy affected the way they behaved.
     Whereas, by comparison, the sort of life one lives in the College
     here, it made me feel I had been living a sort of double life.

H.   You make it sound much worse than it was.

K.   I mean that on the one hand I liked living here and was happy
     in the community, and wasted far too much time in plays and
     writing songs —

H.   So did we all!

K.   And on the other hand there was my intellectual work and
     troubles, and the two didn't connect. And I feel that if I had taken
     my intellectual work more seriously, I would have seen that I
     shouldn't be ordained, that one shouldn't take on a vocation of

that kind if one is the sort of person in whom the pendulum of belief is going to swing.

H.   Yes, but of course one never knows that sort of thing about oneself until later. How will you live afterwards, you must have given some thought to that — I mean how will you earn your living?

K.   I suppose I shall teach in a university, that would be the natural thing for me to do. In the meantime, for that will take some time, I have some money, and some writing to do, and probably can get part-time teaching. In a university I could teach only things that I felt quite sure of — indeed I have been trying for some time rather to concentrate on things I was sure about, like the bomb and housing, but one is constantly having to preach about other things, and indeed just by wearing a collar one stands for so many things.

H.   Yes, it's quite clear to me that you will have to take off your collar for a while, and earn your living as a layman. But this doesn't necessarily mean taking the irrevocable step of being laicized. Suppose that, as a result of the pressure being removed, say in two or four or ten years, something rekindled in you, then perhaps there would be the possibility of your working again as a priest; but if you are now laicized it will be irrevocable.

K.   The other possibility had not occurred to me: I mean, I had not known that it was possible to live as a layman without being laicized. Is it possible?

H.   Well, let's take an analogy, and it is *only* an analogy: suppose you were a drunk; sometimes, once or twice, I've said to drunks 'I'm not going to spend the pennies of the poor on you; you must take off your collar and earn your living; you must rehabilitate yourself the hard way, instead of being sent to some comfortable cure . . .'

We went on to discuss the question whether I ought to take further advice from any one else about laicization.

H.   There is one man in Rome now who is intelligent and holy and wise and sympathetic; the Abbot of Downside. He is at St Anselmo. He would understand you; and he would have plenty of time; good men always have plenty of time; they don't say 'you can have five minutes'; that's no good for a problem like yours . . . Tell me something — how does celibacy connect with this? How do you feel?

K.   It does connect, I think, but only indirectly. It doesn't connect directly — there isn't anyone that I want to marry —

H.   I wasn't suggesting —

K.   And indeed I don't expect ever to get married. I find celibacy hard, but I imagine that isn't unusual. If it connects with my troubles about faith, the connection is subterranean. I have always understood that it was impossible to get permission to be married if laicized. If I were offered a choice, to be dispensed from celibacy or not, I would choose to be dispensed; but I would not press for this, because I would not want it to appear, to myself or to anyone else, that this was my reason for wanting to be laicized. I know, however, that if I am laicized it is quite likely that there will come a time when I want to get married, and that is how it connects in an indirect way.

H.   And then? I suppose it would depend whether then you had any faith or not; if you hadn't you would get married.

K.   Yes.

I wrote to my good friends the Priors in Manchester about the suggestion that I should live as a layman for ten years without being laicized:

> As usual, when talking to H. I felt 'this is a clever move' — the possibility of such a half-way house had not occurred to me — however I just said guardedly that it was a new idea and I'd like to have time to think about it. What I now feel is this — that if there were absolutely no difference between the conditions in the two cases — I mean if I were genuinely free in the non-irrevocable form — then *perhaps* it might be a good idea to leave the bolt-hole but on the other hand I don't imagine that the conditions could be the same. My instinct really is to make a clean break, but I shall have to work out how to justify this to H.

While I was at the English College to see Heenan, I also met Bishop Pearson, whom I had helped with the *schemata* for the Council. I was worried about what he would think of me. As I wrote in the same letter:

> I told him my position, and said I hoped he didn't feel I'd deceived him by not revealing it when first he asked me. He said that on the contrary he was doubly grateful for me helping when I had a crisis on hand etc. He was altogether most kind, and distressed in a very moving sort of way — also in a rather embarrassing way as he kept on trying to describe to me what a good priest everyone thought I was. But he ended by saying he'd respect me whatever I decided, in a tone of voice which sounded as if he really meant it, and this cheered me a lot because in a way he represents just the sort of person (I mean unacademic clergy who are only fairly slight acquaintances) who I thought might feel I'd acted in a cowardly and treacherous way by being laicized. I'm afraid I'm always finding out that people are much nicer than I expect them to be.

To assist in the translation **work** on St Thomas I rejoined the
Vatican library, though I found that the arrangements there did
not encourage work in medieval philosophy; there was a very odd
assortment of medieval books on the open shelves, only the quite
unportable Leonine edition of St Thomas and hardly any
commentaries.

It was interesting to watch from the sidelines the work of the
second session of the Vatican Council. Everyone I met said that
the standard of discussion had much improved from the first
session; they had changed the procedural rules so that bishops did
not have to give notice in advance for their interventions, and so
there could be genuine debate instead of a sequence of set speeches.
I discovered that most of the points which I had made to Bishop
Pearson about 'divisions in the Church' were made in a speech
by Cardinal Lercaro. I took the opportunity of meeting Heenan
to show him the passage in the Council of Trent where it says that
owing to the heresies of these times the Church has been split into
many diverse parts—he was startled, but not convinced, by this
unexpected support for the Branch theory.

A friend of mine who was an official *peritus* offered me the loan
of his passport to gate-crash one of the sessions, but I did not have
the heart to take up the offer. The English College was full of
bishops, some of whom I knew slightly, but I did not explain why
I was in Rome; 'a working holiday' was my answer to queries.

I took the Archbishop's advice about consulting Abbot Butler
of Downside, and had a friendly but inconclusive conversation with
him at Sant' Anselmo. He was very sympathetic, and wrote warm
letters for quite a while after this first meeting; but we approached
matters from such a different philosophical viewpoint that it was
difficult for our minds really to meet on religious topics. He
regarded linguistic analysis with considerable suspicion, and wrote,
in an exasperated moment in the midst of a very friendly letter,
'I wonder whether you have the patience—humility?—to admit
to yourself that a man who uses words all wrong may yet be trying
to convey a real truth by them?'

A priest friend wrote from Lancashire:

> All sorts of rumours go round about you. Theological adviser to
> Heenan is the favourite. Another is sent to cool your heels because
> of the furore you are supposed to have caused at the missile base. I
> have strongly denied this. Everyone is pretty stubbornly certain in his
> own rumour.

Other friends were getting worried about the delays. One wrote:

> There is a time I think for deciding that one has been over pros and
> cons as far as one can, that to continue is to merely tread, uselessly,
> a treadmill and that a question must be put behind one for good so
> that one can turn one's attention more usefully to other matters. So
> long as you are a priest — even though non-functioning — all these
> questions remain, needling below the surface, sapping away like a
> hidden ulcer.

Arthur Prior, in reference to Heenan's suggested halfway house,
contributed this:

> I can see one big thing to be said in favour of what he suggests,
> provided it really means that 'you can take off your collar' and nobody
> can make you put it on again unless you yourself really want to; and
> one big thing to be said against it. The one big thing pro is that it's
> generally a good thing to take just the steps that one is absolutely clear
> that one ought to take at the time, and not be governed too much by
> thoughts of what might happen later on . . . On the other side there's
> just this, do you not *know*, as clearly as you know anything, that you
> don't want ever to be a priest again, even if you stay a Catholic, and
> even if you become a pretty important Catholic? I may be misreading
> your state of mind, but isn't it the case that you just don't want, and
> won't want, the kind of authority that the priesthood gives? — if you
> become, as you could very well become, a Catholic philosopher that
> Catholics and non-Catholics listen to in a big way, you'll want us to
> listen because of the force and truth of what you say, without asking
> for anything additional the priesthood would give you. If this *is* how
> you feel, then it does seem to me a pretty good argument for being
> laicized completely. The main thing is to do whatever brings you real
> inner freedom; and I just doubt whether the retention of a hidden collar
> would do that, and doubt whether the loophole it would leave for you
> leads into anything you would really want, even as a Catholic.

By the time this letter reached me, I had already seen Heenan
again, had a further frank and briefer discussion with him, and
convinced him that the halfway house arrangement would not
serve. I wrote a brief note on 14 October to tell Arthur I was leaving
Rome.

> Archbishop Heenan has now agreed to my being properly laicized.
> The formalities will have to be gone through with the Vicar Capitular.
> They are likely to take until November, which is the next occasion

on which the Pope gives audience to the Cardinals of the Congregation
of Sacraments for purposes of laicization. But H. agrees there is nothing
to be gained by my staying longer in Rome, and says that it is quite
proper for me to start looking for a job, since the result of the formalities
is a foregone conclusion.

By 18 October I was back with my family at St Vincent's, and
from there I sent the Vicar Capitular of Liverpool my formal
petition for laicization. I told him of the month spent in Rome
and of the conversations I had had with Heenan, which ended with
his agreeing that 'in my present state of uncertainty I had no choice
but to seek laicization'. I concluded:

> The canon lawyer whom I saw in Rome on Archbishop Heenan's
> instructions and who told me how to draw up the enclosed petition,
> suggested that I should request you to ask the Holy See to act with
> all possible speed. It seems that it is the normal practice of the
> Congregation of Sacraments, when a petition for laicization is
> presented, to suggest a period of delay. The lawyer suggested that it
> might be useful to make clear to the congregation, in the letter
> recommending my petition, that such a period of waiting had already
> in this case taken place. It should thus be possible for the Holy Father
> to grant the decree at the next audience with the Prefect of the
> Congregation which I understand is about the second week in
> November. The next ordinary audience is not until January.

The Vicar Capitular insisted on seeing me before forwarding
the petition; the interview was a stiff and awkward one, and I
realized that I had been very fortunate in the response I had had
from Heenan. I was asked to list the articles of faith that I was
doubtful about, and I dutifully went through them, beginning with
the possibility of proving the existence of God. When I came to
'the justification of faith' — the question how faith was a virtue,
rather than a sacrifice of intellectual integrity — the Vicar Capitular
misunderstood and thought I meant 'justification *by* faith' which
led to a rumour travelling round the diocese that I had been
converted to Lutheranism. My hope that the petition might be
granted by the middle of November was wildly optimistic; but it
was indeed placed before the Pope in December, and the rescript
was sent back to me on 3 January. It reads in translation:

> Most Blessed Father,
>
> Anthony Kenny, priest of the Archdiocese of Liverpool, having in the
> course of time experienced that he is unequal to the burden of carrying

out the duties of the priesthood, humbly petitions your Holiness to be allowed to return to the lay state.

Audience of the Holy Father on 16 December 1963

The most Holy Lord Pope Paul VI, having heard the account given by the undersigned Cardinal of the Sacred Congregation of the Sacraments, having attended to the particular circumstances of the case, kindly remitted the above petition to the prudent judgement of the ordinary of Liverpool, who can dispense the petitioner from the burdens of the priesthood, with the exception of the obligation of the law of holy celibacy, which remains; there being no hope of readmission to the clerical state, and the possibility of scandal being removed by opportune means, including, if the case requires, the departure of the petitioner from regions where his clerical state is known, under threat of canonical sanctions.

Nobody, in fact, threatened any canonical sanctions if I should return to places where I had been known as a priest; and indeed one of the first letters which I received on arriving in England was from the chaplain to the Roman Catholics in Oxford University, saying that I would be very welcome if I wished to return there. From the moment of receiving the rescript I was, in the practical details of running my life from day to day, as free from episcopal or other control as any non-clerical Catholic.

It was, however, more agreeable from every point of view not to continue living in Liverpool while I looked around for a job. Several kind friends offered me indefinite accommodation; I finished off the translation of the *Blackfriars Summa*, and looked around for a job. This proved much easier than I had expected. I wrote to philosophers of my acquaintance—Lloyd, who had been my Professor at Liverpool, Quinton, who had been my supervisor in Oxford, and Gilbert Ryle, whose seminars I had attended—and asked if they knew of any vacancies. They were all most helpful. Quinton wrote by return: 'A vacancy at Balliol was advertised the other day. Did you see it?'; Ryle wrote rather cautiously, 'More likely than unlikely that we'll find you a berth before the end of the academic year.' He also tactfully offered to help financially if I was short of funds. He quickly passed word round Oxford that I was looking for a job. On 29 October I received a letter from the Rector of Exeter asking whether they might consider my name for a joint lectureship with Trinity; and about the same time a letter from a tutor at Balliol saying that the philosophers there 'have gathered from Ryle that you are thinking of changing your way of life and that you may now be interested in academic jobs—but that you don't feel yourself in an easy or clear position to make applications. So naturally I am led to wonder whether you might have any interest in our vacant fellowship here'.

So the transition from priest to layman happened, in the end, very swiftly. It was within a week of receiving the official rescript from Rome that I took up my duties as a lecturer at Exeter and Trinity; and almost simultaneously I was interviewed for the Balliol fellowship, and pre-elected into it. So my letter of resignation to Exeter followed closely on my acceptance; and after two terms of teaching there and at Trinity I moved to Balliol, where I have remained ever since.

Epilogue

The profession of clergyman, Lord Macaulay once said, imposes on those who are not saints the necessity of being hypocrites. I think that his generalization was harsh: I have known many priests whom I would not call either saints or hypocrites. But he has described vividly my own experience of the priesthood: having failed as a saint, the best I could do was to gather courage to cease to be a hypocrite.

This book has been a story of failure. I have told how I pursued an ideal, failed to achieve it, and grew disillusioned with the ideal itself. At the time when the story ends I firmly believed that I had thrown away my life. 'I will never be happy again,' I used to tell myself, 'but at least I can stop living a lie.'

To my surprise, my life since that time has been one of ever-growing happiness. My mother and Alec came to accept my decision and to enter into my new life as a scholar and teacher. My mother was particularly relieved to discover that I was not treated, even by pious Catholics, as an outcast. Indeed, I lost hardly any Catholic friends: to this day, of my closest friends, one is a priest with whom I studied at Upholland and in Rome, and another is a senior Catholic administrator whom I first met in the Oxford chaplaincy. When I was laicized an ex-priest was a rarity; during the later sixties and earlier seventies more and more priests returned to the lay state, including several of the most distinguished English theologians of my generation. By 1970 Cardinal Heenan could write, in a letter to Alec, 'The path which Tony trod has now become a great high road.'

It took a while, however, to overcome an initial agoraphobia after laicization. I dreaded the first encounters with friends who had never seen me before wearing a collar and tie; it was some years before I was comfortable in suits not of clerical grey. I was glad that most of my new colleagues at Oxford had never known me as a priest, and grateful that most of them seemed incurious about my past. The Catholic friends of my student days welcomed me as warmly as a philosopher as they had done as a priest.

The life of a bachelor don resembled my happier days in the English College more than the recent sad years as a curate. I was busy mastering the texts I was to teach undergraduates; I had to acquire as a don the arts of a tutor without having been initiated into the tutorial mysteries as a pupil. Writing papers for seminars and lecture courses left me, at first, little time to prepare anything for publication. But *Action, Emotion and Will* was well reviewed, and brought invitations to give lectures in the U.S.A. I was also approached to write a popular textbook on Descartes for a mass-market publisher in New York. 'Why would anyone want to write a book on Descartes?' I asked a senior philosopher. 'His whole system could be written on the back of a postcard: he had only two ideas, both of them wrong.' 'If you think that,' was the reply, 'you ought to write a book on him to teach you better.' I accepted the contract, and the cure worked. It was 1968 before the book appeared, but long before that I had come to revere Descartes' greatness: his major ideas—that mind is private consciousness, and that matter is extension in motion—were indeed demonstrably wrong; but they so underlie the thinking of philosophers, scientists, and laymen to this day that he deserves his status as father of the modern mind.

During the Easter vacation of 1965, two terms after I had moved from Exeter to Balliol, I was invited by the wife of a colleague, a graduate of Vassar, to attend a concert given as part of a tour by the Vassar madrigal singers. The concert was in Holywell music room, and was followed by a party for the performers in my colleague's house. At the party I met one of the sopranos, a final-year student from Swarthmore, Pennsylvania, named Nancy Caroline Gayley. We liked each other, and saw each other again from time to time during her tour in Oxford and in London. By the time she left with the Vassar group ten days later I, at least, was firmly in love.

During the spring we corresponded regularly, and in the summer, when I took up the invitation to lecture at a number of American universities, I spent some weeks with Nancy at her parents' home in Swarthmore. For the rest of the year we corresponded almost daily, and at Christmas Nancy stayed with my mother and Alec at Hale Barns, and we became engaged, fixing the date of the wedding for the following Easter.

When I had been laicized, I had not been released from the Church's law of celibacy. Hence, the date of my marriage was also the date of my—automatic—excommunication from the Church. We were married, on 2 April 1966, in the house of Nancy's parents, by a Presbyterian minister of the church where my father-in-law was an elder. My mother and Alec were present and Alec, after the service, read over bride and groom a blessing he had composed himself. Since that date, my marriage, and the family which came from it, has been the keel on which my happiness has been built.

In the 1970s many ex-priests received permission from Rome to marry or had their marriages recognized by the Curia. I have never wished to do so, for however much the pendulum of faith and disbelief may swing within my mind, I can never again imagine accepting the infallible authority of the Catholic Church and the full panoply of Catholic teaching. It is true that many of the things which I objected to in Catholic practice have altered since the Vatican Council, and it is true that many priests will now cheerfully deny in the pulpit doctrines which I could only doubt in solitary guilt. But I am old-fashioned enough to believe that if the Church has been as wrong in the past on so many topics as forward-looking clergy believe, then her claims to impose belief and obedience on others are, in the form in which they have traditionally been made, mere impudence.

This does not prevent me from placing great value on many things in the Catholic tradition, or from feeling nostalgia for membership of the Christian community. There are points on which I identify much more closely with the Church I have left than with the liberal agnosticism of the world in which I live. Thus, I believe that the Church has been fundamentally right in opposing abortion no less firmly than I believe that it has been fundamentally wrong in opposing contraception. In so far as abortion is the termination of the life of an actual, identifiable, human individual it is wrong for the same kind of reasons as the killing of non-combatants in war is wrong. It is a pathological feature of the intellectual climate of our time that so few people are consistent in their attitude to the killing of the innocent. When I am with people who share my opposition to nuclear deterrence, I commonly find I am alone in disapproving of abortion; if I want to find company which opposes abortion it is easiest to do so among those who are hawks on the arms race. This is true not only of secular society but of the Catholic Church: the strengthening of the opposition among bishops to nuclear warfare has gone hand in hand with a weakening among priests and nuns of their abhorrence of abortion.

Since being laicized and excommunicated I have continued to attend church fairly regularly—Anglican more often than Catholic, since the liturgical reforms of the Vatican Council and its aftermath. But I prefer to do so as an agnostic than to simulate faith: I never receive Communion or recite the Creed. When I say that I am an agnostic I am not using the word, as some do, merely as a bland synonym for 'atheist': I mean that I do not know whether there is a God or not. Some philosophers believe that it is impossible for anyone to know whether there is a God or not: they claim that agnosticism about the existence of God is something built into the human condition rightly understood. I do not find their arguments convincing, any more than I find the arguments for theism or for atheism convincing. The agnosticism which I profess is, in philosophical terms, a contingent and not a necessary agnosticism: the agnosticism of a man who says 'I do not know whether there is a God, but perhaps it can be known; I have no proof that it cannot be known.' Contingent agnosticism of this kind is bound to be a restless agnosticism: on a topic so important one is bound to prefer knowledge to uncertainty. So I have never ceased to be concerned about the philosophy of religion, the status of natural theology, and the relations between reason and belief.

In order to resolve the uncertainties of agnosticism the most important step—or so it seemed to me when, after laicization, I 'came out' as an agnostic—was to examine the proofs of the existence of God to see whether any of them was valid. I felt that I could now do so in a more dispassionate manner, having rejected the Catholic discipline which insisted that the existence of God was provable no matter what fallacies I might discover in the arguments offered. Having come to have a great respect for St Thomas Aquinas as a philosopher I decided that the best place to start would be with an examination of the five ways by which he says, in his *Summa Theologiae*, that the existence of God can be proved. If anyone was likely to have offered a really convincing proof of the existence of God, I reasoned, St Thomas, with all his genius, must surely have done so. So I studied his proofs with great care, trying to understand their historical genesis and examining their philosophical validity, attempting to supply suitable presuppositions to fill in gaps which appeared in the argument. I presented the examination in a series of lectures, and eventually in a book, *The Five Ways*, published in 1969. None of the arguments, on close examination, seemed to be successful in demonstrating the existence of God. I tried to pinpoint the move where each of the five ways was guilty of fallacy. I was surprised, and rather disappointed, to discover how much of Aquinas's argumentation depended on a background of outdated Aristotelian cosmology. I learned much from writing the book, but at the end of it I began to question my initial supposition that Aquinas was the best spokesman to choose in favour of the thesis that God's existence could be proved.

While writing *The Five Ways* I was saddened to watch Alec's life coming to a close. The Jerusalem Bible had been published in 1966, just after my marriage; at the end of that year, Alec came to stay in Chicago, where I held a visiting professorship during a sabbatical leave. The success of the version brought him contentment and renown: but he had hardly begun to enjoy it when it was discovered that he had cancer. With my mother he delighted in the birth and babyhood of our first child, Robert; but he died at the end of 1970 just after the birth of our second son, Charles. Impatient at first of illness, in his last days he bore with dignity and even serenity the loss of his strength and the fading of his wit and curiosity. After his death my mother moved to Oxford, to live near Nancy and myself and to share in the raising of our family.

Among the score of books I have had published, more have been concerned with the history of philosophy than with philosophy itself. Within pure philosophy — apart from the philosophy of religion — almost everything I have written has been concerned with the cluster of problems around the traditional theme of freedom and necessity. My first book, *Action, Emotion and Will*, presented a theory of human action and voluntariness without attempting to relate it to the traditional problems of determinism. I attempted to make that link in a second book, *Will, Freedom and Power*, which argued that while there is no reason to believe that any form of determinism is true, some forms of it are not incompatible with genuine freedom. There remain gaps in the overall account I gave; some day I hope to fill them in by writing a third part to the trilogy, with the title *Power, Control and Action*.

In a book entitled *The God of the Philosophers* I brought together my work on freedom and determinism with the inquiry into the arguments for and against the existence of God. If God is to be omniscient, I argued, then he cannot be immutable. If God is to have infallible knowledge of future human actions, then determinism must be true. If God is to escape responsibility for human wickedness, then determinism must be false. Hence, in the notion of a God who foresees all sins but is the author of none, there lurks a contradiction. Hence, there cannot be a God with all the attributes which theologians and philosophers have traditionally assigned to him.

That does not mean that there cannot be a God of some other kind; and I concluded the book with a defence of agnostic prayer in language echoing the conversation I had had with Heenan twenty years before:

> One thing seems clear. There is no reason why someone who is in doubt about the existence of God should not pray for help and guidance on this topic as on other matters. Some find something comic in the idea of an agnostic praying to a God whose existence he doubts. It is surely no more unreasonable than the act of a man adrift in the ocean, trapped in a cave, or stranded on a mountainside, who cries for help though he may never be heard or fires a signal which may never be seen.

Most recently, I gave the Bampton lectures on *Faith and Reason* at Columbia University. I described the virtue of rationality — the virtue of right belief, standing between the opposed vices of credulity (which believes too much) and scepticism (which believes too little). I concluded:

> When I, from my agnostic viewpoint, look at my theist and atheist colleagues, I do not know whether to envy them or pity them. Should I envy them for having a firm belief on a topic on which it is important to have a firm belief and on which I myself have none? Should I pity them because of the flimsiness of the arguments which they use to justify their theism or atheism? From my viewpoint, they appear as credulous; from their viewpoint I appear as sceptical. Which of us is rational, I do not know.

Index

212 *A Path From Rome*

OXFORD

MORE OXFORD PAPERBACKS

Details of a selection of other books follow. A complete list of Oxford Paperbacks, including The World's Classics, Twentieth-Century Classics, OPUS, Past Masters, Oxford Authors, Oxford Shakespeare, and Oxford Paperback Reference, is available in the UK from the General Publicity Department, Oxford University Press (JN), Walton Street, Oxford OX2 6DP.

In the USA, complete lists are available from the Paperbacks Marketing Manager, Oxford University Press, 200 Madison Avenue, New York, NY 10016.

Oxford Paperbacks are available from all good bookshops. In case of difficulty, customers in the UK can order direct from Oxford University Press Bookshop, 116 High Street, Oxford, Freepost, OX1 4BR, enclosing full payment. Please add 10 per cent of published price for postage and packing.

AQUINAS

Anthony Kenny

Anthony Kenny writes about Thomas Aquinas as a philosopher, for readers who may not share Aquinas's theological interests and beliefs. He begins with an account of Aquinas's life and works, and assesses his importance for contemporary philosophy. The book is completed by more detailed examinations of Aquinas's metaphysical system and his philosophy of mind.

'It is hard to see how such a book could be done better.' *London Review of Books*

Past Masters

THOMAS MORE

Anthony Kenny

The place of Thomas More in the intellectual history of Europe is secure, but a fair judgement of the man and his works is made difficult by the varied and biased criticism to which they have been exposed. Dr Kenny argues in this book that Thomas More's life presents a coherent character whose qualities can and should be admired, even by those who do not share his beliefs.

'a small masterpiece' Norman St. John Stevas, Books of 1983, *Sunday Times*

'a magnificent essay' Ronald Blythe, *Listener*

Past Masters

DOCUMENTS OF THE CHRISTIAN CHURCH

Selected and Edited by Henry Bettenson

First published in 1943, this book won a world-wide reputation, so that 'Bettenson, *Documents*' is now referred to as a sourcebook in many important works. It is also fascinating reading, containing 'the hard facts of many disputed questions, the ammunition for controversy, the corrective to loose thinking and idle speech'. It is currently in a second edition, so that it now covers an additional twenty years of Christian history, from the earliest documents after the New Testament, down to the eve of the Second Vatican Council. It spans the periods of the Fathers and the Middle Ages, Roman Catholic and Protestant Churches, the Reformation, the Churches in Great Britain, and the beginning of the Ecumenical Movement, giving an indispensable background to history and current events.

'That invaluable Christian reference book.' *Church Times*.

'Covering the whole range of Christian history, it is especially valuable to the young Student.' *Church Quarterly Review*

'This source book can be used to make your own Do-it-yourself Church History. Here is varied material about which you can make up your own mind, with no partisan scholar coming in between.' *Methodist Magazine*

THE CATHOLIC FAITH

Roderick Strange

'a first-class summary of the teaching of the Catholic Church, which will serve enquirers, students, teachers, and the general reader for some time to come . . . Throughout his book, the author performs the same task, time after time; he put old doctrines—and indeed new ideas as well—into a renewed and spirit-filled context . . . We have been waiting for a little book like this for a long time.' John Redford in *The Universe*

'*The Catholic Faith*, is written with precision and lucidity but above all with absolute conviction. These qualities make it not only informative but also a very spiritual book assuring it of a much wider readership than that which the author initially intended.' Virginia Barton in *The Catholic Herald*

CHRISTIANITY IN THE WEST 1400–1700

John Bossy

Impatience with conventional histories of the Reformation led Professor Bossy to write this book. His aim is to improve our understanding of what happened to Western Christianity at the time of the Reformation by concentrating on Christianity as a way of life, and not just on the institution of the Church. He also renounces the use of the term 'Reformation' and its associated values, and contrary to views now widely held, assumes that the population of the West consisted of Christians throughout the centuries in question, and that the social history of Europe and the history of Christianity were in this period substantially the same thing.

An OPUS book

THE INTERPRETATION OF THE NEW
TESTAMENT 1861–1961

Stephen Neill

'it is probably his attention to the personalities of the scholars involved in the debate which makes Bishop Stephen Neill's history of a century of New Testament interpretation of such absorbing interest. By any standard his grasp of the technical details of a highly complex subject is enviable, and the extent of his knowledge of the major works of New Testament criticism in five languages is astonishing . . . Altogether an excellent book.' *Times Literary Supplement*

AN INTRODUCTION TO THE PHILOSOPHY
OF RELIGION

Brian Davies

Does rational inquiry show religious doctrines to be false, incoherent, or meaningless? Are there logical arguments for thinking that God exists or does not exist? And what, in any case, does 'God' mean? Does it make sense to postulate a good God, given the reality of evil? Does the idea of 'miracles' have any meaning? Can there be a rational basis for ethics which takes no account of God? Is the notion of human survival after death coherent?

This book is written for all who have been puzzled by these and similar problems, not just for students and professional philosophers. None of the questions is new, and Brian Davies examines critically the way they have been treated in the past by such philosophers as Anselm, Aquinas, Descartes, Leibniz, Hume, and Kant, as well as looking at the work of a number of modern thinkers.

An OPUS book

THE EARLY CHRISTIAN FATHERS

Edited and Translated by Henry Bettenson

There is now a wide and growing appreciation of the value
and relevance of the writings of the Fathers of the early Church,
even for non-academic readers, and particularly for all who
wish to understand Christian doctrine. The authors represented
in this volume, first published in 1956, are the principal writers
of the Church in the Roman Empire from the period
immediately after the New Testament down to the age of Con-
stantine and the Council of Nicaea (AD 325). They include
St Ignatius of Antioch, St Justin, Tertullian, St Irenaeus, St
Clement of Alexandria, Origen, St Cyprian, and St Athanasius.
Mr Bettenson has selected passages to display as fully as
possible the thought of the early Fathers, especially on the
great doctrinal themes, and has himself translated them afresh,
with brief annotation where necessary.

'the extracts are sufficiently numerous and full to give the
authentic flavour of Tertullian or Origen or Irenaeus or Cyprian. Notes are provided where needed, and the introductions
are full and up to date.' *Guardian*

THE LATER CHRISTIAN FATHERS

Edited and Translated by Henry Bettenson

The century and a quarter following the Council of Nicaea has been called the 'Golden Age of Patristic literature'. It is this period that Henry Bettenson covers in this companion volume to *The Early Christian Fathers,* selecting from the writings of Basil the Great, Gregory of Nyssa, Jerome, Augustine of Hippo, Cyril of Alexandria, and other Fathers of the Christian Church. Their central concerns were formulating the doctrine of the Trinity after the Nicene conclusions, and enunciating the doctrine of the divinity and humanity of Christ. The writings served to clarify if not to solve the issues and they continue to be valuable and relevant for all who wish to understand the Christian doctrine. As in *The Early Christian Fathers,* Mr Bettenson has translated everything afresh and provided some annotation and brief sketches of the lives of each of the Fathers represented in the selection.

THE CONCISE OXFORD DICTIONARY OF THE CHRISTIAN CHURCH

Edited by E. A. Livingstone

This is the abridged version of the second edition of *The Oxford Dictionary of the Christian Church.* It makes available for the general reader the vast majority of the entries in the parent volume. The range of the *Concise Dictionary* is considerable. It includes the major Christian feasts and denominations, historical accounts of the lives of the saints, résumés of Patristic writings, and histories of heretical sects. It also outlines the opinions of major theologians and moral philosophers, and explores many related subjects.

Oxford Paperback Reference

MODERN THEOLOGY:

A Sense of Direction

James P. Mackey

Late Western civilization has seen an atheistic materialism become the dominant option for the first time in history. Modern Christian apologists have sought to combat this movement by using arguments that have often been turned to better account by the materialists themselves. This book seeks a more promising sense of direction for modern theology. It depicts Christianity as a 'way' (much as Marxism and some Eastern religions are thought to be 'ways' rather than doctrines), and looks for the concrete spirit of Jesus in practice, in truly eucharistic communities. It seeks to understand, on the one hand, how such communal practice could reconcile a belligerent race, and, on the other, how it can be thought to be indicative of a divine spirit moving in the world.

An OPUS book

JESUS

Humphrey Carpenter

Humphrey Carpenter writes about Jesus from the standpoint of a historian coming fresh to the subject without religious preconceptions. He examines the reliability of the Gospels, the originality of Jesus's teaching, and Jesus's view of himself. His highly readable book achieves a remarkable degree of objectivity about a subject which is deeply embedded in Western culture.

'Mr Carpenter has obviously made a thorough study of the latest New Testament scholarship: but he has also read the gospels with great care, pretending to himself that he was doing so without preconceptions, as a historian newly presented with the source-material . . . the most extraordinary achievement.' *Observer*

Past Masters

A DIARY OF READINGS

John Baillie

'That daily quarter of an hour, for now forty years or more,
I am sure has been one of the greatest sustenances and sources
of calm for my life . . . Such reading is, of course, meant as
directly as possible to feed the heart, to fortify the will—thus
by the book to get away from the book to the realities which
it suggests.' It was with the words of Baron von Hügel in mind
that Dr Baillie gathered together the 365 pieces from authors
in the mainstream of Christian thought contained in this diary
of daily readings for use throughout the year.

'one appreciates again both Baillie's gentle certainty of spirit
and the fine literary style of his own theological writing' *Reform*

RELIGION AND THE PEOPLE OF WESTERN EUROPE 1789–1970

Hugh McLeod

In the years between the French Revolution and our own times
there has been a widespread revolt against the various official
churches that emerged triumphant from the turmoil of the
Reformation and the Counter-Reformation. Religion became
an integral part of the conflict between Right and Left, and
economic change widened the gulf between the religious life
of rich and poor.

   Dr McLeod looks at the religious movements that flourished
in these conditions and at the increasing difference between
the religious life of the working class and that of the urban
middle class in the growing towns and cities, and in the
countryside. Finally, he considers how the religious patterns
established in the period are gradually fading and changing.

'It is a wholly absorbing and valuable work, industriously
researched, well written and with excellent and bibliography.'
Church Times

An OPUS book

CHRISTIANITY AND THE WORLD ORDER

E. R. Norman

This book, based on Dr Norman's 1978 Reith Lectures, considers a subject of great significance: the implications of the contemporary politicization of Christianity. Ranging from the political radicalism of Latin American Marxist Christians to the problems encountered by Christianity in the Soviet Union, Dr Norman identifies and presents a critical analysis of the social and political ideas to which the modern Church is attaching itself.

THE OXFORD DICTIONARY OF POPES

J. N. D. Kelly

Based on careful research and eminently readable, *The Oxford Dictionary of Popes* provides revealing vignettes of the extraordinary variety of men who have claimed to be successors of St Peter. It reveals their varying involvement in the great power politics, personal or family aggrandizement, patronage of the arts, theological controversy, or spiritual leadership. It also presents a graphic and moving picture of the fluctuating fortunes of the Christian Church centered on Rome, sometimes submerged by secular forces, but also at other times, under popes of determination and vision, staging a spectacular revival and confronting the world (as today) with a daunting challenge.

'scholarly and objective . . . well-researched, extremely well-written, a delightful exercise in its own right' *Church Times*